THE COKESBURY

STUNT BOOK

THE COKESBURY
STUNT BOOK

Revised

ARTHUR M. DEPEW

*More than 500 Stunts for the
Stage, Banquet, Luncheon, Party,
Boys' Camps, and Other Occasions*

ABINGDON PRESS
Nashville • New York

THE COKESBURY STUNT BOOK

Dedicated to My Parents

HUGH J. and SARAH VIRGINIA DEPEW

*Who left me a rich heritage
in their noble example
and high idealism*

PREFACE

WITHIN the last quarter of a century the demand for stunts has become widespread. I have many times searched books and magazines for appropriate stunts to meet this demand.

The various youth movements have helped to increase the demand for stunts. Frequently young people's groups hold general conferences or assemblies at which each group is requested to produce a stunt.

Within the last few years stunt night has become popular with the high schools. In many high schools where several groups of the school, such as the Latin club, the science club, the music club, the athletic club, and others, contribute a stunt, the stunt night has become popular.

At civic club conventions, both national and district, stunts are always in order at the programs and luncheons. Any such convention would be incomplete without them.

In many cities some civic club has established a custom of having an annual stunt night in which all the other civic clubs in the community participate; and the program on this stunt night is produced as a benefit to raise funds for that organization.

In one city such a program is put on annually by one of the women's clubs, and all other clubs contribute a stunt. The program always attracts large crowds, and one evening when it was given as a free program in the city park, it was attended by as many as seven thousand persons.

Church groups also have taken up the stunt idea, and without stunts many city Christian youth groups or other young people's gatherings would be incomplete.

Stunts are demanded for the weekly luncheons of civic clubs and for banquets. Parties are incomplete without them. In fact, the stunt has taken its place permanently, it seems, in the thinking of the American people.

While several stunt books have been published, a need for stunt material still exists. As far as I know, no book that covers the whole field of stunt demands has heretofore been produced.

I have collected material during a period of years while I was active in the various types of organizations for which stunt nights are most frequently needed. I have been a member of the program committee of a civic club and a member of the faculty of young people's conferences in several states; and I have directed the social life and assisted in putting on stunt nights at these meetings. I have attended state and national conventions of civic clubs and in several instances have had a part in the planning and working out of the district convention programs.

The stage stunts given in this volume have been tried out before large audiences and have all gone over in a big way. Many of them are prize-winning stunts. No stunt is included in this volume merely to fill space, for in order to avoid using too much space I have had to leave out many that I would gladly have included.

A majority of the stage stunts have been given to me by their authors, and to these several authors I express my sincere thanks. More than one hundred persons have contributed to the writing of this volume.

We have written at all times with the idea of satisfying the following needs:

First: The need of high schools, conference groups, church organizations, city Christian youth groups, summer camps, and civic clubs for stage stunts. More than fifty carefully selected stunts for the stage have been included.

Second: The need of civic clubs, chambers of commerce, men's clubs, women's clubs, and other organizations for stunts that will be appropriate for more formal dinners and banquets. Also I have included stunts to be used in entertaining guests at informal luncheons, such as civic club luncheons. A large number of initiation stunts have been included. When new members are initiated into the club, this should be done with appropriate ceremony, but there should always be something humorous in conjunction with the more serious side. I have also included a large number of stunts designed to promote attendance at civic club luncheons.

Third: I have included musical stunts and parodies, as well as a section on Group Action Stunts and Songs.

Fourth: While this book is not a party book, it may be used in connection with any good party book. The party stunts in this volume will liven up any entertainment.

Fifth: I have included one hundred stunts for Scouts or camps. Many of these stunts may be used by other organizations, and are appropriate for civic club and luncheon stunts.

Sixth: The last sections of this book deal with mental stunts, problems, and conundrums. This will render the book usable for small groups and for the home. Children will find many interesting things in these last sections. The brain twisters and conundrums are both amusing and instructive.

I send this volume forth with the hope that it will help program and entertainment committees to do their work in a more satisfactory manner. I hope that the suggestions contained in it will result in producing entertaining and wholesome programs, and that the burdens of life will be lightened and our courage to meet the more serious problems of life will thereby be renewed.

ARTHUR M. DEPEW

CONTENTS

SECTION I

Stage Stunts

MEMORIES

A Stunt in One Act—8 Characters

Stage is set with radio on left. A man of about 40 years in appearance sits by the radio. He wears house slippers and a dressing gown. A magazine is in his hand. He sits musing for a moment, and then turns the dial of the radio as he repeats slowly and distinctly the words of the following poem:

> I sat alone with my radio
>   In a place where time had ceased,
> And I turned the dial of memory
>   As the years of my life increased.
> And the thoughts of forgotten love scenes
>   Came flooding before my sight,
> And the retrospect o'erwhelmed me
>   With its scenes so clear and bright.

Chorus off stage sings "Memories."

> I saw my dear young mother,
>   The first lover that I knew,
> Bending o'er my trundle-bed
>   With eyes that love shined through.

Chorus off stage sings "Pal o' My Cradle Days" or some other mother song. A drop curtain in the center of the stage rises, showing a young woman bending over a child's bed. She holds the pose until the chorus finishes the song.

> As years passed on 'twas dear old dad
>   Who was my pal and friend.
> The hours spent upon his knee.
>   I'll remember to the end.

Scene with small boy and man. The boy climbs upon his

15

knee as he sings "Sonny Boy." If one cannot be found who can sing this solo, the chorus may sing the song.

> When six years old, like other boys,
>   I scuddled off to school,
> And ah, those days I'll ne'er forget,
>   Days of the golden rule.
> Then years passed on, as all years will,
>   But memories will never go
> Of the little lass who wrote on her slate
>   Those words, "I Love You, Joe."

Small boy and girl appear at back of stage. She is dressed in calico and he in overalls. A toe tied up with a rag will add to the effect. She has a slate on which is written, "I Love You, Joe." If they can do so, let them sing, otherwise have the chorus sing "School Days."

> Years passed on swiftly now
>   As an eagle in her flight,
> And there comes before my memory now
>   My graduation night,
> And now my girl of high-school days,
>   My sweetheart with endearing young charms,
> Is most as near to me just now
>   As the day she was held in my arms.

Girl enters as chorus sings "Believe Me, If All Those Endearing Young Charms." She is the principal character and later appears as Sweetheart back home and as the Bride.

> But years rolled on and then there came—
>   It seems most like a trance—
> The great World War—the tragic years—
>   And I find myself in France.
>
> The war has ended—peace has come,
>   Thanks to the great God above;
> But memories linger, not of the war,
>   But the French girl I'd come to love.

French girl enters as chorus sings "Memories of France."

> My soldier life is over now,
> And home I'm glad to be;
> And there I find my dear old girl
> Is waiting still for me.
>
> My youth is passing swiftly now,
> Youth's indecisions past;
> The one who's loved me through the years,
> I'll love her to the last.

She enters as the young man takes his place beside her and sings "Let Me Call You Sweetheart." This may be sung by the chorus if this character is not a soloist. The young man takes his place again at the radio as the drop curtain falls.

> But fondest of all memories,
> As I look back o'er the days,
> Was the day that she became my bride
> And I promised to love her always.

Girl takes place at back of stage—the same girl in the graduation scene, and the last scene. The man takes his place beside her and sings "Always."

This, too, may be sung by the chorus. The curtain falls on all characters except the man, who reads the following:

> What joy to recall these memories
> Of scenes so long ago,
> It makes us forget the sorrows
> We all must bear here below—
>
> And look to a brighter future
> Filled with love just as full and true
> As any we've known in bygone years
> As the time so swiftly flew.

But before we say our "Au revoir,"
Let us hear one more refrain—
A song of reverence for the past
Ere we face the future again:

The curtain in center of stage rises on all the characters. The man joins them and all sing in chorus "Auld Lang Syne." As the curtain falls the chorus back of stage sings "Memories."

MARS VIEWS THE EARTH

BY PROF. H. A. NEWELL, PALM BEACH HIGH SCHOOL

JUST before the curtain is drawn back two people are seen on the stage. One is looking through a large telescope made of galvanized water spouting, such as is used to bring water from the roof of a house, while the other stands by.

The one who is looking through the telescope shouts, as he jumps up and down greatly excited: "Eureka, Eureka. It works."

Then, becoming more calm, he continues: "I have worked for months on this telescope to make its magnifying power more than 100 times greater than any other telescope on earth. I have just been looking at the planet Mars, and this telescope is so powerful that it shows people full size on that planet. Just look. [*The other one looks.*] What do you see?"

"It looks like a group of people gathered for a meeting. Gee, aren't they funny?"

"Let's tune the radio attachment and see if it works, and maybe we can hear them talk."

"I think I hear something."

"Sure, they're talking. Let's swing the telescope around so that everyone can see and hear the people of Mars."

(They swing the telescope around as for the audience to see, and a secondary curtain is drawn back revealing several people seated and an old man standing in front of them as if making a speech.)

The old man begins to speak: "Fellow Martians, this is the time of stupendous achievement. Through the magnificent coöperation, untiring efforts, and multitudinous benefactions of our munificent governments we are on the brink of discoveries of far-reaching and astounding importance. Throughout the past half year we have laboriously and diligently watched the maneuvers and antics of our protégés on the planet Earth. Though it is greater in size than our own, the inhabitants seem to do things of which a Martian might well be ashamed. We have assembled a number of these scenes and will present in pantomime for your inspection some of the most notable events in this weird place called Earth, inhabited by what seems to be a ridiculous race. These events are inexplicable to us; perhaps someone may make a suggestion as to their meaning. Let the scenes be shown."

The first scene is the grandstand of a baseball field. From back stage the voice of the umpire calls, "Play ball" and "Batter up." Part of the crowd yells, "Knock it over the fence." The other part yells, "He couldn't swat a fly." The umpire's voice calls, "Strike one." Part of the crowd yells, "Kill the umpire." Part of the crowd yells, "Strike him out." A boy comes in selling soft drinks, and another selling popcorn.

Some girls come in selling apples for the benefit of a high school club. Add yells and boos.

The second scene is a football parade. Some suggestions for characters are: a drum majorette with a baton, football players in uniform, and a group of cheerleaders in fancy dress, who would lead a yell. Also have some students carrying placards such as "Down with Middletown High" or "Beat the Bears" or some similar slogan. The parade could move across the stage and behind the curtain two or three times. A group of students from the band or orchestra could be in the parade and play the high school or college song of the group putting on the stunt. Also a group of singers from the glee club could sing the school song.

The third scene is a prize fight. Two contestants and referee. The fighters have large gloves, and do not really fight at all. Instead they spar a little and go into a clinch and dance around and chase one another around the ring. A sign should announce that this is the fight to decide the world's championship. Finally one falls down; the referee counts him out, then holds up the hand of the other and pronounces him the winner.

The next scene is a bridge game. A placard should announce that this is a part of the "Ely Culbertson Competition to Decide the Best Bridge Hand." The cards are dealt and the following conversation takes place:

First Player: "This makes ten evenings this week I've played bridge."

Second Player: "Business is getting so bad that my husband has started smoking the cigars I gave him last Christmas and our house smells something awful."

Third Player: "My husband doesn't like for me to go and play bridge every day, so I always take a spool of thread with me and if he gets home before I do I let on that I've been shopping."

Fourth Player: "Aren't husbands the limit anyway? They expect dinner to be ready every evening when they get home from the office."

The next scene is a Marathon Dance. A placard should announce that it had been going on for 922 hours. About five couples dance in. The girls are almost asleep and the boys support them. The dance is very draggy and slow and the dancers move as if they were almost dead on their feet.

The next scene is in the Legislature. The speaker announces: "The honorable member from Miami ties with the honorable member from Tallahassee. Each has introduced one thousand three hundred and thirteen laws at this session."

After these scenes have been shown the professor then asks the class: "What do you make of these fantastic performances?"

First Student: "My opinion is that the people on Earth are people of many religions and that these antics are part of their many religious ceremonies."

Second Student: "My theory is this. You know that here on Mars from time to time, people are affected by the heat. Now the earth is much nearer to the sun than we are, consequently they must receive much more heat, so that more of them are affected by it. My theory is that these people are 'crazy with the heat.' If these people were on Mars, they would probably be inmates of one of our hospitals for the mentally unbalanced."

[*Curtain.*]

THE GRIPE EXCHANGE

Characters:

Judge Odman Ben Abou
The Recording Imp
Poor Man
Vain Woman
Rich Man
Telegraph Boy

The stage is set up like a courtroom with the Judge on the bench. A black robe and a large gavel will add to the effect. If there are not properties for an elaborate setup, put the Judge behind a desk in the manner of an informal court. The Judge and the Recording Imp are on the stage when the curtain opens.

Scene I

Imp. I have listed all the miseries which people want to exchange, and a fine lot they are. Everything from bunions to nagging wives of which some of the men wish to rid themselves.

Judge. People are never quite satisfied with their miseries. They always want to change their miseries, but never give up their vices. Everyone thinks he has a heavier cross to bear than any other. At the same time he minimizes his own weaknesses and shortcomings and thinks that they are not half as bad as his neighbors'. While I have been given the power to aid distressed humanity by permitting people to exchange their miseries, I am growing very tired of it. People need a lesson, and they are going to get it today.

Imp. Your Honor, here comes our first case.

[*Enter Poor Man.*]

Poor Man. Your Honor, I am miserable. I have been poor all my life. I don't ask for a lot of money, but I would like to have some swell clothes and enough money so that I could eat, drink, and be merry for a while.

Judge. I am willing to exchange your poverty for some other misery. I can offer the following: paralysis, fallen arches, a glass eye, indigestion.

Poor Man. [*Deliberates, scratches head.*] Well, if this is a list of what you have, I'll have to take the indigestion I guess, as this would be the best in that list.

Judge. Very well, case dismissed. Imp, show this man to the changing room.

Imp. Yes, your Honor. Go to the right and down the hall. First door to the left.

[*Exit Poor Man. Enter Vain Woman.*]

Vain Woman. Your Honor, I hear that you have unusual power to change people's miseries and that you are very kind.

Judge. Go on, Madam.

Vain Woman. I have been noted for my beauty. I have been considered very lovely, and celebrated men have admired me. I cannot live without admiration. But, Judge, horrid wrinkles are beginning to show in my face. Do you have some misery for which I could exchange my wrinkles?

Judge. I could offer you goiter, hay fever, or deafness.

Vain Woman. [*Deliberates.*] I will have to take the deafness, I guess. That will not show and will not spoil my beauty.

Judge. Will you show the lady to the changing room?

Imp. Go to the left and down the hall. First door to the right.

[*Exit Vain Woman.*]

Rich Man. [*Enters and addresses the court.*] Your Honor, I am a very rich man. Life has become boresome. Women about whom I care nothing are always worrying me because they want to marry me for my money. My life has become a burden. I would like to be just a plain, ordinary citizen, a working man.

Judge. I can fix that easily—I can give you a job as a janitor, a postman, or a milkman.

Rich Man. I think I'd like to be a milkman. I'll go to work as a milkman in the morning. I'll get a kick out of this.

Judge. Imp, show this man to the changing room.

[*Imp gives Rich Man directions.*]

Judge. Imp, I'm growing tired of this kind of life. People come in here one day and want to change their miseries for others. In a few weeks they are back and want the old ones back. Imp, where is that travel folder I was looking at yesterday? I think I'll take a little trip pretty soon.

Scene II

[*Imp is on the stage when curtain rises.*]

Imp. Well, here I am back after the weekend. I wonder where the Judge is. He usually gets here before this time.

[*Poor Man enters. This time he is spruced up and looks the part of an affluent person. He addresses the Imp.*]

Former Poor Man. Imp, I want to see the Judge. I want to change back to the miseries I had in the first place. I just can't abide this indigestion. I have plenty of money. I go into a fine restaurant and order a real dinner: shrimp cocktail, steak, salad, asparagus tips, mince pie à la mode, and do you think I can eat it? No, the very thought of it turns my stomach. I'd rather be poor and be able to enjoy my meals.

[*Enter Vain Woman.*]

Vain Woman. Where is the Judge? I want to see him at once.

Imp. The Judge hasn't come down yet.

Vain Woman. What did you say? [*Puts hand to ear.*] I want to see the Judge at once. I can't hear a word that anyone says to me. No one seems to want me around. And I am ashamed to wear a hearing aid. No one invites me out any more.

Imp. [*Speaking very loudly.*] If you will be seated, Lady, I think the Judge will be in before long.

[*Enter former Rich Man.*]

Former Rich Man. I must see the Judge at once. It is most urgent.

Imp. You can't see the judge at once, for he is not here. He hasn't come in as yet this morning.

Former Rich Man. I hope I don't have to wait long. I have been abused, insulted, overworked. I can't stand it, I won't stand it. I want back my former place of wealth and influence.

[*Enter telegraph boy with telegram. Imp opens telegram and looks at it with amazement. Other characters rise and say in chorus, "What is it? Don't keep us waiting like this."*]

Imp. [*Reading telegram.*]

"Dear Imp. I have tried for years to help people by exchanging their miseries for the miseries of others. I have found that people are never satisfied. I have come to believe that Shakespeare was right when he said, 'Better bear those ills we have than fly to others that we know not of.' So I have decided to take a sea voyage and go to a foreign land and perhaps never return. I am going to write 'Finis' to the ledger of miseries and shut up shop. The exchange is closed forever. Yours in disgust, Judge Odman Ben Abou."

[*Curtain.*]

BILL TELL

WRITTEN AND PRODUCED BY A YOUNG PEOPLE'S
CONFERENCE CLUB

ALL speaking is done by the reader and the characters act in pantomime as he reads. Besides the reader the characters are:

Bill Tell
Pray Tell
Do Tell
King Louie De Monster
Rosie the King's Daughter
Soldiers (from 2 to 8 in number)

The stage is set as illustrated by the diagram below:

Reader: Twice upon a time dere vas a guy by de name of Bill Tell. [*Bill Tell walks across stage.*] Now Bill Tell had two sons, Pray Tell and Do Tell. [*They enter from opposite sides and stand with their father.*] Dot Bill vas a goot shot mitt de Bo-Bo and Harrow, so he got a chob down in a shooting dump. [*Bill Tell, followed by Pray Tell and Do Tell, enters the Shooting Dump.*] Now, in dere same country dere vas a King by the name of Louie De Monster, und Louie, he was a goot shot mit de Bo-Bo und Harrow too. [*The King strides out and takes his place upon the throne.*] Now de King had a gal what vas named Rosie, und she worked down in de Shooting Dump along mit Bill Tell. [*Rosie crosses stage to King.*] Und Rosie, she goes to de King and says: "Louie, do you know dot guy Bill Tell what works down in de Shooting Dump? Vas you aware of de factry dat he was dragging your goot name in de mud? [*Bill Tell crosses stage dragging a placard with "Good Name" written on it.*] No? Vell, he vas." Now dis makes the King werry, werry hangry and he calls out his soldiers da-da-da-da-da. [*Soldiers romp out.*] Und de King says: "Get on your horses and fly chust as fast as your motorcycles can walk and get dot Bill Tell and his cross-eyed keed and bring 'em to me." Und so de soldiers da-da-da-da-da get on their horses and fly chust as fast as their motorcycles can walk und dey got Bill Tell and his cross-eyed keeds and take 'em to de King. [*Soldiers gallop to Shooting Dump, enter and get Bill Tell and keeds.*] Und de King says: "Bill, vas you aware of de factry dat you vas dragging my good name in de mud? No? Vel you vas. Now, Bill, I tell you what, see dis pea [*produces pineapple, peach, or some large fruit*]; set it on your cross-eyed keed's coco and shoot yer harrow thang through it or suffer the quincyse conses." Now dis makes Bill Tell werry, werry hangry and he sets dot pea on his cross-eyed keed's coco and draws back with his Bo-Bo and Harrow and shoots it off without touching a hairs of his head. [*A pea-shooter is used for the Bo-Bo and Harrow. As Bill Tell shoots, the keed shakes his head, causing the "pea" to fall off.*] Und der moral, my children, iss diss: If you find a hair in your split pea soup, don't blame it on the cook. Blame it on Bill Tell."

THE ELBERTA: A PEACH OF A TEA ROOM IN GEORGIA

BY MRS. J. Y. ARNOLD, PALM BEACH, FLA.

SCENE: *Interior of a tea room. Tables, chairs, counter with coffee urn, cash register, candy stand. If this is given as a banquet stunt, have the tea room on raised platform in center of the room.*

CHARACTERS:

Mary and Eleanor, who run the tea room, and characters to represent:

Clark Gable	Dorothy Lamour
Lana Turner	Tarzan
Betty Grable	Chauffeur of the Mills Brothers
Lauren Bacall	Bing Crosby

Eleanor. [*Looking disconsolate and counting change.*] Just 20 cents in the cash drawer. One year in this old tea room, hard work, no money, and never any thrills.

Mary. [*Arranging flowers on table.*] Cheer up, Mary. It's getting cold in the north now, and folks will soon be stopping on their way to spend the winter in Palm Beach, Fla.

Eleanor. Yes! And they will be just folks, too-stingy, on-a-diet, middle-aged, unromantic. Look, we haven't even made enough to go to the movies tonight, and I did so much want to see Clark Gable and Lana Turner.

Mary. Don't give up, old Indigo; my ears have been burning all day, and now by nose is itching. I have a feeling that we are going to have some romance and witness some thrills before this day is over. [*Car honks on outside.*]

[*Enter Clark Gable and Lana Turner. They are seated and give their orders.*]

Clark. Bring me cabbage cooked with ham hock and a big dish of onions, corn bread, and buttermilk.

Lana. Bring me a big juicy steak cooked with garlic, a hot dog with onions, and a glass of root beer.

[*Mary and Eleanor start out with the order.*]

Mary. Gee! They look familiar to me. Who could they be?

Eleanor. [*Nodding head.*] I know I have seen them some place. [*Exit. Car honks outside.*]

[*Lauren Bacall and Betty Grable enter. They are seated and examine menu. Lauren wears goggles. Clark recognizes Lauren, rises, takes off her glasses, and exclaims:*]

Clark. Lauren! The great Lauren Bacall herself.

[*Mary and Eleanor return with order just in time to hear these words from Clark.*]

Lauren. And Clark Gable, the great lover himself. [*Mary drops waiter.*]

[*Lana recognizes Betty.*]

Lana. And there is Betty Grable, more beautiful than ever.

[*Clark turns to Betty.*]

Clark. And Betty Grable—kiss me girls, before I eat my onions.

Betty. [*Kissing Clark.*] And you are kissing as well as ever, Clark. Think of the millions of women who would like to have had that kiss.

Lauren. Well, here is another one of that million that gets hers. How I'd love to be your leading lady! [*Kisses Clark.*]

Lana. Won't you sit with us?

[*All are seated.*]

Clark. Well, what are you doing to make a living now, Betty?

Betty. [*Rises and parades and dances around.*] My next picture will be grand. I have to be beautiful and sophisticated. I don't worry about that, but I have to sing.

Clark. Well, practice on us. Maybe you can take some of Lana's appetite away. She is a pound overweight now.

[*Betty Grable sings. Select a song that has been featured in her latest picture.*]

[*A great noise is heard outside; laughter, Tarzan yelling, honking of horn, and other commotion.*]

[*Enter Dorothy Lamour with Tarzan on chain. Tarzan should have little on except a fur coat wrapped around him, and of course should be muscular and wild looking.*]

All arise and exclaim: Dorothy Lamour and that wild Tarzan! [*They all seem a bit afraid of Tarzan, but Dorothy speaks.*]

Dorothy. Don't be frightened. I have him under perfect control. [*Ties his chain to post.*] Boys and girls, I am happy. Listen, I have got a job. Celebrate with me. Yes, sir, I'm going to sing at the Colony Club this winter. How do you think the millionaires will like this song? [*Dorothy sings a popular song.*]

Lauren. [*Rising and pointing to Tarzan.*] But who is the animal with you?

Dorothy. [*Petting Tarzan, who tries to bite Lauren.*] This? Well, he's my pal.

Lauren. [*Speaks to Tarzan.*] When you want me, just grunt.

[*Horn blows outside, and chauffeur enters.*]

Chauffeur. I want supper for four to be served outside. [*Picks up menu card and orders.*] Swiss steak, Russian dressing, French rolls, English tea, American cheese, Danish pastry. Italian spaghetti, Mexican chili, Turkish coffee—

Tarzan goes wild during this order and yells: Bring me some Idaho potatoes and Tennessee ham.

Mary. Won't your people come in and get a hot supper?

Chauffeur. No, ma'am, they won't come in in Georgia. It might be too hot, lady. [*Singers start getting pitch out-*

side, and male quartet sings off stage. Everyone rises and exclaims:* The Mills Brothers!]

[*Have a male quartet take this part and sing some new and popular song.*]

Clark. Order something to eat, Lauren—or do you eat, you skinny thing?

Lauren. Very good. Bring me a soft, very soft-boiled egg.

Dorothy. Well, of all things. Bring me a hard-boiled egg, and when Dorothy says hard-boiled, she means hard-boiled.

[*Mary and Eleanor start out.*]

Mary. I am woozy. Pinch me. Clark Gable, Lara Turner, Betty Grable—

Eleanor. Lauren Bacall, Dorothy Lamour, the Mills Brothers, Tarzan. Now I would love to see Bing Crosby.

Mary. You greedy pig.

[*Car honks outside. Much laughter. Enter Bing Crosby, wearing loud plaid coat and pants.*]

Bing. Hello, everybody. Girls, bring me a big, juicy steak, fried chicken, french fries, corn on the cob, cake and ice cream. Now girls, give ole Bing a great, big hand. [*Starts singing one of his latest hits.*]

[*Mary and Eleanor fall over in a faint as the lights go out.*]

AND THE LAMP WENT OUT

BY MRS. MABEL ALDRICH, SARASOTA, FLA.

Stage has screen near back and other furnishings as given throughout text. One person reads. All action in pantomime. Exaggerate all actions.

Fiercely the storm raged, the rain fell in torrents, the trees were lashed by the fury of the storm [*shakes branch of tree above screen*], the thunder crashed and roared [*hit pans together behind screen*].

But within the softly lighted library silence reigned. Presently the door opened and Evelyn DeVere tripped [*actually trip over something*] into the room. Gracefully sinking into a chair, she was soon engrossed in the latest novel of the day.

Footsteps were heard [*stamp loudly before coming in*], and tossing her book aside Evelyn sprang to meet the newcomer, but disappointment was written plainly on her face when Herbert Vanderslice stepped over the threshold [*steps very high*]. Although it was not he whom she expected, she greeted him pleasantly.

That young Vanderslice was nervous was evident. He paced the floor rapidly for a moment, then dropped on his knees at Evelyn's feet. Clasping her hand in his, he cried: "Evelyn, Pride of my heart, I love you. I cannot live without you. Say you will be mine and make me the happiest man in the world."

Evelyn answered: "Herbert, I cannot. I am very sorry for your sake, but I do not love you." Withdrawing her hand [*exaggerate*] from his, she rose and walking over to the table gazed lovingly at a framed photograph there. [*Kisses the photo.*] Springing [*actually springs*] to his feet, Herbert cried: "Ah, ha! I see it all! You love Ralph Grayson, but I swear it now, you shall never be his."

Evelyn was greatly frightened by his manner and her tears fell fast [*squeeze tears from sponge*]. Herbert, turning, saw Mrs. DeVere standing in the doorway. Giving him a look of scorn, she swept into the room. [*Sweeps in with a broom.*]

"So! You would threaten my child, you cad, you scoundrel," she cried. "Leave this house and never darken our doors again!" Bewildered by her great wrath, he stood, nailed to spot [*trys to pull up own feet without success*]. Time passed rapidly by [*Evelyn turns hands on clock hung on screen or standing on the table*], still he did not move; then Evelyn, with never a glance in his direction, took her mother's arm and left the room [*takes stuffed arm her mother is holding*].

"Go!" said Mrs. DeVere. Herbert attempted to speak but she silenced him with a gesture. Just then the clock struck. [*The property man may drop or strike something with it*]. Vanderslice took his hat and staggered through the doorway.

Weeks flew by. [*Mrs. DeVere tears leaves off the calendar.*]

It was a beautiful night, the moon rose [*pie tin*] and its silvery beams [*flash light*] played about the room. Mrs. DeVere was sitting in the library doing a dainty bit of punch work [*punch holes in an old ragged cloth*], the picture of placid industry, when, with a hearty laugh, Ralph Grayson slid [*actually slide*] into the room.

Dropping her work with a glad cry of welcome, she rose to meet him with outstretched hands: "Ralph, my dear boy, I am so glad to see you! When did you return? We have missed you sadly during your travels."

"Mrs. DeVere, I am here on the most important of errands. I have come to ask you for Evelyn's hand." Taking a deep breath, he showed his heart [*big red heart pinned in-*

side his coat] to her mother. Mrs. DeVere, pointing to the Conservatory, said: "You will find her there."

Evelyn's mother, memories crowding, rocked thoughtfully, but was soon startled by the sound of someone creeping softly into the room [*actually creeps in*].

Startled to see that it was Herbert Vanderslice, she rose from her chair and, drawing herself to her full majestic height, said in a haughty manner: "Pray to what do I owe this unexpected intrusion? Have I not forbidden you to enter this house?"

"Mrs. DeVere, I must and shall see Evelyn and naught—" Just then the door opened and Evelyn and Ralph danced gaily in [*actually dance*], smiling and happy. When Evelyn saw Herbert there she turned a little pale [*turn upside down a small pail*]. "Did you wish to see me?" she asked.

In the midst of the warmth and light he shivered, chilled by the frosty tone of her voice. He then frowned darkly and, striding toward her, attempted to pass Ralph who, quickly stepping forward, placed himself as a barrier between them while Mrs. DeVere whisked her daughter from the room [*with a whisk broom*].

Herbert, in his great anger, strode back and forth, tearing his hair [*throws excelsior about which he has in his pockets*]. The room seemed intensely hot and the thermometer rose rapidly [*pull thermometer up by string*].

Evelyn, watching the scene from the doorway, caught her breath with fear. Ralph emitted a low whistle [*toy whistle*] as he gazed upon the insane fury of Herbert. Then, hoping to placate the man, he placed his hand on his shoulder, talking to him in a soothing manner. But Herbert turned upon Ralph suddenly and the two grappled in fierce embrace.

Evelyn, chained to the spot, watched the terrific combat. Finally as Ralph threw Herbert to the floor, with piercing scream she ran to him and fell fainting to the floor.

Herbert slowly picked himself up from the floor and stood quiet and subdued while they tenderly placed Evelyn in a chair. Mrs. DeVere glared at him and said: "Now, young man, the tables are turned" [*turn over one or two small tables*].

Evelyn soon revived and gazed scornfully at her rejected suitor. Ralph walked over to Herbert with outstretched hand and said: "Vanderslice, take your defeat like a man. You have lost Evelyn and I have won her. Won't you wish us well?"

Herbert stood motionless for a moment, then extended his hand, which Ralph clasped in a hearty grip. Turning, he took Evelyn's hand and pressed it to his lips, then, with his face drawn with pain, walked haltingly from the room.

Ralph held out his arms and Evelyn ran into them. Presently the lovers sauntered out toward the Conservatory. Mrs. DeVere resumed her dainty work, but, affected by the peace and quiet of the room, soon dropped into gentle slumber [*snores loudly*]. The clock ticked on, the lamp went out. [*Some one comes in and takes the lamp out.*]

ROMAN FOOTBALL GAME

PRESENTED BY THE LATIN CLUB OF A HIGH SCHOOL

The stage is laid out as a miniature football field. There is a grandstand at the rear for spectators. The men wear

*togas and the women are in green costume. An impro-
vised radio sending machine and a microphone are set
up to the left of the stage. The Announcer decribes
the game and gives the plays as they are worked out on
the stage. The Announcer, as the curtain rises, says:*

Well, folks, here we are in the great Coliseum at Rome.
We are all ready for the great battle between the Augustan
Linesmashers and Cæsar's Pillchasers. The crowd is assembling now, it looks like there are fifty thousand people
here to-day. [*Spectators are coming in and taking their
places.*] Well, here come Queen Dido and her train of attendants. She is coming to see her old pal Æneas kick the
old gong around. Now I see her sister Anna with her. You
can see her golden crown shining distinctly above the mob.
[*The Queen should enter at this time, wearing a crown and
accompanied by her train of attendants and her sister Anna.*]
It is a beautiful day today; not a cloud in the sky, except
some fleecy white ones in the west. The sun is shining down
on the Coliseum walls and making them look like gold.

Now, here come the Pillchasers; they are certainly fine
young fellows in their lovely white togas. Here are the
line-ups, folks. Get your styluses ready. For the Pillchasers:
Cæsar, Menelaus, Antony, Cicero, Æneas, Amantius, Didius,
Brutus, Cassius, Lepidus, Cinna. Now here is the line-up
for the Linesmashers: Pompey, Achilles, Marcellus, Len-
tulus, Metellus, Domiticus, Spinther, Scipio, Cato, Octavius,
Flavius. [*If the stage is not large enough for all twenty-two,
cut down the list to five or seven on each side and leave off
the last names in each list.*]

Here come the cheer leaders out of their boxes now.
Let's pick up the cheer—

Hi Cic, Hi Ro,
Hi, Hi, Cicero.

Here come the Linesmashers and the game is about to begin. The teams are lining up. Cicero kicks off for the Pillchasers. The ball is received by Pompey, on the ¾-yard line and he dashes madly up the field to the 1½-yard line. And here's another yell, folks:

> Julius Cæsar, Cicero dear,
> We're the team that has no fear.
> We may be rough, we may be tough,
> But we're the team that has the stuff
> Yeah, Pillchasers!

And now Pompey is back and his teammates go into formation, and he dashes madly between their legs for a ¼-yard gain. But wait a minute, folks; here's a penalty against the Pillchasers, 15 yards for illegal use of hands.

Cæsar shakes his fist at Pompey. Now Pompey takes the ball and when he is about to be tackled by the fierce Antony, gives him the ball rather than be tackled. Now it's the Pillchaser's ball. The Pillchasers go into formation by forming a ring around Æneas, who carries the ball, and play "ring around rosy" down the field as interference while he crosses the goal line for a touchdown. That's a touchdown for the Pillchasers. Listen to that crowd yell. The teams line up for the next kick-off now, folks. Cicero is back.

But look who's coming—Helen of Troy, the most beautiful woman in the world. The players stand stupefied. Ah, Helen, to what lengths will you not drive the souls of men? [*Helen goes before the teams and all the players follow her across the stage. Those in the grandstand begin to leave and follow.*]

Everybody is following Helen. Why should I stay here?

AN EVENING WITH THE AMERICAN GIRL

THIS stunt is a very beautiful pantomime and may be very impressive if the costumes and settings are carefully arranged and carried out. There is no memory work required, as all the poetry is read by a reader and the songs are sung between acts. The stunt, however, should be carefully rehearsed.

SCENE I: THE INDIAN GIRL

The first American Girl, the Indian maiden, is shown. The scene is taken from Longfellow's "Hiawatha." The old Indian Arrow-maker sits with Minnehaha at the door of his tent. He is engaged in making arrow heads, and smokes a pipe. Minnehaha is weaving a mat of rushes. The Arrow-maker should be dressed in Indian costume, his body may be bare down to the waist with spots of red paint smeared on, and a headdress of feathers, beads, etc. Minnehaha is dressed in a long, loose dress, made of khaki, with a belt of beads at the waist, a band around her head with two feathers in it, her hair down over her shoulders. A girl with long hair should be chosen for this part if such a one is available. Hiawatha, when he appears, wears a shirt that comes down almost to his knees, fringed trousers, and a headdress of feathers, and carries a bow and quiver of arrows. As the curtain opens, the Arrow-maker and Minnehaha are seated at the tent door and as the reader reads the words are acted out.

> At the doorway of his wigwam,
> Sat the ancient Arrow-maker,
> In the land of the Dacotahs,
> Making arrow-heads of jasper,
> Arrow-heads of chalcedony.

At his side, in all her beauty,
Sat the lovely Minnehaha,
Sat his daughter, Laughing Water,
Plaiting mats of flags and rushes;
Of the past the old man's thoughts were,
And the maiden's of the future.
  He was thinking, as he sat there,
Of the days when with such arrows
He had struck the deer and bison,
On the Muskoday, the meadow.
  She was thinking of a hunter,
From another tribe and country,
Young and tall and very handsome,
Who one morning, in the Spring-time,
Came to buy her father's arrows,
Sat and rested in the wigwam,
Lingered long about the doorway,
Looking back as he departed.
She had heard her father praise him,
Praise his courage and his wisdom;
Would he come again for arrows
To the Falls of Minnehaha?
On the mat her hands lay idle,
And her eyes were very dreamy.
  Through her thoughts they heard a footstep,
Heard a rustling in the branches,
And with glowing cheek and forehead,
Suddenly from out the woodlands
Hiawatha stood before them.
  Straight the ancient Arrow-maker
Looked up gravely from his labor,
Laid aside the unfinished arrow,
Bade him enter at the doorway,
Saying, as he rose to greet him,
"Hiawatha, you are welcome!"
  And the maiden looked up at him,
Looked up from her mat of rushes,
Said with gentle look and accent,
"You are welcome, Hiawatha!"
  Then uprose the Laughing Water,
From the ground fair Minnehaha,

Laid aside her mat unfinished,
Brought forth food and sat before them,
Water brought them from the brooklet,
Gave them food in earthen vessels,
Gave them drink in bowls of bass-wood,
Listened while the guest was speaking,
Listened while her father answered,
But not once her lips she opened,
Not a single word she uttered.

Yes, as in a dream she listened
To the words of Hiawatha:
"After many years of warfare,
Many years of strife and bloodshed,
There is peace between the Ojibways
And the tribe of the Dacotahs."
Thus continues Hiawatha,
And then added, speaking slowly,
"That this peace may last forever
And our hands be clasped more closely,
And our hearts be more united,
Give me as my wife this maiden,
Minnehaha, Laughing Water,
Loveliest of Dacotah women."

And the ancient Arrow-maker
Paused a moment ere he answered,
Smoked a little while in silence,
Looked at Hiawatha proudly,
Fondly looked at Laughing Water,
And made answer very gravely:
"Yes, if Minnehaha wishes;
Let your heart speak, Minnehaha!"

And the lovely Laughing Water
Seemed more lovely as she stood there,
Neither willing nor reluctant,
As she went to Hiawatha,
Softly took the seat beside him,
While she said, and blushed to say it,
"I will follow you, my husband!"

This was Hiawatha's wooing!
Thus it was he won the daughter

Of the ancient Arrow-maker,
In the land of the Dacotahs.
[*Curtain.*]

While the stage is being arranged for the next scene, have
someone sing one of the Indian songs, as "Indian Love
Call" or "The Land of Sky Blue Waters."

SCENE II: THE COLONIAL GIRL

Priscilla is at the spinning wheel and John Alden sits
near her. Study the costumes of this period and imitate
them as nearly as possible. There should be a skein of yarn
among the properties, which Priscilla fixes on Alden's hands
and untangles during the reading of the following selection
from Longfellow's "Courtship of Miles Standish":

So as she sat at her wheel one afternoon in the Autumn,
Alden, who opposite sat, and was watching her dexterous
   fingers,
As if the thread she was spinning were that of his life and
   his fortune,
After a pause in their talk, thus spake the sound of the
   spindle.
"Truly, Priscilla," he said, "when I see you spinning and
   spinning,
Never idle a moment, but thrifty and thoughtful of others,
Suddenly you are transformed, are visibly changed in a
   moment;
You are no longer Priscilla, but Bertha the Beautiful
   Spinner.
She was so thrifty and good, that her name passed into a
   proverb.
So shall it be with your own, when the spinning wheels no
   longer
Hum in the house of the farmer, and fill its chambers with
   music.
Then shall the mothers, reproving, relate how it was in their
   childhood,

Praising the good old times, and the days of Priscilla the
    spinner!"
Straight uprose from her wheel the beautiful Puritan maiden,
Pleased with the praise of her thrift from him whose praise
    was the sweetest,
Drew from the reel on the table a snowy skein of her
    spinning,
Thus making answer, meanwhile, to the flattering phrases of
    Alden;
"Come, you must not be idle; if I am a pattern for house-
    wives,
Show yourself equally worthy of being the model of hus-
    bands.
Hold this skein on your hands, while I wind it, ready for
    knitting;
Then who knows but hereafter, when fashions have changed
    and the manners,
Fathers may talk to their sons of the good old times of
    John Alden!"
Thus, with a jest and a laugh, the skein on his hands she
    adjusted,
He sitting awkwardly there, with his arms extended before
    him,
She standing graceful, erect, and winding the thread from
    his fingers,
Sometimes chiding a little his clumsy manner of holding,
Sometimes touching his hands, as she disentangled expertly
Twist or knot in the yarn, unawares—for how could she
    help it?—
Sending electrical thrills through every nerve in his body.

[Curtain.]

Between the scenes have pianist or orchestra play "Minuet
in G."

SCENE III: GIRLS OF REVOLUTIONARY DAYS

The scene shows a girl and young man dancing the
Minuet. Powdered hair and costumes should depict the
styles of the times. The man should wear a long coat cut-

away at the sides. Cambric or sateen would make excellent material for this garment. The color should be blue. The coat should be double-breasted with four buttons, cutaway across the front, with the waistcoat in a buff color showing below the front of the coat. The trousers should fit the legs tightly and over them should be pulled striped stockings or Hessian boats. If striped stockings are worn, low shoes with buckles and high tongues should be worn with them. The woman should wear a high-waisted dress, with low-cut neck and a long skirt reaching the floor. The sleeves should have a puff at the shoulders. Gloves reaching to the sleeves should be worn. It will be necessary to make a study of the dress of this period to reproduce it accurately.

During the scene soft music should be played and the couple should dance the Minuet while the reader reads "The Minuet," by Mary Mapes Dodge:

> Grandma told me all about it,
> Told me so I couldn't doubt it,
> How she danced, my Grandma danced, long ago;
> How she held her pretty head,
> How her dainty skirt she spread,
> How she slowly leaned and rose, long ago.
>
> Grandma's hair was bright and sunny,
> Dimpled cheeks, too, oh how funny.
> Really quite a pretty girl, long ago.
> Bless her, why she wears a cap,
> Grandma does, and takes a nap
> Every single day: and yet
> Grandma danced the Minuet, long ago.
>
> "Modern ways are quite alarming,"
> Grandma says, "but boys were charming"
> (Girls and boys she means, of course) "long ago."
> Brave but modest, grandly shy;

She would like to have us try
Just to feel like those who met
In the graceful Minuet, long ago.

[*Curtain.*]

SCENE IV: THE WESTERN FRONTIER GIRL

While the dress of the Western Frontier girl was far different from our conception of it, and consisted of a long skirt and waist that buttoned down the front, and to some extent patterned after the Eastern styles of that day, yet this scene would best be depicted by a girl in laced boots, short skirt, shirt or blouse opened at the neck, with a bandanna about the neck and wearing a sombrero. There should be also a brace of six-shooters. The man should be dressed in typical cowboy costume. Have the reader read the poem "Lasca," and during the course of the reading the girl and boy come in. The places for the entrance and exit are indicated in the poem:

I want free life, I want fresh air,
I sigh for the canter after the cattle,
The crack of the whip like shots in battle.
A medley of hoofs and horns and heads,
That wars and wrangles and scatters and spreads,
The green beneath and the blue above,
And dash and danger and life and love,
    And Lasca.

Enter Western girl and boy and seat themselves on a bench as the reading continues:

Lasca used to ride
On a mouse-gray mustang, close to my side,
With blue serape and bright bell spur;
I laughed with joy as I looked at her
She was as bold as the billows that beat,
    She was as wild as the breezes that blow,

And from her little head to her little feet
  She was swayed in her suppleness to and fro
At each gust of passion.

  Like a northern pine
That grows on the edge of a Kansas bluff
And wars with the wind when the weather is rough,
So was this Lasca, this love of mine.
She would hunger that I might eat,
She would take the bitter and give me the sweet.
But once when I made her jealous just for fun

At something I'd said, or whispered or done,
One Sunday down in Antonio,
To a glorious girl on the Alamo,
She drew from her garter a dear little dagger,
The sting of the wasp—it made me stagger,
An inch to the left, or an inch to the right,
And I wouldn't be maundering here to-night.

  But she sobbed;
And sobbing, she so swiftly bound
Her torn reboso above the wound
Till I quite forgave her,
As scratches don't count in Texas,
Down by the Rio Grande.

  Her eyes were brown, a deep-deep brown,
Her eyes were darker than her hair,
And something in her smile or frown,
Curled crimson lip, and instep high,
Showed that there ran through each blue vein,
Mixed with the milder Aztec strain,
The finest vintage of old Spain.

  She was alive in every limb
With feeling to the finger tips;
  And when the sun is like a fire,
  And the sky one shining blue sapphire,
One does not drink in little sips.
The night was heavy, the air was hot;

I sat by her side and forgot, forgot—
Forgot that the herd was taking its rest,
Forgot that the air was close and oppressed,
That the Texas norther comes sudden and soon
At the dead of the night or the hour of noon.
And once, should the herd in their course take fright,
Nothing on earth could stop their flight,
And woe to the rider, and woe to the steed,
That falls in front of a mad stampede.

[*Exit.*]

At this point the girl and boy hastily leave the stage in a state of agitation.

Was that thunder? I grasped the cord of my swift
mustang
Without another word and sprang to the saddle.
She clung behind, away on a mad chase down the wind.
Never was fox-hunt half so hard,
Never was steed so scarcely spared,
For we rode for our lives, and you shall see how we
fared
In Texas down by the Rio Grande.

Our mustang flew, we urged him on.
"There's but one chance left, and only one—
Halt, spring to the ground, shoot your horse,
Crouch under his carcass and take your chance,
And if the steers in their frantic courses
Do not crush you both to pieces, you may thank your
stars."
If not, good-by to the quickening kiss and the long-
drawn sigh,
The open air and the open sky,
In Texas down by the Rio Grande.

The cattle gained on us.
I felt for my old six-shooter in my belt.
Down came the mustang and down came we, clinging
together—

And what was the rest? A figure that folded me to
   its breast,
Two hands that shielded my dizzy head, two lips that
   to my lips were pressed.
And then came blows, blows, blows that beat blood in
   my eyes,
And when I could rise, Lasca was dead, dead, dead.

   I dug her a grave a few feet deep,
And there in earth's arms I laid her to sleep;
And there she is lying, and no one knows,
The summer suns and the winter snows,
After many days, the flowers have spread,
A pall of petals over her head.

   The little gray hawk glides aloft in the air,
The sly coyote trots here and there,
The rattlesnake glitters and glides and slides
Into a rift in the cottonwood trees,
The buzzard sails on and comes and is gone,
As stately and still as the ship at sea.
I wonder, O, I wonder, why it is
That I don't care for things that are as things that were.
Does half my heart lie buried there,
In Texas down by the Rio Grande?

SCENE V: GIRLS OF THE 60'S. GIRLS OF THE BLUE AND
GRAY

Between the scenes the piano or orchestra plays "Tramp,
Tramp, Tramp, the Boys Are Marching," or "Darling Nelly
Gray," or "Tenting To-night on the Old Camp Ground," or
some of the old Southern melodies, as "Swanee River."

The scene opens with a group of Northern girls wearing
high-neck dresses and scoop hats such as those worn in 1860.
Study the styles of this period and imitate them as nearly as
possible. As the girls enter and cross the stage the pianist or
orchestra plays "Yankee Doodle."

The next scene shows a group of Southern girls, wearing

ruffled muslin dresses, wide hats, and with their hair curled. As they enter and cross the stage "Dixie" is played by the pianist or orchestra.

[*Curtain.*]

SCENE VI: GIRLS OF THE GAY 90's

Costumes of this period should be carefully studied. It should not be hard to find original dresses of the 90's among your older friends. The following descriptions may assist in preparing these costumes: The skirt of the dress should be cut in gores, lined and stiffened around the bottom with crinoline. Several starched petticoats could be worn to help distend it. The waist should fit the figure snugly and the sleeves, which must be quite large, should be lined with crinoline to give them the proper set. Many of the sleeves of the gay 90's were a revival of the leg-o-mutton sleeve of the earlier days, except that in the 90's they were attached to the normal armholes. The hat should be turned up in the back and profusely trimmed. Ruffled umbrellas were always carried as accessories.

During this period the shirtwaist, also, became popular. At first it was a tailored waist, with a high stiff collar and stiff cuffs. With this should be worn a skirt, such as the one described above. These separate skirts were usually black or dark in color.

If an evening dress is desired, it should be made of sheer material. The neck of the dress should be cut low and round, with tiny puff sleeves hanging below the shoulder.

Songs that were popular in this period were "There'll Be a Hot Time in the Old Town To-Night" and "After the Ball Is Over." Have these songs played or sung as the girls stroll across the stage once or twice.

Between the scenes, and while preparations are being made

for the appearance of the Modern Girl, have a soloist sing "There's Something About an Old-Fashioned Girl That Brings Back the Long, Long Ago."

SCENE VII: GIRLS OF TODAY

The girls of today may come in by groups of two or three, and by their dress represent their different activities. Some suggestions would be sport costumes, yachting costumes, bathing suits, blue jeans, riding habits, golf togs, tennis attire and rackets, afternoon dresses, evening dresses.

USING THE ABOVE STUNT FOR A MONEY-MAKING STUNT

This would be a good stunt for a church organization to give for a benefit. Invitations may be sent out, and with them a little bag or envelope and with the bag this poem:

> We're having a play and want you there,
> To look upon the ladies fair;
> Girls of the present and of the past,
> From the first American to the last.
> We want some money in exchange for our play,
> So we're sending a pocket to collect what you pay.
>
> Our ladies, you know, all require money;
> The ways to get it are often funny.
> Read this over and if you're willing,
> Open the pocket and drop in your shilling,
> And help us to see the happy day
> When there's no building fund to pay.
>
> For every letter of your name
> A penny take and cast the same
> Within this little pocket;
> Then do not quickly shut and lock it,
> But if you would be very nice,
> Go through this operation twice.

Place your name within the sack
And bring or send it quickly back.
And be sure and don't forget
That on . . . . the play date is set.
It surely will be very fine
To see you there, and right on time.

THE PRESIDENT'S DREAM

BY LUCY C. MARCHANT, BUSINESS AND PROFESSIONAL
WOMEN'S CLUB

SCENE: *Ordinary room. Necessary properties; two chairs, and table.*

ENTER: *Jimmie and another club-member. C. M. sits down. Jimmie paces restlessly around.*

C. M. What *is* the matter?

Jimmie. Oh, I'm feeling low—here it is nearing the end of the club year, and I've a feeling that it has been sort of a flop—looks to me as if we hadn't accomplished anything during the entire year.

C. M. Why, Jimmie, I wouldn't say that. If we haven't done anything else, we *have* kept the Club out of debt, we have a balance to our credit with which to begin the new year, and we have kept our membership up to sixty. That is something to be proud of.

Jimmie. I suppose so. But it isn't enough.

[*C. M. goes out. Jimmie sits down, yawns, and goes to sleep.*]

[*Enter—from the right; girl dressed in softball uniform, with bat, etc.*]

Jimmie. Why, where did you come from?

Girl. I'm one of the girls who played on the Club's pennant-winning softball team. I came to thank you for what you have done for me and for the other girls. They asked me to come. There are a lot of the girls on our team who, without your help, would not have been able to buy their uniforms and equipment. My father has been sick for a long time, and three of the girls do not have fathers. I think that one of the finest things your Club has done this year was to sponsor the softball team. The team has given us an interest and an outlet that we all needed so much. Again I want to thank you for financing, helping, and encouraging us.

Jimmie. I will admit I hadn't thought of it from that angle; I thought of the softball team only from the viewpoint of a civic benefit. I am glad you visited me.

[*Girl exists from one side, and there enters from the other side a poorly dressed woman, very shabby.*]

Jimmie. Where you looking for somebody?

Woman. Yes, I was looking for you. I wanted to tell you how much the circulating library which your Club sponsored for the rural areas of our county has meant to me and my family. My husband's crop was almost ruined by the drought this year, and he was very despondent. Then I learned through the Home Demonstration Agent about your Club using your books as a nucleus for a circulating library. From that time things have been much better in our home. I borrowed some books from the library, and now my husband spends most of his spare time reading. He does not worry so much about the loss of his crops. My children are reading good literature which helps them in their schoolwork and gives them something to occupy their minds while school is out. My entire family is cheered and helped by this opportunity to use good books. Many of the women in my neighborhood, when I told them that I was going to thank you, asked me to express their thanks as well. We are all very grateful.

Jimmie. When we started this circulating library, we had in mind only the opportunity which it offered to the children in your section, but it makes me very happy to realize that the benefits have not been limited to your children alone.

[*Woman exits from one side, and a man comes in the other. He also is shabbily dressed.*]

Jimmie. Is there something you wanted?

Man. Yes, I wanted to tell you how your Club helped me during this past year. I was feeling mighty blue and down-at-the-mouth, and I wasn't caring much what happened when I joined a big crowd in the Central City Park of the city. There must have been five or six thousand people there—I didn't know what it was all about, but I thought, "Well, here's something to do, anyway, to kill time." That was the night that your Club put on Civic Stunt Nite, and gave that wonderful entertainment in the park, free, so that every person in the community could see it without cost. You don't know what that meant to hundreds of people in that community—people who hadn't seen a show or a movie of any kind for months—people who were hungry for amusement, for entertainment, for laughter—people who were hungry and realized that there was more in life than just to eat and sleep. That was a wonderful thing to do; the music, the colorful scenes, and the humorous stunts bolstered up my morale, gave me a different outlook on things, and sort of gave courage to go on in the face of everything. I thought that if your Club considered all the work and expense of that Stunt Nite to be worth while for other people, then it was little enough for me to do to tighten up my belt and get going.

Jimmie. That's grand. Whatever benefits the community is bound to benefit the club too.

[*Man exits on one side, and a nurse enters from the other.*]

Jimmie. Is somebody ill? What are you doing here?

Nurse. I don't believe anybody ever expressed to your Club just exactly how grateful some of the unfortunate children of this county are to your organization. You know, it is a great problem with the school nurses and doctors as to what is best to help those children who do not have a proper, balanced diet at home. We examine the children and list those who need to have their diet supplemented. Then the P. T. A. endeavors, in each community, to raise funds to meet this need; and the school then distributes either milk or fruit-juice to the children who are unable to be taken care of at home. This year we were desperately short of money, and at the opportune moment your Club gave its benefit play, "For the Love of Ann," and donated the proceeds to the milk fund of the P. T. A. In one community alone, in a school of 142 students, there were 29 pupils on the list to receive milk. When this particular school received its quota from your club's donation, it was found that there was then just enough money to carry them through the school year. I do not believe that you have ever thought of the particular part your Club has played in this helping our coming generation.

Jimmie. Perhaps we fed a future President! Who knows?

[*Nurse exits. Jimmie is asleep still. Club member comes in hurriedly. Shakes Jimmie and wakes him up.*]

C. M. Say, Jimmie, when you said we hadn't accomplished anything this year, you forgot about the work we have done on our ten-year objective. We have had at each of our weekly luncheons a speaker who has talked on various phases of our government and our political subdivisions; each of these speakers has been well qualified to handle his subject, and I am sure the Club itself has been immensely benefited by this course of study.

Jimmie. Well, to tell you the truth, since you left I have had occasion to change my mind about what we have done. I believe we have had a good year, and I hope the next year we will do as well.

[*Finis.*]

LONG DISTANCE

Arrange three tables on the stage with a desk telephone on each. There are four actors: Leading Man, Lady, Man, and Bellboy.

Leading Man meets Bellboy on stage. Bellboy is carrying a suit case. Leading Man spots him and speaks.

L. M. Say, boy, won't you run over to the Breakers Hotel and give a message to my mother? I left her standing in the lobby, and I cannot get back for my dinner engagement with her. You will know her; she is a motherly lady with gray hair. Just tell her that she should not wait any longer for me, as I am delayed and am rushing now to meet a very important engagement. Tell her that it is so impor-

tant that my future happiness depends on it. Have you
understood all that you are to tell her?

Bellboy. Yes, I understand; but I can't go to the Breakers
now. I am tied up with my work. I would suggest that
you call her by telephone. You can get her much quicker
that way than I would be able to see her.

L. M. That's a good idea. Why did I not think of that?
Here is a tip for you. [*Reaches in pocket to get coin as the
bellboy extends hand. He does not give tip, but says:*]
Don't play the horses.

[*Leading Man goes to telephone.*]

L. M. Give me the Breakers Hotel—phone 2525. Yes,
the Breakers. Right over there, just two blocks away. Let
me see if I can see it from here. Yes, there it is, that
building over there on the beach with a round dome on the
top. I want to talk to my dear mother; she has been standing in the lobby waiting for me the last half hour, and I am
late for an appointment. This appointment is a very important one; my future happiness depends on the outcome
of it. So won't you please rush the call? [*Starts to sing
"Mother Macree" or "Pal o' My Cradle Days."*] Say, wonder what is the trouble. [*Looks at watch.*] Gee! I'm late
ten minutes already. [*Starts to sing "Darling, I Am Growing Old." Rattles telephone.*] Hello! Hello! Say, operator
get me the Breakers Hotel; my poor mother has been waiting
for me for the last forty-five minutes. She is an old gray-
headed lady, a motherly sort of lady. Won't you please ring
the Breakers Hotel and let me talk to her.

Lady enters and uses other phone. Hello, I want to get
the Savoy in Paris. *Hello!* Est ce le hotel Savoy? Je veux
parler avec M. Jean Valev. C'est vous Jean? Comment allez
vous, ma chere? Je suis en Palm Beach. Tous est tres
jolie. J'ai beaucoup jolie temps. Je tu telephone a dit! Je
vous aime, je vous adore. Au revoir.

Leading Man. [*Rattles the phone during conversation. At its conclusion he says:*] Pardon me, Mademoiselle, but were you actually talking to Paris?

Lady. Oui, oui, Monsieur.

Leading Man. Say, operator, will you please ring the Breakers Hotel again? It is only across the way. It is important that I get them at once. My dear old mother is waiting for me in the lobby. She is a motherly sort of lady with gray hair. [*Whistles "Mother Macree" or "Pal o' My Cradle Days."*]

Man Enters. [*Goes to other phone.*] Hello, I wish to get Prague, Czechoslovakia, and speak to Anton Musrat. Hello— Nazdar Anton, jak se mate? Ya sem Dobre. Zchnecte Pani Nina, ya man rad. Nazdar.

Leading Man. Pardon me, sir, but were you really talking to someone in Prague, the capital city of Czechoslovakia?

Man. Certainly I was.

Leading Man. [*Rattles phone again.*] Hello, will you get me the Breakers? Why can't I get the Breakers? My poor mother is waiting for me. She will be so disappointed. [*Jumps up and down and says:*] Eureka, Eureka! I have it. [*Hangs up and rings again.*] Hello, operator, get me the liner United States at sea. I wish to speak to the captain. [*Pause.*] Hello, captain. This is Ikey Wookie Woo at Palm Beach. Will you do me a favor? I am in Palm Beach, and my poor mother is waiting in the lobby of the Breakers for me. It is not very far from here; in fact, I can see it through the window, but I can't get the bellboy to go over there, and I want to get a message to my poor mother. She will be alarmed about my delay. Won't you please call her and tell her that I am late for an important engagement, and explain that it is a matter on which my future happiness depends? Tell her that I am sorry. Then kindly ring me back as soon as you have given her the message. I will hang up for just a moment and await your call. [*Hangs up and whistles for a moment; the phone rings.*] Hello, captain. Oh, you talked with her, did you? Thank you very much, captain. I hope to be able to reciprocate sometime. If you are ever in Palm Beach, I will let you come to see me play in a Charity Benefit Show.

UNITED BY LOVE

A One-Act Melodrama

BY AUDREY BURDELL CONK

CAST

Samantha Tompkins .... The Mother
Ebenezer Tompkins .... The Father
Ivy Tompkins .... Their Daughter
Caleb Strong .... The Hero
Obadiah Slithers .... The Villain

Time: The Old Showboat Days
Scene 1: The Tompkins' front porch on a summer afternoon
Scene 2: That same night at the lighthouse

SCENE 1

[*Discovered: Ma is rocking and knitting. Pa hobbles about on a cane, worried expression on his face.*]

Ma. Ebenezer Tompkins, what's a-ailin' ye? Prancin' up and down here like ye didn't have good sense.

Pa. Now, now, Samanthy, ye know I need a little exercise to get this stiff ole knee limbered up a mite.

Ma. [*Noticing Pa's expression, stops knitting, leans forward in chair.*] Why, Paw, ye look a little worried about somethin'. What's the matter? Bess hasn't had another calf, has she?

Pa. No, Maw, 'tain't nothin' wrong with Bess. [*Brief silence.*] Maw, ye know how we've been a-savin' every penny so's we could pay the last of the mortgage?

Ma. Yes, Paw.

Pa. Wal, that money's gone.

Ma. Gone?

Pa. Yep. Lost, strayed, or stolen. I've sarched all over the farm fer it an' it ain't to be found. And today's the day Obadiah Slithers comes to collect.

Ma. Oh, Paw!

Pa. Maw, we've lived here nigh unto forty years now, but I'm afeerd we'll have to go. That yaller, black-mailin', low-down—

Ma. Paw!

Pa. Wal, anyhow, ye know what he'll do about it. He's jest bin a-achin' to throw us off the place an' take over the old homestead. We've fought hard to save it, Samanthy, but I reckon we've lost.

[*Ma weeps into her apron. Pa looks very crestfallen.*]

[*Villain enters with a flourish. Removes his derby and bows overpolitely to Ma.*]

Obadiah. Ah, my dear Mrs. Tompkins. Well, Tompkins, you should be in higher spirits. After today this old place is yours once more. Heh, heh, heh!

Pa. I—wal-l—

Ob. Ah, you have the money all ready, I presume.

Pa. Wal, uh, Slithers, the truth of the matter is—I can't pay ye to-day. I've had a little misfortune. Can't ye give us—say a month longer?

Ob. [*Aside.*] Aha! My plans are working out fine! [*To Pa:*] Now, Tompkins, don't worry about the money; I have a subject much nearer my heart which I would like to talk over with you.

Ma. Oh, Mr. Slithers, you are kind!

Ob. Tut, tut, Mrs. Tompkins. Now this other matter—it's about your fair daughter, Ivy.

Pa. Eh?

Ob. Yes. Permit me your daughter's hand in marriage and you need never worry about mortgages again. [*Strokes mustache.*]

Pa. You—you scoundrel! You marry my daughter? Never! Git out before I—[*Raises cane as if to strike Obadiah.*]

Ob. [*Aside.*] I'll fix this old man. [*To Pa:*] You seem to have forgotten the mortgage. Your daughter or the money or you go! Heh, heh! Threaten me, will you? We'll see about that. I'll return in an hour for your answer. Ah, how I'd hate to see little Ivy perish from the cold, or homeless and starving. [*Exits laughing.*]

Ma. Oh, Paw, Paw, what shall we do?

Pa. There, there, Maw, don't cry. I'll think of something. [*Singing is heard off stage.*] There comes Ivy now, singin' and as happy as a bird. We mustn't let her know anything's wrong. Here, Maw, dry yer eyes an' be busy with yer knittin'. [*Ivy comes skipping in, sunbonnet thrown back, arms full of flowers.*]

Ivy. Hello, Paw; hello, Maw dear. [*Kisses Ma.*] Oh, Paw, look what I found. A wallet, your wallet.

Pa and Ma. Ivy! [*Ma jumps up, Pa rushes to Ivy and takes wallet.*]

Pa. Child, where did you find this?

Ivy. Out in a field, under a clump of daisies.

Ma. Oh, Ivy dear, you've saved us. That's the mortgage money. [*Pa beams as he counts the money with shaking fingers.*]

[*Off stage Caleb is heard calling "Yo-ho, Ivy."*]

Ivy. Oh [*silly giggle*], it's Caleb.

Caleb. Hello, Ivy. Oh, how do you do, Mrs. Tompkins and Mr. Tompkins? Jest thought I'd drap by to see Ivy a minute, if you don't mind.

Ma. Not at all, Caleb. Paw, let's go in and let these children have their little tetti-tetti.

Pa. [*Absorbed in his money.*] Eh? Oh, shore, shore, leave the youngsters to themselves fer a spell.

[*Exit Ma and Pa.*]

[*Caleb peers into the house to be sure no one is looking, then gropes shyly for Ivy's hand. Both grin.*]

Ca. Uh, er, that is—Ivy—I—uh—we—I mean. [*Falls on his knees.*] O Ivy, my beloved, will you marry me?

Ivy. [*Silly giggle.*] Oh, Caleb, this is so sudden. I hardly know what to say.

Ca. Say yes, light of my life, or life won't be worth living for me.

Ivy. Not now, Caleb; tonight maybe.

Ca. Will you meet me down at the end of the lane to-night, heart of my heart, and give me your answer then?

Ivy. Y-yes, Caleb.

Ca. Well, I hafta be running along, darling, but I'll see you tonight at seven-thirty. Ah, until then the minutes shall be as years to me. Farewell, Ivy, farewell. [*Exits.*]

Ivy. [*At center stage.*] Ah me, I am so happy I fear I shall swoon.

[*Obadiah rushes in; when he sees Ivy he stops suddenly.*]

Ob. [*Aside.*] Aha, she is alone. Perfect! [*To Ivy:*] Ah, fair Ivy, what a pleasure to find you here, and alone, too.

Ivy. [*Frightened.*] Oh! Oh, you want to see father, Mr. Slithers? I'll call him. Paw!

Ob. [*Aside.*] Curses!

[*Pa enters; Ivy backs into the house.*]

Pa. So, Slithers, ye've come fer your answer, eh? Wal, here's yer money. Now—GIT OUT!

Ob. See here, Tompkins, I want your daughter and I'm going to have her. Nothing shall stop me!

Pa. [*Brandishing cane over Obadiah.*] Git out, you scala-wag!

[*Curtain.*]

SCENE 2

[*Semi-dark stage. Scene—rocky shore and lighthouse. Obadiah is seen dragging Ivy over rocks toward light-house. Ivy falls and looks as though she will swoon any minute.*]

Obadiah. Heh, heh! So you were going to meet your lover, eh? But he was a little late and I got there first. How fortunate for you, my pretty.

Ivy. Oh, pul-lease let me me go, Mr. Slithers, I beseech you—take me back to my dear parents.

Ob. Your dear parents, bah! You will never lay eyes on them again or that handsome sweetheart either. You are mine, little Ivy, and I shall keep you my captive princess in the old lighthouse yonder. Just like a fairy tale, isn't it? Heh, heh!

Ivy. Oh, I can't go another step; the rocks have cut my feet and I am weary, so weary.

Ob. Then I shall be your dashing knight and carry you, little one. [*Makes an attempt to lift her in his arms.*]

Ivy. No, no! Don't touch me! I'll go on. Ah me! I feel I am going to die; if so, my death be on your hands, you villain. [*They enter the lighthouse, which is just a suggestion of one made of cardboard. They go round and round, as if ascending winding stairs.*]

Ob. Here we are, my pretty, at the end of our journey. We shall be very cozy here—just you and I. Heh, heh!

Ivy. Oh, why must you torture me in this way?

[*Caleb enters stage, followed by Pa and Ma.*]

Ca. I'm sure he has brought her here to the old light-house. That is the only place where he could safely hide, the scoundrel!

Pa. The blackguard.

Ma. Oh, my poor little girl! Hurry, hurry, Caleb boy.

[*Caleb enters lighthouse. Pretends to run upstairs. Pa and Ma remain outside.*]

Ca. [*Calling.*] Ivy! Little Ivy! Where are you?

Ob. So, your lover has come at last! I shall make away with him in short order. [*Grabs a club.*]

Ivy. Oh, Caleb, I'm here, up here, but you mustn't come up. He'll kill you! Oh, my darling!

[*Ivy wrings her hands and weeps; Caleb reaches top, grabs club out of Obadiah's hands, and pushes him down the steps. Obadiah tumbles to the bottom, dead.*]

Ca. You viper! Kidnapper! [*Turns to Ivy.*] My beloved! [*They embrace very dramatically.*]

Ivy. My hero!

[*They descend the steps muttering endearing phrases.*]

Ca. [*As he throws Obadiah into the sea, and a great splash is heard off stage.*] Food for the sharks!

Ivy. My hero! [*They embrace again.*]

Ca. [*Very dramatically.*] United by love.

Ma and Pa [*Beaming.*] Bless you, my children.

[*Curtain.*]

THE CASE OF JOHN IMBECILE
BY C. E. WYATT

THE stage is set up like a court room, with the Judge's bench and twelve chairs for the jury.

The characters are:

The Judge, who should wear a black robe and whiskers.

Attorney for the State, to represent Daniel Webster.

Attorney for the Defense, to represent Mrs. Harriette Beecher's Toe.

The Sheriff, comic dress with large badge.

The Jury, six men and six women dressed in as funny a manner as possible.

John Imbecile, a dummy made by stuffing a pair of trousers and a coat with straw or other material. The Sheriff carries him in, slung over his shoulder.

The scene opens with the Judge on the bench and the jury in their seats.

The Judge hits the desk with a large gavel.

The Sheriff opens court in a bombastic manner: Oyez! Oyez! This honorable court is now met for business.

The Judge. Sheriff, bring in the prisoner.

The Judge then reads:

> COUNTY OF BUNCO
>
> STATE OF SUSPENSE
>
> Henry Clay, Judge presiding.
>
> State of Suspense versus John Imbecile.

Judge. Officer, bring in the Jury and let everything be done quickly, for it is my purpose to go fishing. . . . Gentlemen, be seated. Officer, bring in the prisoner and the attorneys. Daniel Webster, Attorney for the State, Mrs. Harriette Beecher's Toe, Attorney for Defense.

[*Note.—Lawyers and prisoner come in and stand in front of the Judge's bench.*]

Judge. John Imbecile, you are accused of the heinous and atrocious crime of living in ——. Are you guilty or not guilty? I am not surprised at what you have done, if you come from such a place.

Charge to the Attorneys: Stick strictly to your manuscript, gentlemen, so that we will not be reversed when this case goes to the Supreme Court, as I am sure it will.

Judge. Attorney for Defense, as John Imbecile cannot answer for himself, how does he plead to the charge of living in ——, guilty or not guilty?

Attorney for Defense. Not guilty, Your Honor.

Judge. Not guilty? On what grounds?

Attorney for Defense. Insanity, Your Honor.

Judge. Daniel Webster, Attorney for the State, what have you to say?

Attorney for State. Your Honor, it is not necessary that we put on the stand any witness for proof; it is unnecessary because in every way this man loudly admits that he is from ——. I have heard that he made the remark that one could not buy a thermometer in his city because the needle always pointed to the north where the fair city of —— is located. [In case location is west, substitute "They never use the expression 'Go west, young man,' for fear he might go to our fair city."]

Judge. Attorney for Defense, what have you to say?

Attorney for Defense. Your Honor, there are mitigating circumstances. We admit that this man is from ——, but that it is not his fault. He was taken to that city by his parents, who fell for the publicity that it is a decent place to live. Another thing that Your Honor should take seriously into consideration, he was dropped on his head while just a boy and since that time has been, like most citizens of ——, not level-headed, but flat-headed; therefore we expect you to find the prisoner NOT GUILTY.

Judge. Gentlemen of the Jury, you have heard the evidence and testimony in this case. Retire and consider your verdict and return immediately, for the Judge is very nervous on account of his contemplated fishing trip. [*Jury leaves for a moment.*] While the Jury is deliberating, I would like to say a good word for the city of ——. [*Describes his own city in glowing terms.*] [*Jury returns.*] Gentlemen of the Jury, have you come to a decision?

Jury. We have, Your Honor.

Judge. What is your verdict, guilty or not guilty?

Jury. Guilty, your Honor.

Judge. John Imbecile, stand on your feet and receive the verdict of the Court. John Imbecile, a Jury of very much your peers, having found you guilty of the atrocious charge of living in ——, makes it the pleasant duty of this Court to pronounce sentence on you. I sentence you to live the balance of your natural life in —— [*Rival city*].

[*The End.*]

HORACE, THE FAMILY PET

THIS stunt is performed by two persons, preferably a man and a woman. A man and his wife would be ideal. The woman stands behind the man and extends her arms under his armpits so that they appear to the audience to be his arms. The man, of course, must put his arms behind him and around the woman so that they will be out of sight. This may just as well be done by a boy dressed as a girl, who in the same way stands behind the front man. He should be smaller, however, so that his arms would fit under the armpits of the front man.

The man recounts the following story while the woman, or the person behind him dressed as a woman, makes appropriate motions with the hands. If the man in front can keep an extremely blank, doleful, or ludicrous facial expression, the stunt will be more effective. As the story is told, the woman behind must keep her hands moving with gestures to fit the story and make it appear that the words and actions are willed by the same mind.

After the two persons have taken their positions, and before the story begins, have them stand silently while the woman's hands familiarly pull the man's watch out of his pocket, straighten his tie, push back his hair, examine his pockets, etc. Then she pauses and raises her hands, and the story begins. The suggestions for the actions of the woman's hands are in brackets.

We've got a family pet at our house [*pats left hand with right hand*]. He's a great big German police dog [*indicates height with hands*]. Horace is always hungry, and when Ma don't give him enough food to eat he kills the chickens, and he even killed and ate the old cat [*takes out handkerchief and wipes man's forehead*]. But we never did expect what happened [*wrings hands*]. One day as I was a'comin' home from school, just a'runnin' and a'runnin' along [*fingers make motion of running*], I looked [*hands fixed to forehead in attitude of looking*], and there was Ma [*pointing*] standin' on the front porch [*wrings hands*] just a'wringin' and a'wringin' her hands. And I said, "Ma, what's the matter?" And she said, "You'll see." [*Hands beat chest.*] I rushed in the house to find little brother had disappeared. There stood Horace with a satisfied look on his face. I was so mad I could have killed Horace [*hands clasp man's throat in act of choking*]. But then I couldn't do that, for Horace was the family pet.

The story is repeated beginning, "Another day as I was a'comin' home from school," and ending, "I rushed into the house to find my baby sister had disappeared."

With the third repetition of the story it is father who has disappeared.

With the last repetition of the story the ending is as follows: "I looked, and Ma was not standing on the front porch as she allus did. I rushed into the house, and there was Horace. He was licking his chops [*hands wipe man's mouth*]. I was so mad that I could have killed Horace, but Horace was the family pet."

Other versions of the ending of this stunt are: "But Horace is the family graveyard," or "But that would be too much like disturbing the family burying ground."

On the fourth repetition it is advisable to increase the violence of the motion of the woman's hands. For instance, ruffling the man's hair when he says, "I was so mad," or actually choking him when he says, "I was so mad I could have killed Horace."

[*Finis.*]

HUMOROUS DIALOGUE

CHARACTERS: Two men in costume. These costumes may be "hick" costumes, "zoot suits," or almost any fancy costumes.

[*Both men enter stage together. One has some paper which he is tearing up and throwing on the floor as the dialogue begins. First man has a black eye painted on his face.*]

First man. Why in the world are you tearing up all that paper?

Second man. Why man, I'm playing hookey.

First. How do you get you are playing hookey by tearing up paper?

Second. I'm cutting classes from a correspondence school.

First. By the way, where were you going with that lantern I saw you with the other night?

Second. Man, I was going courting.

First. Going courting with a lantern? Why, when I was your age I never took a lantern with me when I went courting.

Second. Yes, and look what you got. And by the way, how did you get that black eye you are wearing?

First. My wife hit me with some tomatoes.

Second. You don't mean to tell me that hitting you with tomatoes would give you a black eye.

First. Well, you see, she didn't take them out of the can.

Second. Did you know that a man can have sixteen wives?

First. What do you mean, sixteen wives?

Second. For better, for worse, for richer, for poorer. Sixteen wives.

First. Did you know I had a dog?

Second. No, do you have a dog?

First. Sure, I have a dog.

Second. Well, what kind is he?

First. Why, he is a Heinz dog.

Second. What kind of a dog is a Heinz dog?

First. You know, fifty-seven varieties.

Second. Is he part spitz?

First. He did, but we broke him of that.

Second. Will he follow a scent?

First. No sir, that dog won't follow anything less than a dollar.

Second. Well, has your dog a pedigree?

First. Man, I hope to tell you he has. Say, you don't know who my dog is?

Second. Well, that is just what I am asking you.

First. My dog is Strongheart's little brother.

Second. Strongheart's little brother?

First. Yes, he is Weakliver.

Second. You must not become too attached to that dog, you know—every dog has his day.

First. Yes, and the cats have the nights. You know, a dog fills a place inside of a man.

Second. Yes, I know—especially a hot dog.

First. What happened to your dog?

Second. He ate a tape measure and died.

First. Then he died by inches, did he?

Second. No, he went out in the alley and died by the yard.

First. Boy, I sure am tired.

Second. How'd you get so tired? I thought you always rested before you got tired.

First. Well, man, my heart beat 3,283 times today, and my blood traveled 168 miles. I breathed 2,340 times and inhaled 438 cubic feet of air. I ate 3½ pounds of food, drank 3 pounds of liquid, perspired 1½ pints, gave off 86 degrees of heat, and generated 450 tons of energy. I spoke 4,800 words, moved 750 muscles, my nails grew .000,046 of an inch, and my hair grew .01714 of an inch, and I exercised 7,000,000 brain cells.

First. Say, what do you think of all these "isms" we hear about? Nazism, Fascism, Communism. What do you think about these "isms?"

Second. You know what I think about them. I think we ought to make them all "wasms."

First. I hear you are a poet.

Second. Sure, I'm a poet.

First. Well, would you mind giving me one of those poems?

Second. Sure, I'll give you one.

The Sultan got sore at his harem,
So he thought up a way to scare 'em.
He caught him a mouse,
Which he loosed in the house.
The result was sure Harem-Scarem!

First. Do you know, I heard them use your name three times in a song last night?

Second. They did? What was the name of the song?

First. "Tramp, tramp, tramp, the boys are marching."

Second. I sure was embarrassed at you at that great big dinner we went to last night.

First. Well, what did I do now?

Second. When the lady said her father had money to burn, you said he couldn't take it with him when he died.

First. Well, look what you did when the lady passed around the olives. You said, "Lady, how long do you have to keep green peas in vinegar before they get to be that size?"

Second. You know, I have a new coat.

First. A new coat, boy, that is fine. What is it made of?

Second. It is made of skunk fur. Don't you think it will look good on me?

First. Sure I do. It should look as good on you as it did on the other skunk.

Second. I hear you have been studying English.

First. Sure I've been studying English. I just learned the other day why they call it the mother tongue?

Second. Why do they call it the mother tongue?

First. Father never gets a chance to use it.

Second. Say, do you know what a recession is?

First. No, what is a recession?

Second. That's when you have to tighten your belt.

First. Well, do you know what a depression is?

Second. No, what is a depression?

First. That's when you don't have any belt to tighten.

Second. Well, do you know what a panic is?

First. Well, go ahead and tell me what a panic is.

Second. That's when you don't have any pants to hold up.

[*Finis.*]

THE LIE DETECTOR

THIS stunt is done by two persons, a man and a woman. The more beautiful the woman and the more handsome the man, the more effective the stunt will be.

Almost any stage setting will do. The only necessary properties are a large vase on a table against the back curtain and a large coin with a hole pierced in it so that a black silk thread may be tied through it. A confederate behind the curtain is necessary. The coin should be tied on a long thread so that it may be carried a few feet from the vase and passed from the man to the woman. When the man places the coin in the vase, the man behind the curtain must draw in the thread, which is invisible to the audience. It is this man also who, at the proper time, smashes the jar with a hammer or overturns the table so that it will be broken.

It would add to the interest of this stunt if the characters who play the parts would work out additional dialogue that would in some way include certain facts about persons in the audience and weave this into the conversation.

[*Man is on stage as curtain opens and is holding in his hand a large coin. He stands near the back of the stage, not too far from the vase, to make it easier for the assistant behind the curtain.*]

Man. I do not see anything unusual about this coin, and yet my friend who gave it to me insisted that it has magic power. He said that if it is placed in a vase it serves as a lie detector. I think that he was kidding me. He said that the bigger the lie, the more agitated the coin became, and if an unusually big lie was told, it might even explode and break the jar. Well, I am going to drop it in this old vase and see what happens. [*Takes coin over and drops it in vase, while man behind curtain takes up the slack in the thread.*]

Woman, entering. Oh, I beg your pardon I did not know that there was a man in here. [*The coin begins to jump up and down in the jar as the man behind the curtain pulls the thread.*]

Man. Oh, that's all right. I have just returned from Arabia and know only a few people here. I am glad to have the opportunity of meeting you. Are you married?

Woman. Oh, mercy no. [*Coin jumps up and down a little harder than before.*] I suppose you are married?

Man. Oh, no. [*The coin starts jumping up and down again.*] Being a scientist I have always been so busy with my studies and travels that I have never had time to think about women. [*Coin starts jumping up and down vigorously.*]

Woman. Haven't you ever been in love?

Man. No, not until this minute. [*Coin jumps up and down.*] I suspect that you have had many suitors.

Woman. Oh, not me. I have always been rather shy about men. [*Coin jumps up and down excitedly.*]

Man. Lady, you have been lying to me.

Woman. What do mean, saying I have lied to you?

Man. In that vase on the table I have placed a magic coin which a friend of mine picked up in Mesopotamia. He gave it to me when we came on the same boat from the East. He told me that it would become agitated and jump up and down when anyone told a lie. I did not believe it, but I placed it in the vase just before you entered, and each time you have told a lie it has jumped up and down in the vase. [*Man takes coin from the vase and shows it to the woman. After she examines it, he places it back in the vase.*]

Woman. I do not believe that this is a magic coin, and I do not believe that it is a lie detector. I would not lie to a tall, dark, and handsome man like you. [*Coin becomes very much agitated, and the woman gives a start.*]

Man. Woman, this coin is truly a lie detector. You should be very much ashamed of yourself to go about telling lies about not being married and never having been in love. Why, I never told a lie in my life. [*At this point the man behind the curtain breaks the jar with a hammer or upsets the table so that the jar is smashed.*]

[*Curtain.*]

SUNDAY A.M. IN THE AVERAGE HOME

BY REV. G. HUBERT STEED, ST. PETERSBURG, FLA.

THE lines for the players in this stunt are not given in full, as it is the intention that they "ad lib" their parts.

The one who carries the part of the mother should be the cleverest of the players, as she has to carry most of the conversation. This was originally produced by the Faculty at a Young People's Conference.

The players are: Mother; Father; the Baby; Junior, the Bad Boy; Prissy, the teen-age Daughter; Percy, the Good Boy; Grandma and Grandpa; Auntie; Prissie's Beau; Sunday School Superintendent (a voice from behind curtain); a Group of Singers to sing song at climax.

The stage is set with a dining table, an easy-chair, a baby high-chair and other chairs. As the curtain opens Mother is arranging the breakfast table, Father sits in chair near table and Baby in high-chair.

Mother. Junior, Prissy! Come downstairs this minute. Breakfast is waiting. [*Aside.*] Just looks like they would come down without being called for once. And it is nearly time to go to Sunday school. Pa, you call them. Perhaps they will come for you.

Father. Can't a man read his paper on Sunday morning without being bothered to call his offsprings? You go ahead and call 'em. [*Pause.*] I did want to finish my paper so that I could get out to the golf course early this morning.

Mother. Why, Pa, it seems as though you could give one day to the family. Besides, you ought to go to Sunday school with the children.

Father. Here I have to work all week. I ought to have one day to myself.

[*Baby starts crying and Father goes over and moves him up to the table. Gets him settled and puts a napkin around his neck. Auntie comes in. Looks at Father with the paper and turns up her nose, for she knows that she had better not try to take it away from him. Junior enters without his face being washed and his hair combed. As soon as he enters Mother looks him over and sends him back upstairs to finish dressing, while he is trying to get the funny paper away from Dad.*]

Auntie. It seems as though it was about time that someone else had a bit of the paper. Let me have a piece. [*Father reluctantly gives her part of the paper. She looks through it, then exclaims:*] I can't find that article by Mary Haworth anywhere. Have you seen it?

[*Father looks in his section and finds it on the back of his sport page. With a growl he gives it to her. Baby starts to cry and hammers with his spoon on the chair. He wants his breakfast. Enter Prissy and Junior. They wrangle over the funny sheet. They end up by Junior getting it after he has rumpled up his sister's hair. She leaves to fix it. Enter Good Boy, all ready for Sunday school, carrying his Bible over his heart. Mother commends him and they all sit down to the table. All bow their heads as though offering the blessing and Junior takes something. The Good Boy discovers him and tells Mother. A fight almost starts, and Father quiets them. Daughter reenters. She starts to eat when the doorbell rings. She rushes out and calls to someone that she will be ready in a minute. Dashes back and demands her food.*]

Grandma and Grandpa enter: Good morning! Land sakes. It is time for Sunday school to start. Aren't you ready yet? Well, we will see you children later.

[*Whole family begins to get ready for Sunday school. They besiege Father for money to give in Sunday school. During this confusion the girl's beau comes in and they leave with Mother cautioning them to be sure and go to Sunday school. After much wrangling they all start out. Mother calls Father back to get the baby and take him to Sunday school. After they leave Mother starts to pick things up. She finally sits down exhausted with the confusion.*]

It is presumed that the church is so close to the house that the services may be heard. Off stage the voice of the Sunday School Superintendent is heard saying: "We will open our Sunday school by singing Hymn No. 234." This song turns out to be "Sweet Peace, the Gift of God's Love," or "Peace, Peace, Wonderful Peace," or "Peace, Perfect Peace."

THE SPIRIT CABINET

THIS is a stunt that can easily be done by two amateur magicians and with only a little practice. We will first tell something of the illusion and then tell how it is done.

Construct the spirit cabinet as follows: Make a frame out of wood, 1x2 inches, firmly bracing it at the corners. This frame should be about 5½ feet high, 5 feet wide, and 2½ feet deep. This can be made so that it can be quickly constructed, and it should be constructed on the stage in the presence of the audience. This frame should then be covered with a heavy black cloth, cotton flannel, which has been cut to fit the frame and sewed together in such a way that it will cover three sides and the top. Across the front of the cabinet there should be a curtain of heavy black cloth suspended from a rod placed seven or eight inches below the top of the cabinet and leaving an opening about eight inches wide across the entire front of the cabinet and at the top of the front curtain.

The front curtain should be made out of heavy black material and should have slits in it which overlap. It would be best to make it out of six-inch strips of cloth and let these overlap three inches, leaving slits in the cloth about a foot or a foot and a half in length. There must also be a slit large enough for a man's head to pass through in the center of the front cloth and far enough from the floor for a man to stick his head through while seated on a chair in the cabinet.

All curtains used in covering the cabinet should be large enough to completely cover all parts of the cabinet and the corners of the side curtains should overlap the front curtain.

Two people are needed for the act, one on the outside of the cabinet and one on the inside. The outside man or woman may wear any kind of clothing, but the inside man should have on a black shirt of wool cloth and a black pair of trousers. The shirt must not be too tight, as will be explained later. The cuffs of the shirt must fit tightly to the wrists, so that long stitches will be necessary in sewing.

Properties needed, besides the cabinet, are a needle and black thread, four strips of white cloth about two feet in length, three small dinner bells, a water glass and water, a tambourine, pad and pencil, two dozen carnations, a large pair of scissors, and a razor blade (a Gem single-edge blade is better). All properties, except the flowers and the razor blade, are on the table on the stage and are to be used by the outside man. The carnations are concealed in the bosom of the inside man's shirt. The razor blade is stuck in the side of the inside man's shoe.

After the cabinet is constructed, the outside man uses the following patter: "The Spirit Cabinet is a copy of the one used by Harry Houdini, and this power which I possess to attract the spirits to it was given to me by one of the associates of Houdini. It can only be bestowed upon such a one as I happen to be, for I am the seventh son of my mother and she was the seventh daughter of her mother, and it cannot be passed on by me unless I have six more sons, etc., etc."

After this is said, two judges are selected from the audience. In case this stunt is given at a civic club luncheon, two judges should be selected in advance, and told that they are not to question too much, but cooperate to make the illusion a success. They are to judge things as they appear to them to be, and not go too thoroughly into the details of the case. When the stunt is given from the stage, two or three should be selected who will cooperate and not embarrass the performers by trying to get smart.

After the judges have been selected, the inside man takes his place on a chair in the cabinet and the judges are asked to tie his hands to his thighs, just above his knees, with one of the white cords; also to tie his feet to the legs of the chair. When this has been done they are then asked to sew the two ties together with a needle and black thread. The judges are then asked to sew the cuffs of the inside man's shirt to his trousers with the needle and black thread. When this has been done the curtain is dropped and in a moment the inside man sticks his head through the hole. (A little time is necessary here for the inside man, as will be explained later.)

After the inside man has stuck his head through the hole in the front curtain, the outside man has some more patter: "Now I will ask you all to be very quiet, as spirits like quiet, and I will summon the spirits." The inside man begins to stick his hands through the slits of the curtain, thrusting both hands through at once, sometimes at the top of the curtain and sometimes at the bottom, sometimes one hand high and the other low, and sort of waving his hands like an Egyptian dancer. This should not be done too rapidly, but is more impressive if done slowly and rhythmically.

After this has been done the curtain is raised and the judges asked to examine and see if the cuffs are still sewed and the hand tied. They find him to be (apparently) tied fast and sewed.

After this in rapid succession do the following stunts: Pass in three bells, just holding the handle of the bell below the left side of the opening at the top of the front curtain. These bells are taken in one at a time and are vigorously rung and thrown out either through the slits in the curtain or over the top of the front curtain. Then carnations begin to come through the curtain and are given to people in the audience by the outside man. There should be a lot of these, and the more there are the more impressive the stunt. Allow a little time after this, and the outside man should put in some patter to give the inside man a little time: "In just a moment we are going to open the cabinet and let you see that the inside man is still tied and sewed, but I want first to get a glass and some water." (If this stunt is done at a luncheon or banquet, one may be taken from the tables; otherwise he must have water and a glass among his properties.) The curtain is raised and the hands of the man are still tied and his cuffs are still (apparently) sewed. The outside man places a glass about a fourth full of water on the chair between the legs of the inside man and drops the curtain. In just a moment the curtain is raised, the inside man has the glass in his mouth, has drunk the water, and is holding the glass in his teeth.

The curtain is dropped again. The inside man should be

allowed a few seconds of time (the purpose of which will be explained later) and the outside man must go on with his patter: "We will have to have some music for this next part of our program and I will ask the orchestra to please play softly. In just a moment I am going to pass the tambourine in to the spirits and see what they do with it." The inside man sticks his head through the curtain again, and the tambourine is passed into the cabinet, the outside man holding it so that about half of it shows over the top of the front curtain. The tambourine then begins to move across the cabinet and keeps time to the music striking the cabinet to mark time. It moves all the way, slowly, across and back and then is thrown out.

The outside man then says: "Now is the time to release my helper, and I am going to drop these scissors into the cabinet and let the spirits release him." The scissors are dropped and immediately the curtain is raised and the inside man is found to be released, with the ties heaped in a pile on one side.

The explanation of this stunt is very simple. To the judges his sleeves only appear to be sewed to his trousers after the curtain is raised. In reality they have already been cut loose, and only appear to be sewed because the thread is there and it is very hard to see in the cabinet with a black shirt and trousers and the white cloth ties which are around his hand. (This is the reason that it is suggested that judges be selected who will not be too inquisitive, for the average man would think the inside man was still sewed, as he appears to be. Of course he must hold his hands tightly in place all the time that the curtain is open. The sewing is the only thing that really holds him. It is no difficult matter to slip his hands out and back when he is not sewed. How does he get unsewed? He has a Gem single-edged razor blade in his left shoe, and immediately after the front curtain is dropped and before he sticks his head through he raises his left foot, takes out the razor blade with his right hand and cuts the threads and releases both hands, slipping his hands out of the ties. He then sticks his head through the curtain, and after the outside man's patter he begins to stick his hands through the front curtain. When the examination is made, or before the curtain is raised, he must get his hands back into the original position so that they will appear to be sewed.)

When the bells are passed in, the inside man feels up the side of the cabinet, on his right, until he touches the pole that holds the front curtain and in this position his hand takes hold of the bells. The carnations are taken from his shirt and passed out through the slits in the curtain. Before the curtain is raised again the inside man must get his hands back into position and do the water-drinking stunt. This could be followed by the writing of answers to questions that are asked by those in the audience, and answered by the inside man in writing. After this the inside man cuts himself loose and cuts the bandages off his feet and hands and piles them to one side. The curtain is then raised and both actors are ready for the final applause.

A DAY IN SEVILLE

BY MRS. CAMILLA ATTANASIO BAKER, PALM BEACH, FLA.

THIS stunt is a representation of a Spanish bullfight, and if put on cleverly is very interesting and entertaining. Have the stage arranged according to the diagram below:

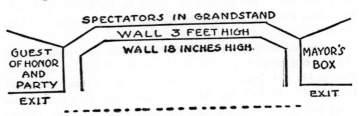

There should be a wall about three feet high in front of the grandstand and boxes. This should be white, and may be built of boards and covered with white paper. There should be a second wall about eighteen inches high, and about two feet in front of the first wall; over this wall the toreador may jump if hard pressed by the bull.

The main wall should be draped with Spanish shawls, tapestries, ribbons, and flowers to make it colorful.

In the Mayor's box, to the right of the stage, are seated the Mayor's family, to represent a wife and at least three children. The Mayor should be wearing a regular Spanish costume and the woman should be wearing a black lace dress and mantilla (a shawl that covers the large comb in her hair) or a large Spanish shawl. The children's clothing should duplicate to a great extent that of their parents. They may wear boleros (tight-fitting vests).

The box at the left is occupied by the guest of honor, who is generally a young lady. She has with her a party of young men and women. These may be dressed in American or English style, as oftentimes the guests of honor are from other countries. Anyone may be a guest of honor at a Spanish bullfight by paying for the privilege.

The spectators at the rear of the stage may be dressed in typical Spanish costumes, and should cheer and yell during the fight. There should be a peanut vender and there may be a musical number introduced before the beginning of the fight. The introduction of a Spanish dancer would not be out of place. During the performance the "Toreador Song," from Carmen, should be played by the orchestra.

The trumpet blows off stage; it announces the coming of the cuadrilla. From the opposite side of the Mayor's box march the following people in military fashion: Two banderilleros, two picardors, and one toreador. They march up to the Mayor's box, and the Mayor presents them with the key of the bull pen. This he gives to the toreador. They bow and march off the stage. The trumpet sounds again, announcing the coming of the bull. The bull and the two banderilleros come out together.

The bull is formed by the bodies of two boys or men covered with burlap. The head of the bull will be the most difficult part to construct, and it should be made so that the front man's head can see through the bull's eyes. There should be horns and the boys inside the bull should wear brown leggings. The bull must have ears, as one of these has to be cut off by the toreador.

The banderilleros tease the bull by waving a red banner and they shoot darts into the bull's sides. These darts may be fixed so that they will explode, as in a real bullfight these darts are made to explode in the bull's side and enrage him. After the banderilleros have teased the bull until he is enraged they leave and the picadors come out.

In the real bullfight they ride horses, but in this instance they may ride wooden horses or sticks with horses' heads on them. If the stage is large enough, two horses may be im-

provised like the bull, with boys inside of them. The picadors carry lances and pick at the bull. Have one of these
picadors killed with his horse during the fight.

During all this the spectators are cheering madly and
wildly. When the picador is killed, have some cry and some
faint. The remaining picador exits and the one that is supposed to have been killed is carried out, while the bull stands
and paws the earth. The toreador enters carrying a red
banner or cloak, and he enrages the bull still more. At the
logical time or moment he draws his sword, which is hidden
in the folds of his cloak, and kills the bull. The crowd yells.
Then the toreador cuts off the right ear of the bull, walks
over to the guest of honor, and graciously presents it to her,
and receives a kiss from her.

[*Curtain.*]

BURYING JACKSONVILLE

THIS stunt may be put on by any of two rival cities. It
requires a little rehearsal and is amusing and entertaining.

The characters are as follows:

1. The preacher
2. The undertaker
3. Six pallbearers
4. A number of mourners
5. Man from Miami

Use a box somewhat in the shape of a casket for the coffin and cover it with black crepe paper. Improvise a wheeled carriage like those used by undertakers. Any kind of wheeled machine will do for this, even a wheelbarrow. A toy wagon would be good if large enough. If such a wagon is not available, the pallbearers may carry the casket. If a carriage is used, cover it with black paper.

The procession enters from the back of the auditorium and the preacher leads it down the aisle. Any kind of clever costume on the part of the preacher will make the stunt more effective, such as a robe or a long coat. The mourners should weep and wail, and should have wet handkerchiefs from which they wring water to represent tears shed for the deceased.

As the procession moves down the aisle the preacher reads slowly the following words:

> A voice is heard in Florida,
> Weeping and great lamentations,
> The people weeping for Jacksonville,
> And they will not be comforted,
> Because she is not—she is DEAD.
> > [*Mourners weep and wail.*]
> For the lack of pep, cities must perish.
> > [*Mourners weep and wail.*]
>
> Go to now you that say, To-day or to-morrow
> Or on such a day we will go to Jacksonville.
> You know not what you say, for why
> Should you seek the living among the dead?
> When you go to a city, go to a good live city.

When the procession reaches the front of the auditorium the mourners and pallbearers group themselves around the coffin. The mourners weep occasionally and wring their handkerchiefs. The preacher reads the obituary: "Jackson-

ville was born in the year 1493. Death came in 1953, and
was caused by its being so overshadowed and overawed by
the marvelous progress of Miami. The approach of death
was first evidenced by their inability to win athletic con-
tests, they having been defeated by [*fill in here local matter
known to the group*]. The approach of death was shown
again by their failure to send a large group of young people to the Young People's Conference, and by the lack of
pep on the part of those who did come.

> Dead, a city of 250,000 people,
> Filled with business blocks and houses.
> There is no hope of resurrection,
> For it is gone forever.
>
> [*Weeping.*]

Does anyone have anything further to say?"
[*Allow time for a sort of awkward pause.*]
The man from Miami comes forward and says: "If no one
has anything further to say about the deceased, I would like
to say a word for Miami. Miami is not dead, but very much
alive. She stands upright, full-statured, and equal to any
city in the country, breathing the keen air and looking out
upon the expanded horizon and sees there the promise of
even brighter days in the future than we have witnessed in the
past. Anyone looking for a live city that is full of pep and
enthusiasm need look no further; come to Miami. Our
athletic teams are unbeatable, a fine group of young people
comes to conference each year, and we have plenty of push."
The preacher then says: "The undertaker will now take
charge."
The undertaker takes the lid off the box. In the box is
a large placard which reads: *"Miami Remains."*
The audience is asked to come and view the remains. If
it is not practicable, on account of the size of the crowd or

the time allotted for the stunt, to have them pass by and view the remains, the undertaker may hold up the box in such a way that the placard can be read by the audience.

The group may either march out down the aisle or retire behind the stage.

ATHLETIC TABLEAUX

THIS stunt may be very beautiful if the lighting is right. The idea is to show different athletic activities by players in tableaux. There should be no movement at all, but each one should hold his position while the curtain is open.

Basket ball is represented by four or five players in tableau as they might appear on the court.

Baseball may be represented by a player sliding a base, while the baseman is catching the ball.

Football may be represented by a player that has just been tackled with the ball.

Girl's volley ball by a girl's team; girl's softball; deck tennis; tennis; archery; golf; tumbling; wrestling; boxing; and expression gymnastics.

The positions should be carefully rehearsed and care taken to see that the lighting effect is right, and the stunt will be very beautiful and interesting. Care should be taken in changing the scenes so that there will be a minimum of confusion so that it can be done quickly.

IDENTIFYING ARTICLES BLINDFOLDED

THE following stunt may be worked by two amateur performers, with little or no rehearsal, and will be very mysterious.

The leading man announces that he will have his assistant blindfold him, and that he will sit with his back to the audience while various articles are collected, and when they are held above his head he will identify or describe them.

It would be well to have a cap that would pull down over the eyes and extend to almost the end of the nose, made of black material with a strap to fasten under the chin. Pass the blindfold so that any who desire may examine it.

The assistant then blindfolds the leading man and seats him in the chair with his back to the audience, and collects various articles in a hat. These are held over the leading man's head, one at a time, and he describes them.

How is this done? In a very simple way. The leading man has in his pocket a small round mirror, which, when he is seated, he takes out and holds in the palm of his right hand. By looking down his nose, under the bandage, he is able to see in the mirror the reflection above his head. When the stunt has been finished he slips the mirror back into his pocket and rises. He holds out both hands so the palms are plainly seen by the audience.

Throughout the stunt there should be continual patter by the leading man or the assistant. A few bits of humor will add to the effect. Make it appear that by some unusual power the leading man is able to describe the article when the assistant concentrates on it. He should ask the assistant to concentrate on the article, or the one in the audience who gave the article should be asked to concentrate on it.

SPIRIT READING

THE performer asks anyone in the audience to take a blank piece of paper or card with which he supplies them and write a brief sentence on it. He should limit the writer to five words, and ask him to write or print his name plainly. He might suggest some sentences, such as "That's nothing but applesauce," or "You're a big hunk of cheese," or "Am I in love?" "What's on my mind?" etc. There should be about 12 or 15 cards and envelopes passed out, and each person who receives one should be asked to write his message on the card and seal it in an envelope.

The performer then announces to the audience (while he is still among the crowd) that he will read the messages without opening them and return them sealed to the writer. This he does in effect in the following manner:

There must be an assistant who is always out of sight and the stage must be arranged in the following manner:

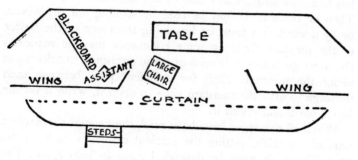

As the performer returns to the stage with the tray of letters in his hand he passes by the chair; holding the tray in his left hand, he uses his right hand to move the chair slightly. As his back is to the audience and he is so close to the wing that no one can see it, the assistant reaches out his hand and takes the messages from the tray and places other sealed envelopes on the tray. These dummy envelopes must be the same size, and each should have a card in it. The performer then sets the tray of dummy letters on the table.

The envelopes and cards that were passed out in the audience should have been numbered from 1 to 12 or 15, depending on the number used. The performer should first announce that he is going to rearrange the messages by number. This will take sufficient time for the assistant to open message number one and write it plainly on a blackboard so that the performer can see it. Additional time should be allowed for the assistant to replace the message in another envelope and reseal it. This time may be gained by the performer filling in with patter and jokes, etc.

The performer, when he is ready to read a message, should take the message and place it on his forehead and walk up and down and back and forth on the stage until he has had time to read and understand the message given him. Then he reads it. It may be read by spelling out the words, or by a word at a time, or by giving the name of the writer of the message first, or some comments may be made on the message before it is read or some amusing remarks made about the message. Stall for sufficient time between each message to give the assistant time to open it, write it on the blackboard, and reseal it.

When all messages have been read, then comes the hardest part of the trick, getting the original messages back on the tray. The chair must be depended upon to help again. The performer should hold the tray of letters in his right hand, and as he walks around the chair his hand and the tray are out of sight for only a second, but this is sufficient time for the assistant to change the letters on the tray and put back the original letters in new envelopes with similar numbers and all.

This stunt should be carefully rehearsed, and every detail worked out and timed so that there will be no suspicion of an assistant being used at all.

It would be well to have soft music played during the act, and much better if this could be music of the weird type.

Do not attempt too many messages or prolong the stunt. Ten or fifteen minutes will be sufficient.

LIVING PICTURES

THIS stunt may have twelve or more characters in it, depending upon the number of songs selected to be acted out. Among these characters should be:

A Boy and Girl for School Days
Mother, with baby or doll in cradle
Old Man and Lady
Mother and Son
College Campus Group
Young Man and Girl

Living pictures make a very beautiful and impressive stunt. We are assuming that these stunts will be on a stage. Have a large frame constructed about eight feet high and about ten feet wide, with hidden lights around the border. Raise this frame up a foot or more from the floor of the platform. A hidden chorus or quartet furnishes the music while the pictures are given in a tableau. After each song that is given in tableau the quartet or chorus sings "Memories."

1. *School Days.* The tableau would be a small boy and a small girl holding hands, the girl carrying in her hand a slate on which is written "I love you, Joe," and thus they stand while the chorus or quartet sings.

The curtain is then drawn and the picture is changed, but the chorus continues singing "Memories."

2. *Rock-a-Bye Baby.* This picture might be a mother with her baby. If an old-fashioned cradle can be obtained, have a doll or a baby in the cradle. The mother rocks the cradle while the chorus sings.

3. *When You and I Were Young, Maggie.* An old couple are on the stage holding hands.

4. *Campus Scene.* A mixed group of students in sweaters or cheerleaders' costumes sing "Alma Mater," "Boola Boola," or the song of their own university. End up with a rousing college yell.

5. *Mother Macree.* An old lady, dressed in black or lavender with white lace and cap, is seated in a rocker. A young man stands by her. He looks down at her as the song is sung.

6. *My Wild Irish Rose.* A girl with summer dress, wide-brimmed hat, garlanded with roses, and a boy are on the stage. The boy is dressed in summer sport clothes, white trousers, sweater, white hat in hand. The girl takes a rose and puts it in his buttonhole during the singing of the music. The action should be carefully timed to fit the scene.

Other songs that might be used are: "Let Me Call You Sweetheart," "Auld Lang Syne," "Comin' through the Rye," "Gypsy Love Song," "I Want a Girl Just Like the Girl that Married Dear Old Dad," "Silver Threads among the Gold."

BRAIN-TESTING MACHINE

THE Brain-Testing Machine may be used as a stage stunt, and would be a good stunt for a group of Conference or Summer Assembly young people to pull on the faculty. It would work, also, at a banquet or luncheon and would be a clever stunt to put over on the officers or distinguished guests.

Construct the brain-testing machine as follows: Make a box with boards about nine inches wide and about one foot square and as high as the width of the boards. Put a board over the top and on the bottom, boring a hole about a half inch in diameter through the top and bottom boards. It is necessary for this box to set about two inches off the table, so around three sides of it there should be a board, one by two, nailed up edgewise, so that the bottom of the box will appear to be on the table. Get a piece of rubber hose about a half inch in diameter. This should be ten or twelve feet long. Put this through the holes in the bottom and top of the box, so that one end of it just projects over the top of the box. It will be necessary to get a small tube, glass or brass, which may be procured either at a hardware store or a plumbing shop. This should be just large enough to slip the end of the rubber hose over and to make it fit tight in the hole and in the box. Then get a toy rubber balloon and slip over the end of the tube. This box is placed on the table with the tube sticking out on the back side, and then the tube is placed behind the curtain, with one person behind the curtain to make the balloon large or small at will by inflating it. It would be well also to have some sort of a dial, either drawn on the side of the box or purchased and put on the box. Also have some kind of a crank that will turn other little apparatuses on the box. On the top side there should be driven a nail on each corner, and a small wire tied around the entire edge of the box and also to the top of the nails. One person stands on the stage and announces that very recently a wonderful machine has been invented which will test brain capacity and that it operates electrically. He puts one hand on the head of an individual and the other hand on the wire of the Brain-Testing Machine, and the balloon will indicate the capacity of the brain. This is a very humorous stunt if carried out properly. As soon as the hand is placed on the wire, if it is desirous to indicate that the person is a man of brain capacity, the balloon is immediately made large. If not, it might be made to just barely move, and perhaps just to flop over.

Another variation of this is to get a bald-headed man and put lampblack on the fingers and make some black spots on his bald head. This will cause much merriment. If it is desirable to especially honor someone, the one who is blowing the balloon might blow it until it bursts, or the one on the stage might puncture the balloon with a pin or touch it off with a cigarette.

HICKVILLE COMES TO CONFERENCE

MANY times there will be a group which will desire to put on a stunt that will require little rehearsing and no memory work. The following will get a good laugh:

An automobile is represented by ten boys or girls. Four represent the seats, four more represent the tires, one the engine, and one the spare tire.

Four or five young people come out on the stage and seat themselves in the car. One has to get out and crank before he can get the car started. When he gets back in car, the engine dies out—that is, the noise made by the boy representing the engine stops. He has to do the cranking all over again. The car goes for a few feet and then a tire goes flat. The chauffeur gets out and pumps up the tire and starts again. A blow-out occurs. This is made by one representing a tire, inflating a paper bag and bursting it. The chauffeur goes through the business of taking off the spare tire, jacking up the car, and changing the tire.

This could be made to look more like an automobile, by covering those who take part with large black cloths or blankets. Make it look as much like a car as possible.

Do not let the stunt last so long that it will get monotonous.

CHICAGO

This stunt may be worked on the stage, but may be used in front of the curtain between acts.

If it is done in front of the curtain, two characters come from opposite sides of the stage and run into a third who comes between the curtain in the center of the stage.

First Character. Oh, excuse me, but your face looks familiar. Where have I seen you before?

Second Character. Well, I don't know; but I'm from Chicago. Perhaps you have seen me there.

First. So, you're from Chicago. Well, I sure am glad to meet yer. I happen to be from Chicago myself.

Third Character. Well, gentleman, I see you are both from Chicago. That is quite a coincidence, for I happen to be from the Windy City myself. It is unusual that three of us from Chicago should run into each other by accident.

[*At this point all draw guns, start shooting, and make hasty exits.*]

THE EMPLOYMENT OFFICE

THE scene is laid in an office. There should be a desk, a typewriter, and a few old chairs. A woman is seated at a desk reading a magazine. A man faking a foreign accent enters and says: "Is this the employment office?" The woman says: "Yes, it is; what can I do for you?" He says: "I want to get a job." As a man enters, the woman says: "Here is my husband. He will take care of you." The man speaks and then goes to the desk and takes out a form, a questionnaire, and starts to ask the man questions: "What is your name? How old are you? Where were you born? Are your father and mother living?" The applicant interrupts: "I do not want to buy life insurance. I want a job."

The employment agent then asks: "What can you do?"

To which the applicant replies: "I can cook, or superintend the kitchen. I am a butler, or a chauffeur. I am a general handy man around the house."

The employment agent then says: "How much salary do you want?" The reply is: "Oh, about a hundred dollars a week would do."

The employment agent then says: "If you will leave me your address and pay me five dollars, I will let you know if I find anything in your line." The money is paid and the applicant starts to leave.

The telephone rings and the woman answers it. She says: "Oh, you want a butler and a man to superintend the kitchen. There is one here now." The agent takes the telephone from her and starts talking. He says: "You want a butler and a man to superintend the kitchen? I have a good man. How much will you pay? A hundred dollars a week? Is the job permanent?" Meanwhile the applicant is nudging him and saying: "I'm just the man for the job." The agent then says: "Give me the address and I will have a man right over."

The address is written down, and the applicant beams at the prospect of getting a job. The agent, however, reaches for his hat and coat and starts for the door. The applicant says: "Where are you going? Why don't you give me the address?" The agent answers: "I'm going after that job. This is the first call I've had in two years."

STYLE SHOW

THE stage should be set to represent a Ladies' Ready-to-Wear Shop. Any sort of background will be all right. The scene is supposed to be laid in a fashionable ladies' shop. The characters should be:

The Shopkeeper

The French Maid, assistant to the Shopkeeper

The Bride-to-Be

Mother of the Bride-to-Be

The shopkeeper and her assistant are on the stage busy at anything they desire when the bride-to-be and her mother come in. The bride-to-be is shopping and the shopkeeper displays different kinds of dresses. These are worn by models, who should be boys dressed up as girls.

First there should be a street dress, then an afternoon dress, an evening dress, a sports outfit, pedal pushers, and lounging pajamas. There might be two or three of each displayed, depending upon the number of boys available to take part.

Do not have too much conversation or let the stunt last too long. The main feature will be the laughs when the models enter.

This is a very effective stunt and one that needs very little rehearsal.

INDIAN MEDICINE

HAVE a person dressed as an old Indian Medicine Man. He has bottles of medicine for sale.

Two women come on the stage. They have large sheets thrown around their shoulders and pinned down the front. One of these looks like a very large woman as she enters, because she has an umbrella raised under the sheet. The other woman is thinner and should be as slim as it is possible to represent her.

They ask the old Indian about his medicine and he tells them it is wonderful medicine and that it will make fat people thin and thin people fat. They buy a bottle of the medicine, and the one who has the umbrella raised takes a dose. After a moment she lowers the umbrella to give a very humorous impression of rapidly losing weight. The thin one then takes a dose of the medicine and in just a moment she raises the umbrella under the sheet to give the impression of rapidly gaining weight. This stunt will bring down the house if properly carried out.

WHAT IT TAKES TO MAKE A MAN

BY MRS. E. RICHEY CLAWSON

PROLOGUE

[*The stunt opens with the sounding of a bugle call. The curtain is drawn and a herald reads the Prologue.*]

"Oh where are the young folks,
Where are the young folks,
The young folks who hail from Miami?"

[*A large group enters from the back of the auditorium and marches down the aisle as one of the group answers the herald.*]

"Here we come.
We're ready to do our stunt.
We hope you'll like it
And not think it the bunk.
We'll do our best
With what we find
And leave the rest to your keen mind.
Now watch us make a man without a flaw,
And when we've finished you'll stand in awe.
                                    [*Curtain.*]

Act I

[*When the curtain is opened again the stage is set with a table on which are test tubes, a tube holder, some bottles, spoons, a medicine dropper, scales, and anything else to make it look like a chemical laboratory.*]
[*Two chemists enter, discussing an experiment one is about to make.*]

First Chemist. Surely you would not be so foolish as to think you can make a man. You are assuming the prerogative of God. Only God can make a man. He made him in his own image and breathed into him the breath of life. Such an attempt is foolish indeed.

Second Chemist. I believe that God made man originally. But we scientists know by this time what he is made of. Repeatedly we have taken the body of a man and analyzed it and we have ascertained all the ingredients that go into a human body. I have it here and will read it to you: "Here is what a man is made of: It all can be bought for about one dollar. To be exact it is a shopper's dollar, 98 cents. In a human body there is enough fat to make seven bars of soap, enough iron to make a sixteen-penny nail, enough sugar to fill a sugar bowl, enough lime to whitewash a chicken coop, enough phosphorus to make 2,200 matches, enough magnesia for one dose of milk of magnesia, potassuim enough to explode a toy cannon, and enough sulphur to rid a dog of fleas, enough iodine to fill a thimble, and enough water to water a horse." Now what I purpose to do is to take all of these ingredients, mix them in their proper proportions and let them stand for a while, and see if the chemical action will not set in and produce a man. I have ordered the ingredients and they will be coming very soon.

First Chemist. Well, I do not believe that you will be successful, but I will help you mix the ingredients.

[*At this point different ones enter with the above-mentioned ingredients—soap, a nail, sugar, lime, matches, milk of magnesia, sulphur, iodine, big bottle of water. These in turn are measured and put into a large container, such as a large jar or tub. When all the ingredients have been mixed the container is left to precipitate, the curtain is drawn, and the first act ends.*]

Act II

[*The curtain opens with a young man lying on the table that the chemists were using. He lies still with eyes closed and appears to be asleep. The chemists enter and examine the man, and are convinced of the success of their experiment, but face the fact that he lacks life. They decide that some higher power or intelligence must be invoked to give him life.*]

[*The Fairy Queen Enters.*]

Fairy Queen. I am the Fairy Queen. I came in answer to your desire for a higher power. I see you have made a lifeless man. If you desire, I will try my power on giving him life.

Chemists. Surely, you may attempt to give him life.

Fairy Queen [calls the other fairies].

Haste, ye fairies,
Bring with you
Gifts that will this man imbue.
With life, activity, and growth,
Intelligence and reasoning,
The power to love, the power to hope,
With faith and loyalty as seasoning.
No longer then a clod to be,
But a glorious personality.

[*The fairies enter, any number of them, dressed in flowing costumes. They dance around, some of them lay their hands on the man, others take hold of his hands, one may kiss him as he begins to awaken. Finally he rubs his eyes, jumps up, and looks around. After this he may do something to show that he really has life and pep, as lead a yell, make a talk, do a tumbling act, do some shadow boxing, or lead a song. What he does will end the stunt.*]

[*Finis.*]

AU REVOIR

THIS little skit may be used between acts.

Two men meet in center of the stage and talk *ad lib.* for a moment. They may pass the time of day or talk about the weather, or any current topic of interest just for a moment.

As they separate one of them says: "Au Revoir."

The other says: "What you talking about, au revoir?"

First. Why, don't you know what *au revoir* is? That is good-by in the French language.

Second. Is that so?

They start to separate again and the second says: "Carbolic acid."

First. What in the world are you talking about? Carbolic acid.

Second. Didn't you tell me that *au revoir* was good-by in the French language?

First. Sure I did; but what's that got to do with carbolic acid?

Second. Oh, that's easy, *carbolic acid* is good-by in any language.

KITCHEN CABINET ORCHESTRA

THE kitchen cabinet orchestra is a good stunt, but some care should be exercised in selecting those who have good voices, and there should be some rehearsing. Each player in the orchestra is provided with an instrument, to which has been attached a kazoo. This is a small, inexpensive instrument which can usually be purchased at the five-and-ten-cent store or the music store in any city. Imitations of the sounds of instruments can be made on the kazoo, and a number of good voices, especially mixed voices, give a very pleasing result.

Someone who is very clever at improvising should be asked to make the instruments. A cornet could be made from a rolling pin, with a funnel on one end and the kazoo attached to the handle on the other. A clothes basket with a mop stick and some old wires could be made into a bass viol. A bass horn can be improvised out of an inner tube attached to a funnel and some other kitchen utensil. A long-handled frying pan might be made into a violin. A washing tub would make a good bass drum, and a small dishpan would make a good snare drum. The leader could use a dish mop for a baton.

It would be better to have each one improvise his own instrument. In this way you would get a variety of ideas.

The program should be given from a stage, and old tunes and popular music should make up the program. Lively songs like "The Old Gray Mare, She Ain't What She Used to Be" and "It's a Long Way to Tipperary" would be good beginners. Of course play "Dixie" and "Yankee Doodle." It would be well to put in some of the war songs, like "K-K-K-Katy" or "There's a Long, Long Trail a-Winding" or "Keep the Home Fires Burning." Put in some of the old Southern melodies like "Carry Me Back to Old Virginny "or "My Old Kentucky Home" or "Way Down upon the Swanee River." Get some of the old tunes, like "Just a Song at Twilight." Others that might be suggested are "Silver Threads Among the Gold," "Springtime in the

Rockies," "When Your Hair Has Turned to Silver," "Pal of My Cradle Days," "Mother Macree," and end up with "God Be with You Till We Meet Again" or "Perfect Day." These, however, are merely suggestions; but any musical program would be suitable and very pleasing.

THE QUESTIONABLE WELL

CONSTRUCT out of old boards a box about three feet square and about two and a half feet high. Have board extending into the air from each side and a board nailed across the top from which is hung a rope with a hook on it, so that a bucket can be hooked on the rope and a small part of the top of the bucket can be seen from the audience. Get about two or three pounds of rice and put in the bucket. Fill a dipper about half full of water and set it in the bucket and on the rice.

When the curtain is pulled no one is on the stage, but a couple enters. The girl says: "I am thirsty. Look, here is a well." They go to the well, and the boy picks up the dipper and hands it to her. She smells the water, says "I do not believe that water is good," and puts the dipper back in the bucket taking care not to spill the water. This couple retires and another couple enters immediately. This couple goes to the well, and the boy says to the girl, "Will you have a drink?" to which she replies, "No, thanks." The boy then takes the dipper, tastes the water, says, "My gracious, that water isn't fit to drink," and throws the water on the floor. This couple passes on and a third couple enters and goes to the well. The boy dips down as if to get a dipper of water, puts it to his nose, smells it, says "I don't believe that water is fit to drink," and hands the dipper to the girl. The girl smells it and says, "Good gracious, no." The boy then takes the bucket from the hook and throws the rice into the audience.

As all have received a very vivid impression of water being in the bucket, there will be much dodging to get out of the way of the water, and everybody will be surprised when it is found that the bucket contained rice.

This may be done by three persons instead of three couples, and could be done quite as effectively by two persons.

THE BURIAL OF THE GIANT

THE Burial of the Giant can be easily worked up and will create a lot of good fun.

Affix a pair of large rubber boots to two poles about ten feet long, nailing strips across the poles about two and a half feet long so as to make a sort of litter. Build this up with pillows in such a way that it will look like the body of a giant, and cover this over with a sheet so that when this litter is raised to the shoulders of the ones carrying it, the sheet will hang down on the floor. One man walks behind the sheet with his head thrown back in such a manner that it will look like the giant's head. His face should be whitened with powder, and he should have his eyes closed and appear as one dead.

One man walks behind with the poles on his shoulders and the other in front with the rubber boots over his shoulders. A funeral march should be played while the procession marches across the stage. They may march around behind the back curtain and across the stage two or three times.

THE WHOPPER CLUB

A STUNT FOR SMALL BOYS

Two or three boys sit at the entrance of a tepee tent on the stage. Other boys approach and ask about the meaning of the tent and the costumes of the boys who sit at the door. They get an answer that this is the tent of the Whopper Club. They ask how one can become a member of the Whopper Club and are told that they must tell a story of adventure or experience which, in their estimation, is a Whopper. This will admit them. This they proceed to do. Have each one tell a story and the judges decide whether they are to be admitted or not.

Some stories that may be told are the following:

1. I was coming through the Jungle of Africa one day, where I had gone with Frank Buck, when all of a sudden I saw a lion coming at me with open mouth. I drew back my fist to try and defend myself and my fist landed in the throat of the lion. I decided that I would ram my hand down his throat and choke him to death. I pushed my arm right through his body and got hold of his tail. I pulled on this with all my might. The lion by this time had started to realize his plight and began to back off. I kept hold of his tail and pulled it right through his body. The lion kept backing off and I kept holding on to his tail with all my might. Finally the lion was turned completely wrong side out. I never saw such a funny sight in my life.

2. I was walking in the garden the other day, and I saw two large snakes fighting. They were fighting to the death as if they were mortal enemies. Finally one snake grabbed the other snake's tail and started swallowing. This snake in turn grabbed his tail and started swallowing. I stood right there and watched them swallow each other. I never saw anything quite so funny in my life.

3. I was out in the Rocky Mountains bear-hunting last January. It was fifty degrees below zero. I met this bear, and at first I was so scared that great beads of perspiration came out on my forehead. But these immediately froze. I did not have any buckshot, so I dropped these frozen beads of perspiration down in my gun and fired. The heat from the friction in the gun barrel melted the frozen beads of perspiration; but when the air struck them they froze again, but into icicles, and so a dozen icicles struck the bear in the head and penetrated his brain. They did not immediately kill him, but only stunned him. In just a moment, however, the heat in the bear's body melted the icicles, and he died from water on the brain. That is the funniest way I ever killed a bear.

4. My father used to work in a soap factory and one day when he was working on the tenth floor a fire broke out and all means of escape were cut off. What do you suppose my father did? Well, he didn't stay there and get burned up. Not him. He quickly mixed some soap in some

water and made a big lather. Then he poured this soapsuds out the window and went down the lather.

5. Aw, shucks, that's nothin'. My daddy used to work in a rubber boot factory and one day when he was working up on the twentieth floor a fire broke out and he had no way to escape. An idea came to him. He put on a pair of rubber boots, and then he put on a larger pair over them, and then another pair over them, and so he kept on putting on larger boots until he had on twenty pairs. Then he jumped out of the window. He bounced back up and down again, and he just kept on bouncing back and forth, until they finally had to charter a helicopter and get a man to snatch him from the air and save his life. It was the funniest thing I ever saw when he was bouncing up and down.

6. When my dad was a young man he was out West and stayed at a hotel. When he went to bed he found that the bed was buggy. This made him restless and during the night he took the nightmare. Say, what do you reckon that dad of mine did? Why, he just put the mare in the buggy and got up and took a buggy ride. When he came back he said: "Thanks for the buggy ride."

PEANUT TAKE IT OR LEAVE IT

THE NATIONAL BROADCASTING COMPANY radio program that is called "Take It or Leave It" has attracted so much interest that the expression "the $64 question" is now used around the world. This stunt program is based on that famous program in that the contestants are selected and quizzed, but here peanuts are used instead of money.

The stage should be set to represent a radio broadcasting station with microphones and other paraphernalia usually found on such a stage. There should be a piano to be used in the musical quiz. The arrangement of the stage will do much to enhance the effectiveness of the stunt.

The Master of Ceremonies must make preparations in advance, such as having the list of categories printed on a placard or on a blackboard. He must have the questions and answers printed on cards for his own use so that he will be perfectly familiar with each category. It will add zest and interest if he is able to ad-lib a few humorous expressions into the questions and answers.

As many contestants should be selected as the time allotted will permit. It will probably take about two or three minutes for each contestant. If eight are selected, this will take about thirty minutes together with the Grand Sham question.

If the Master of Ceremonies wants to try the musical category, he will have to arrange to have someone play on the piano, accordion, or some other instrument the tunes he wishes to place in this category.

The contestants are quizzed one by one, and if they fail to answer one of the questions, they may stand by for the Grand Sham Question. Prizes for answering the questions will be 1, 2, 4, 8, 16, 32, and 64 peanuts. The prize for answering the Grand Sham Question may be a box of peanut brittle.

When the categories on which questions are to be asked have been posted and the stunt is ready to start, select eight persons from the audience, or have them selected in advance. It must be understood that everything is unrehearsed. No one of the contestants knows what the categories are to be until the program starts, and no one but the Master of Ceremonies knows the answers, which he should have on cards.

The contestants are introduced one by one and may be introduced in any way the Master of Ceremonies thinks proper. If the group is a young people's summer gathering made up of groups from several cities in the state, it would be well to give the name and the city from which each contestant comes. Here the Master of Ceremonies can ad-lib some questions before the contestant chooses his category.

The following categories are suggested, and the questions and answers are given below.

1. Historical and Fictional Characters by Clues
2. Tables, Measures, and Dates
3. Animals and Insects
4. Questions about Games and Sports
5. Questions about Historical Characters
6. Bible Questions
7. Famous Quotations: "Who Said This?"
8. Musical Quiz

Given below for the information of the Master of Ceremonies are questions that may be asked under each of the above suggested categories. You will note that while only seven questions are necessary if all are answered, in some cases the contestant may miss the first or second one, and by having a few extra questions the Master of Ceremonies may be able to use the same category again if he has seven questions left.

HISTORICAL AND FICTIONAL CHARACTERS BY CLUES

1. What character is suggested by a rainbow? Noah.
2. What character is suggested by a kite? Benjamin Franklin.
3. What character is suggested by a slingshot? David.

4. What character is suggested by a hatchet? George Washington.
5. What character is suggested by a steamboat? Fulton.
6. What character is suggested by a rail fence? Abraham Lincoln.
7. What character is suggested by a burning bush? Moses.
8. What fictional character is suggested by a wolf? Red Riding Hood.
9. What fictional character is suggested by a footprint? Robinson Crusoe.
10. What fictional character is suggested by a bow and arrow? Robin Hood.

Tables, Measures, and Dates

1. How many states are there in the Union? 48.
2. How many original English colonies were there in America? 13.
3. How many men are on a football team? 11.
4. How many pecks are in a bushel? 4.
5. How many days are there in September? 30.
6. How many square inches are in a square foot? 144.
7. How much is a gross? 144.
8. When did Columbus discover America? 1492.
9. When was the Declaration of Independence signed? 1776.
10. On what day of the month was Pearl Harbor bombed? December 7 (1941).

Animals and Insects

1. Are a cow's ears before her horns or behind them? Behind.
2. Do fleas have wings? No, they hop.
3. What baby animal has a cow for a mother, a bull for a father, and is known as a pup? Seal.

4. What animal carries its home on its back and has its eyes in its horns? Snail.
5. What is a baby elephant called? Calf.
6. From what animal do we get venison? Deer.
7. From what animal do we get veal? Calf.
8. What animal sleeps all winter? Bear.
9. What animal mother carries her baby in a pouch on her body? Kangaroo.
10. What does a cat have that no other animal has? Kittens.

QUESTIONS ABOUT GAMES AND SPORTS

1. What game is called "the national sport" in the United States? Baseball.
2. What famous baseball player holds the home run record? Babe Ruth.
3. How many points does a football team score on a touchdown? Six.
4. In tennis what is meant by the term "love"? It means no score.
5. What club does a golfer use to knock the ball into the hole? Putter.
6. In basketball how many points are scored by a field goal? Two.
7. In baseball what is meant by a "hit"? A ball hit so that the batter gets on base and the fielder does not make an error.
8. How many holes are there on a regulation golf course? 18.
9. In croquet are there 7, 8, or 9 wickets? Nine.
10. In golf what is a birdie? A hole played in one under par.

QUESTIONS ABOUT HISTORICAL CHARACTERS

1. Who was called the "Father of our Country"? George Washington.
2. Who was called "Old Hickory"? Andrew Jackson.
3. Who was called "Silent Cal"? Calvin Coolidge.
4. What president served longer than any other? Franklin D. Roosevelt.
5. Name one of the presidents who was assassinated? Lincoln, Garfield, McKinley.
6. What queen of England reigned longer than any other ruler of that country? Queen Victoria.
7. Who used the expression "blood, toil, tears and sweat"? Winston Churchill.
8. What was Woodrow Wilson's vocation before he became Governor of New Jersey and President of the United States? College Professor and President of Princeton University.
9. What father and son have been presidents of the United States? John Adams and John Quincy Adams.
10. Who discovered the Pacific Ocean? Balboa.

BIBLE QUESTIONS

1. Who had a coat of many colors? Joseph.
2. Into what did Moses' rod turn when he threw it to the ground? Serpent.
3. Name one of the three Hebrew Children who were thrown into the fiery furnace. Shadrach, Meshach, and Abednego.
4. Who saw the handwriting on the wall? Belshazzar.
5. Who killed a lion and made a riddle about it? Samson.
6. What was the name of Abraham's wife? Sarah.
7. Where did the source of Samson's strength lay? In his hair.

8. What two women were friends of Jesus at Bethany? Martha and Mary.
9. What disciple was a tax collector? Matthew.
10. What books in the New Testament are called the Gospels? Matthew, Mark, Luke, and John.

FAMOUS QUOTATIONS—"WHO SAID THIS?"

1. Who said, "I came, I saw, I conquered"? Julius Caesar.
2. Who said, "Give me liberty or give me death"? Patrick Henry.
3. Who said, "The British are coming"? Paul Revere.
4. Who said, "Why don't you speak for yourself, John?" Priscilla.
5. Who said, "I do not choose to run"? Calvin Coolidge.
6. Who said, "Fourscore and seven years ago our fathers brought forth upon this continent a new nation"? Abraham Lincoln.
7. Who said, "We must all hang together, or assuredly we shall all hang separately"? Benjamin Franklin
8. Who said, "Go west, young man"? Horace Greeley.
9. Who said, "Old soldiers never die; they just fade away"? Douglas MacArthur.
10. Who said, "Friends, Romans, countrymen, lend me your ears"? Mark Antony in Shakespeare's *Julius Caesar*.

THE MUSICAL QUIZ

The Master of Ceremonies should arrange in advance to have someone play the category of tunes on the piano or some other instrument. The musician and the Master of Ceremonies should have duplicate cards on which the tunes are written by number. Some familiar tunes suggested are:

> "The Missouri Waltz"
> "The Caissons Go Rolling Along"
> "Anchors Aweigh"
> "A Perfect Day"
> "The Wedding March" from *Lohengrin*
> "The Bells of St. Mary's"
> "I Love You Truly"
> "Onward, Christian Soldiers"
> "God Bless America"
> "Alma Mater"

THE GRAND SHAM QUESTION

All who have participated in the quiz program should be allowed to try to answer the Grand Sham Question and win the Grand Sham Prize, the box of peanut brittle. Each contestant should be supplied with paper and pencil and should be told that the first one to write the correct answer will get the prize. There should be sufficient helpers to be judges in this case. A more difficult question should be asked for the Grand Sham Question, one that everyone is not likely to know. One of the following is suggested:

1. Which city is farther north, London or New York? London.
2. What is the capital of Portugal? Lisbon.
3. What percentage of the earth's surface is covered by water? 30%, 40%, 50%, 60%, or 70%? 73.39%.
4. In what state is the most easterly point in the United States located? Maine.
5. What was the slang name for cattle thieves in the old West? Rustlers.
6. Who wrote "The Raven"? Edgar Allan Poe.

7. What president of the United States served two non-consecutive terms? Grover Cleveland.

The following are some pointers for the group that arranges this stunt:

1. There should be no delay or fumbling around in getting the contestants. This may spoil the stunt. It would be better to select a number of contestants in advance and have them sit in the audience. By prearrangement they should resist momentarily when they are invited to come to the stage, as if reluctant or unwilling to participate.

2. It would be a good thing to encourage some audience participation. If the contestant fails to answer a question in a category, the Master of Ceremonies might turn to the audience and ask for an answer from them before he asks the contestant to stand aside for the Grand Sham Question. The audience shouting in unison gives the sense of playing the game.

3. The tone of the quiz should be informal, intimate, and personal. It is up to the Master of Ceremonies to attempt to control the audience so that they will have a sense of mass play and a sense of individual worth as members of a group.

4. The contestant must never be made to feel foolish or inadequate. The Master of Ceremonies should encourage and help with clues as much as possible. When a wrong answer is given, the Master of Ceremonies should say something of a consolatory nature to keep the contestant from losing face.

BURYING THE SENIORS

THIS is a good stunt for the Freshmen or Juniors to use in school or in Young People's Conferences.

Someone is placed on a stretcher and covered with a sheet to represent the corpse and on the sheet is printed, in large letters, "Seniors."

The procession comes in with the pallbearers carrying the stretcher, marching to the funeral march. They come down the aisle and onto the stage of the auditorium. There should be weeping and wailing. When they reach the stage the leader reads:

In all solemnness we have assembled ourselves together for the purpose of burying the Seniors and not praising them. Speaking from the standpoint of the Freshmen, who have had an opportunity of observing the conduct of the Seniors for the past year, we attribute their demise to malnutrition in that they have had too much starch in their diets and have become big stiffs.

Even the President, Dave, although he has had many cares on his shoulders, has found time to try to scare one of the poor Freshman girls, but the joke turned out to be a joke on himself. You see, Dave got a frog one morning with the intention of scaring a Freshman girl with it. That afternoon he came running up to one of the Freshman girls and said, "Here, my dear, is a nice slimy green frog for you." Then he pulled a paper bag out of his pocket to shake out the frog and out fell a ham sandwich. After a moment's hesitation Dave said, "Gee, that's odd. I ate my dinner." So this was the last of poor President Dave and the Senior class, for they died of grief for him.

Even though you are big stiffs, we love you and hope that our departure will be as glorious as yours.

THE JIG-SAW PUZZLE

THE following stunt is adapted for a stage stunt from a skit in the *Saturday Evening Post* by Norman R. Jaffray.

As the curtain opens the "First Addict" and the "Second Paranoiac" are seated at a table working a jig-saw puzzle.

First Addict. Look out! Look out!

Second Paranoiac. I'm only moving this section over. It fits right in here.

First Addict. Don't be silly; it's not even the same color.

A Kibitzer. Hello, folks. Doing a jig-saw puzzle?

Third Maniac. What does it look like?

Kibitzer. I think it's upside down.

Another Kibitzer. It must be Washington Crossing the Delaware. No, wait. Isn't that a horse? Maybe it's a hunting scene.

First Addict [*wearily*]. Harry's doing the horse.

First Kibitzer. I'm sure it's a horse. Where's his left hoof?

Second Addict. Who ever saw a green horse?

Second Kibitzer. Look; this fits! Give me some more red pieces. [*Leans heavily over table.*] Well, that's funny. I was sure it would fit.

First Kibitzer [*drawing up a chair*]. Move over, Harry, will you? [*Shoves him roughly aside.*] We'll just finish this up in a jiffy. Doesn't that round section go in here? [*Lifts it up; it falls to pieces.*] Oops!

First Addict [*darkly*]. We worked two weeks on that section.

Second Kibitzer. It won't take a minute to put it together again. [*Picks up pieces and fumbles with them desultorily— none of them show any inclination to join.*] That's very strange.

Three More Kibitzers. Hello, folks. Doing a jig-saw puzzle? [*They draw up chairs and sit down. The original solvers rise wrathfully to their feet, upsetting the table.*]

NAPOLEON'S FAREWELL TO HIS GRAND-MOTHER

PROLOGUE: Someone comes on to the stage and announces that the next scene will depict Napoleon's Farewell to His Grandmother. He requests the audience to be very quiet and pay strict attention because it is a very sad and heart-rending scene.

SCENE: Dress up a boy like an old woman. The cleverness of getting up a costume will add largely to the success of the stunt. This boy is seated in an easy-chair on the stage. Napoleon rushes in wearing a long coat that comes down to his knees and the sleeves of which almost cover his hands. He also wears a cocked hat and, if it could be obtained, a sword. If not, make a sword out of wood. He rushes on to the stage, waves at the Grandmother, says "Good-by, Granny," and then rushes madly out. This is the sad farewell.

THE RETURN OF MOTHER GOOSE

THE return of Mother Goose is given here for characters who are small children. However, the same program can be used with grown-ups, in which case it would be rather a burlesque or a humorous take-off. On one occasion it was used for a stunt for a group of high school boys. Each character improvised his own costume, and some of these were very clever, particularly Old Mother Hubbard's dog and Mary's little lamb.

SCENE: *The home of Mother Goose. She has been away for a long time, and the room is dusty and untidy. Many articles are piled about the room, and dusty toys belonging to Mother Goose characters are piled upon a mantel or high shelves, or on tables at sides of stage. A row of kindergarten chairs is in a circle at rear of stage.*

TIME: *Present, and in your own locality.*

CHARACTERS: *Mother Goose, a girl about twelve to fourteen years old. King Cole, a boy a little larger than the girl. Old Woman Who Lived in a Shoe, a girl about twelve years old. Use the Mother Goose characters that appear in the second scene, or you may use others if preferred, and you may use as many more as you desire. For the little girls with the dolls and buggies use at least twelve, and as many more as you can secure. If all do not have doll buggies, they may just hold dolls in their arms. They are to be dressed in long dresses made of flowered cretonne or some of the various colors of cheesecloth. The costumes for Mother Goose characters should be made of crepe paper in suitable colors, cambric, calico, or cheesecloth. Use illustrations in any Mother Goose book for copying the costumes. Be sure to rouge the cheeks and lips of all the cast, as stage lights reflect improperly in most auditoriums.*

Scene I

[*Enter Mother Goose, wearing traveling cape, gloves, and quaint hat, with a heavy suitcase in her hands. She enters at center rear door, shines her spectacles as if trying to believe her own eyes, looking about interestedly, and removes wraps. She walks about the stage happily, examining one or two toys, chairs, etc.*]

Mother Goose. [*Facing audience, but as if to herself*] When I left home some time ago, I said I would never return, as the children of today do not need old Mother Goose any more. But my heart yearned so, I just had to come back for a few days. [*To audience*] Now when you were little children, you lived in a world of imagination and believed in toys, dolls, and fairies. But these modern-day children do not believe in me any more or need me and their dolls. I wonder if it could be possible that a few of the children of long ago have remembered me enough to write to me; and it could be possible that Old King Cole—the gay old flirt—has written me. Maybe I should have accepted him. No telling, he and The Old Woman Who Lived in a Shoe may be married by this time, but (*laughing*) imagine Old King Cole as a stepfather to all of her children! [*Goes outside door, returns with her lap full of hundreds of cards, letters, telegrams. Happily excited as she piles them on a table in view of audience.*] Such a lot of mail—and who would have thought they would write me like this? [*tearing many of them open exitedly.*] "Dear Mother Goose: I wonder where it could be that you have gone. Please do come back." Signed by Boy Blue, bless his little heart. Oh, and here is one from Little Miss Muffet: "Dear Mother Goose, I love you so much, and all the children are asking about you. Please come back"—now isn't that just too sweet? Gracious! My cheeks are blushing just like a schoolgirl's—here is one from Old King Cole. Not married yet, I suppose! "Dear, Wonderful Mother Goose: My love for you is still true, and I await your return to ask for the hundredth time the return of my love. Witness the seal of my hand this day—Old King Cole." [*excitedly looking through a great handful*] Well, of all things, one from Jack Be Nimble. It would take me months to answer all of these messages. [*puzzled*] How can I get word to these dear children? I must let them know that I have come back for a visit. [*pondering*] Why, I know! Since I have been gone, these newfangled contraptions called radios have come into style, and folks talk over them and reach many people. Where I have been, I listened in and heard actual human voices. The thing for me to do is to get permission to broadcast—I remember that is what they call it, broadcast—over the land that I have come back for a visit and want all of these dear children to come at once. How stupid of me not to have thought of this while I was away. I could have kept in touch with my friends over the land. Another sign that I am getting old—slow thought. [*Scolding herself as she dons cape, quaint hat, gloves, preparatory to leaving to get in touch with the radio station.*] I have heard that this city has a broadcasting station. What is it they call it? Oh, yes, I remember, they call it WMXQ. But what if the man in charge does not believe that I am the *real* Mother Goose? Stupid! I'll just carry along my lapful of letters and telegrams—that will convince the young gent if he doubts me. [*Piles great mass of mail into her lap and presents a laughable sight as she excitedly goes to door weighted down under the lapful of mail. Turns toward audience.*] There will be extras out when I've finished broadcasting! "Mother Goose has returned for a visit! All children invited to rush at once to her little home!" [*This to be exclaimed in a dramatic, loud tone. She closes door and cur-*

tain slowly falls. Outside, she is heard walking very fast, and the steps fade away as curtain falls.]

Scene II

[*Several days later. Same scene, except Mother Goose has everything shining and clean and dusted. She is still nervously rearranging the chairs as she turns toward audience.*]

Mother Goose. My, such very busy days as I have had! The radio man let me broadcast to my many children, and he said it was one of the most exciting things he had ever put on over his station. Thousands of telegrams came to him asking me to talk again, as everybody is interested in childhood things. I thought that I was entirely forgotten in this modern rush of things, with children who are so sophisticated. [*Takes telegrams from her pocket.*] These have just come [*reads*] "Dearest Mother Goose, I am on my way by airship. Signed Boy Blue!" Another—this is from The Queen of Hearts—"Mother Goose, how wonderful—I am rushing to you in my queen's fastest plane." [*Reads the following and is greatly excited and happy.*] Jack Be Nimble asking if he left his candlesticks here! Humpty Dumpty asking if his large egg is still fresh! The idea, of course! And this looks like the kind of fat message that Old King Cole used to send me [*sniffs at perfume*]. The same kind of violet cologne that he always uses—the old flirt—well anyway, he has been faithful to me [*reads*], "Greatest news ever to come to my kingdom, Mother Goose! I and my three fiddlers are en route in fastest airplane." Now that is just like his spontaneous lovemaking! [*Primping at tiny mirror on wall.*] He may slip in on me, and I must be looking my best! [*The door is excitedly opened with a loud commotion, and in rush Little Miss Muffet, Little Boy Blue, Jack Spratt, and his wife. All grab Mother Goose and whirl her around in a frenzy of happiness, laughing, and exclaiming greetings. The characters are asking questions in a storm of confusion* —"*Where is my platter?*" "*Oh, have you found my horn?*" "*Mother Goose, have you some of those good tarts?*" *Clapping her hand to get attention, she goes to center of stage, and children move on each side in attention and with an old time military salute of obedience.*] Listen, dear, blessed children! I am so delighted that you have come! Look about on the shelves and find your own things; they are all dusted and ready for you. [*They rush to shelves, find articles that go with their Mother Goose rhymes, and at once there is a bedlam of exclamations as they try them to see if in good condition. Outside there is heard loud auto horns and enter Mary, Mary, Quite Contrary, Old Mother Hubbard and her Dog Tray, and The Crooked Man Who Walked a Crooked Mile. All rush and greet Mother Goose. Amid exclaiming greetings, she continues.*] You newcomers hurry and get your things from off the shelves, and all of you be seated. We must have a review of our rhymes. I feel sure you have forgotten them. [*All are seated in row of kindergarten chairs facing audience in semicircle, while Mother Goose sits at table or stands in center front of circle to be seen and heard. She then takes her large roll book of names and with a very large pencil begins to call the roll of Mother Goose characters. Make a long, written list for the girl taking this part to have in her roll book. Those not present are answered for by original comments by others who are present or by Mother Goose. As names of those who have arrived are called, they answer "Present" and Mother Goose says, "Repeat your rhyme." This is done each time with great gusto by the little folks who answer present. Have them memorize correctly the rhyme suitable to their own characterization. She brags on each one with a comment of "Fine, fine."*] Now, that finishes the roll, and we are ready to await the arrival of the other children.

Little Boy Blue. [*alertly*] But Mother Goose, whatever made you think that we had forgotten you or forgotten our rhymes?

Mother Goose. Well, you can scarcely blame me, when all I heard for a year before I left was mothers and fathers talking about how grown-up their children are. I decided that the modern-day children did not need me any more, and so I went away for a long while just to see if I would be missed and invited back.

Chorus of all. For shame! You should have known better. Real children love you and need you just the same as ever before.

Mother Goose. Well, it makes me very happy to have all of you here and to know that others are coming! The— [*listens for a very loud commotion is outside*] That must be some of the others. [*Door is thrown open with a flourish, and in dance lively Old King Cole and his Fiddlers Three. Wild exclamations of delight by all on stage as he embraces Mother Goose, musses up her air, and whirls her around in a mad dance, with the fiddlers jigging wildly and screaming with delight.*] Stop! Stop! King Cole! Your manners are quite shocking for one of your age and great dignity! [*Timidly arranging her hair.*]

Fiddlers Three. Where are our fiddles, Mother Goose?

Mother Goose. Look on the shelves and find them. Children, all of you be seated! [*Claps hands for quiet. All take seats, while Old King Cole tags at her heels lovingly and with ridiculous pantomime of loving despair of winning her attention. Just the second that quiet is restored, another commotion is heard at the door. (Keep up keen enthusiastic movement of all on the stage, and do not let the*

*excitement die down one second. Rehearse this until the
children can keep it up to a high pitch. Let them be
natural in their costumes and gleefully enter into the spirit
of the occasion of the joyous homecoming.*) *Mother Goose
rushes to the door, and children stand up in their chairs,
looking excitedly toward the door as there bustles in with
many joyous exclamations The Old Woman Who Lived in
a Shoe. She and Mother Goose loudly smack greetings and
whirl each other round and round as Old King Cole looks
on admiringly, winking at audience as he says:* "Now I
wonder why women are so excitable!"]

Mother Goose. Oh, I am so happy you have come, dear Old
Woman! Do come in! And where are the children?

Old Woman. They are waiting outside in their big old shoe
that is tied onto a large truck, the dears.

Mother Goose. Well, bring them in at once. [*Watches at
doorway until Old Woman enters ahead of a long procession of daintily dressed little girls with dolls in arms,
some with doll buggies and dolls in buggies. Children
standing on the chairs exclaim with delight and shout,*
"Welcome to the homecoming."]

Old Woman. [*Bustling about getting the little girls in a row
in front of the Mother Goose characters who stand up in
their chairs.*] It is such a task to get so many children
dressed and off in time. I only brought my best little girls.
This crowd of my children never have had to go to bed
without their supper, and this visit to you, Mother Goose,
is a reward for their good behavior! [*The others shout,*
"Oh, how fine to get such a reward!"] Can you make room
for such a crowd of us, Mother Goose? [*She steps aside
to inspect the row of beautiful little girls facing the
audience.*]

Mother Goose. Well, I am dumbfounded over the happen-
ings of the last few days. I did not dream that so many little

girls of this modern day still love their dolls and buggies.

Old Woman. Tut, tut, you are just getting old! [*King Cole interrupts with, "I'd not dare say that to her." All children in the chairs laugh at this to disapproval of Mother Goose, who is teased.*]

Mother Goose. Well, praise be for old-fashioned little girls!

Old Woman. Well, you were just borrowing trouble. Any mother who has only a few children, not half as many as I have, knows that children are just children ages over and the world over.

Mother Goose. [*Weeps joyously as King Cole slyly takes her hand.*]

Old Woman. I want these children of mine to roll their dollies and carry their dollies down the aisle to take their mothers and dads, aunts, uncles, granddads, and grandmothers back to their own childhood. Come, children, follow little Rosie down the steps and show off to your best advantage for me. [*They march down the steps, off the stage, down one aisle, across to other aisle, back to the steps of the stage, to the music of lively marches as the other children then fall in line behind the last little girl, leaving King Cole and Mother Goose in center front stage watching the procession. Have high-school boys to assist the children down and up the steps to prevent anyone falling. Keep the procession moving quietly to lively march; an orchestra, if possible, should be secured for the music. Characters may blow their horns, whistles, etc., as they follow the procession. Fiddlers Three dance down the aisles playing on fiddles. This procession of the doll show can enlist a very large number of little girls and insure you a good crowd in attendance, so do not fail to get just as many little girls as possible.*]

Old Woman. [*When all are in line again*] Fine, fine! But you are staying up way past your bedtime. Get your dollies to sleep, and we will be going back to our dear big, warm, roomy shoe, for Mother Goose has not room for such a crowd tonight. Besides, those noisy Fiddlers there will keep me awake anyway. Sing the rhyme, little children. [*All on stage loudly repeat the rhyme in unison.*]

> We are just little children
> As you used to be.
> We play the same things
> As you did, you see.
>
> Did you think, Mother Goose,
> Fathers and mothers too
> That we were so very different
> From each one of you?
>
> Why of course children love their
> Dollies, and other toys too,
> So don't you worry—
> We are just like you!

[*Mother Goose, Old Woman, and King Cole much pleased as they clap.*]

Old Woman. Come, children, we will go to bed. Good night, all. [*Children repeat their good nights to Mother Goose, who holds the door open. Exit all except Mother Goose, Old King Cole, and Fiddlers Three.*]

King Cole. (*taking Mother Goose's hand*) And now, maybe I can finish my proposal begun so many years ago. You know now that all children need you and love you, and you are going to remain here. We will be married and keep all the children in the land remembering the old-time things of long ago!

Mother Goose. You old dear! The only way to get rid of your proposal is to accept you! [*They embrace.*]

King Cole. Well, I will see you tomorrow, and remember —now the wedding bells will ring for Mother Goose and Old King Cole. [*Fiddlers Three dance about them as King Cole stands in doorway, throwing kisses at Mother Goose.*]

Mother Goose. Never again will I doubt the dear little children. I too must get some sleep for the busy days ahead and tomorrow.

[*Finis.*]

MAN FLOATING IN AIR

THIS is a fake magical stunt which will bring a thrill and a laugh to almost any audience. The effect is that of a man rising and floating in the air. The bench on which he has been lying is taken from under him. As a finale, if desirable, the audience may be shown that it is all a fake.

The following properties are needed:

1. A bench about sixteen inches high and about six feet long, and covered so that an object lying behind it is invisible to the audience.

2. A frame made of pieces of wood 1x2 inches, and so arranged that a pair of shoes may be attached to the ends of the boards in such a way that they will look like a man's feet and legs. This frame should be long enough to fit under

the man's armpits and extend out the approximate length of the remainder of his body. This frame should be padded so that when it is covered, as described later, it will appear to be the man's actual body.

3. Two assistants, with a long sheet to be used to cover the man on the bench. These assistants may be dressed in oriental costume and may carry on a conversation in mumbo-jumbo during the act.

When the curtain opens, the man is lying on his back on the bench with one assistant at his head and another at his feet. Back of the bench and concealed from the audience is the frame with the shoes on it to be used later. After a bit of patter the assistants hold the sheet between the audience and the bench, as if getting ready to cover the man with it. The purpose of this is to give the man on the bench a moment to get fixed. In this brief interim the man puts his feet and legs on the side of the bench away from the audience with his feet resting on the floor. He then lifts the frame with the shoes attached into place on the bench. As soon as he is ready the assistants cover him up with the sheet, leaving an ample portion of the sheet on each side of the bench. The man's head and feet (or rather the fake feet) are not covered. The more carefully the frame is made and padded to resemble the outlines of a man's body, the more effective the stunt will be.

We are now ready for the surprise. As the assistant at the man's feet waves the magic wand the man slowly rises from the bench, and at the same time extends the fake feet and legs in such a way as to make it appear that his entire body is rising. Some practice will be needed for this, as he should arise with his head thrown as far back as possible, so that it will appear to be his real body that is rising. As soon as he is standing on his feet, which must be covered by the over-hanging sheet, the attendant at his head removes the bench from that end of the opening of the sheet so that the man seems to be actually floating in air.

The act may conclude by the man walking off the stage. In this case, as his feet are covered by the sheet he will appear to float off. He should walk straight in front of him and leave by the side exit. If this is done cleverly, it may remain a mystery as to just how the stunt was done.

Another ending, that will probably bring a bigger laugh, is to have one of the assistants step on the sheet, as if by accident, and pull it off the floating man, thus exposing the fake.

DOUBLE SEXTET

ONE of the cleverest stunts we have seen recently was put on by six girls from a Church in College Park, Ga.

The girls were all good singers, which is essential to the success of the stunt. They wore boys' white trousers put on backwards and shirts put on backwards with the neckties hanging down their backs. They wore boys' false faces on the back of their heads.

They side-stepped in from the side of the stage and sang a popular song, stepping to the music and waving their hands. For an encore they turned around, waving their hands behind them in such a way that they appeared to be boys facing the audience, and in this way they sang the encore.

The stunt was so cleverly carried out that they were repeatedly encored. Any six girls who are good singers can make a hit with this stunt.

VICTOR RINGS THE BELLE

AN OLD-FASHIONED MELODRAMA

BY MRS. JAMES STUCKER

CHARACTERS	POSITION OF CHARACTERS	PROPERTIES
Reader	Upstage left	Script
Victor Hero	Off stage right	Ring
Belle Heroine	Off stage right	Cup
Belle's Mother	Off stage left	
Belle's Father	Off stage left	
Hugo Villain	Off stage right	Hat, red scooter
Tree (Arms above)	Center stage	
Moon	On chair behind tree	
Gruff, the dog	Stage right	Dog collar
Pump	Center stage near tree	Cup, bottle of water
Time	Off stage left	Clock
Curtain	Seated near reader	Sign, "Curtain"

THE STAGE SETTING

IF there is a curtain in front of the stage, arrange characters as indicated above before the curtain is opened. If there is no curtain, the actors just take their place on the stage as indicated above and the stunt begins. All characters should have a large placard on their chest to let the audience know what they represent. A little make-up for the dog, Gruff, such as a tail and a burlap sack, would add to the effectiveness of the stunt. The Pump should stand with the left hand extended like a pump handle and should carry a bottle of water from which to pour when the handle is moved up and down. The Moon "beams" by grinning a broad grin, and the Tree expresses emotion by waving the arms like tree branches. Time should have not only a clock, but a placard reading "Time" and another placard, reading "Early Summer Evening," to carry while crossing the stage the first time.

The Reader's Script

The reader tells the story and indicates the actions while the characters pantomime the actions as described. The stunt should be rehearsed a couple of times with the reader so that the characters may fit their actions to the reader's words.

Reader: We now present an old-fashioned melodrama entitled "Victor Rings the Belle."

The Curtain rises. [*Character who is the Curtain stands up.*]

The scene is in the yard of Belle Heroine's house.

The time is early summer evening. [*Character Time crosses the stage with Clock and placards, "Time" and "Early Summer Evening."*]

The big oak tree sways gently in the breeze. [*Tree waves arms gently.*]

The Moon beams brightly through the branches. [*Broad grin from Moon.*]

The Pump creaks lazily. [*Pump moves left arm up and down and makes creaking noise.*]

Gruff, the faithful dog, lying in the yard, yawns and stretches. [*Actions.*]

Belle and Victor enter, hand in hand, gazing amorously at each other.

Victor gets Belle a drink from the pump. [*Victor moves Pump's left arm up and down and holds cup to receive water when poured from the bottle.*]

The Pump gladly yields water for Victor. [*Pump smiles and fills cup.*]

Gruff pants.

Victor pats Gruff.

Belle and Victor bid a fond adieu. [*Exaggerated actions.*]

Belle enters the house where her father and mother are. [*Leaves stage.*]

Victor exits, down the street. [*Leaves stage.*]

Time passes. [*Time walks across the stage with Clock and placard "Time."*]

The old Tree sways in the breeze. [*Tree moves arms.*]

The Moon beams. [*Grins broadly.*]

Gruff goes to sleep. [*Snores.*]

Hugo Villain enters stealthily with his bright red scooter.

He tiptoes past the sleeping dog.

Hugo grins villainously—and twirls his moustache.

He hides the cup by the Pump.

Hugo picks up a rock and throws in the direction of Belle's window. [*Rock must be provided for this act.*]

He beckons to Belle to come out.

The Tree moves its branches angrily. [*Tree moves arms madly.*]

The Moon scowls.

The Pump shakes its handle in rage.

Gruff snores.

Belle enters.

Hugo acts as if famished for a drink. He indicates that there is no cup.

Belle returns to the house for a cup.

Belle returns with a cup. She gives the cup to Hugo.

Hugo pumps with difficulty. [*Pump should hold arm straight out so that it is difficult to move up and down.*]

Pump begrudgingly gives water for Hugo. [*Pours out only a few drops of water.*]

Suddenly Hugo throws cup away, grabs Belle, dropping his hat.

Then he rides off with her on his little red scooter.

The Tree sways violently.

The Moon gasps.

The Pump shakes with rage.

Gruff awakens. He barks.

Belle's mother and father enter from the house.

The father, in great agitation, declares, "Belle's gone!"

The mother rings her hands.

Gruff barks. He brings Hugo's hat to father.

Victor runs in.

He takes the hat, announces that it belongs to Hugo.

The Pump points its handle in the direction of Hugo's departure.

Mother faints into Father's arms.

Victor takes Gruff, who sniffs hat, and they hasten after the Villain.

Time passes. [*Time walks slowly across the stage.*]

Victor soon appears, dragging Hugo. Gruff follows. Belle reappears.

Belle runs to her mother and father. They comfort one another.

Victor shakes his fist at Hugo. Victor points the way for Hugo to leave forever!!!

Hugo takes his hat and shamefully slinks away.

Belle runs to the arms of Victor.

Mother and Father go into the house.

Victor shows a lovely engagement ring to Belle. [*The largest and gaudiest ring that can be obtained.*]

Belle "ah's" in ecstasy.

Gruff pants happily.

The Tree sways delightedly.

The Moon beams.

The Pump nods approvingly. [*Pump bows and pumps arm*] as

Victor Rings the Belle. [*Puts ring on Belle's finger.*]

The Curtain falls. [*Curtain falls to the floor.*]

[*The end.*]

PERSONAL SERVICE TO BOYS

BY PROF. IRVING BAKER

THE following playlet was successfully used by a civic club to show the value of personal service to underprivileged and delinquent boys. The chairman of the committee had asked the Judge of the Juvenile Court to take part. The club member's part was taken by the Chairman of the Personal Service Committee. It could be taken by the Big Brothers' Committee, or whatever committee has charge of this type of work.

CHARACTERS:

A Boy of the Streets

A Policeman

The Juvenile Judge
Club Member, Chairman of Personal Service Committee
One to represent Boy of the Streets three years later
A second Delinquent Boy

Act I

[*Heard off stage the breaking of a pane of glass. Small boy rushes on stage carrying flip and with pockets full of pebbles. Very ragged and dirty in appearance, with suggestion of being undernourished. He looks back to see if anyone is following, then slackens his pace to a walk. At this instant a policeman rushes in and grabs him.*]

Policeman. Here you are! So, it's you that's been breaking all these windows.

Boy. I didn't break the window! Honest I didn't!

Policeman. Quit your lying! Didn't I see you with my own eyes? You'll have to talk with the Judge about this.

Boy. Honest, I didn't mean to break it. I shot at a bird and my hand slipped!

Policeman. Your hand has slipped plenty of times, but I've got you with the goods now. You'll find you slipped just once too often.

Boy. That's the first window I ever broke!

Policeman. Yeah? Tell it to the Judge.

[*Boy makes a desperate lunge and nearly pulls out of policeman's grasp. Policeman yanks him back.*]

Policeman. Come here, you! You're going with me whether you like it or not.

Judge. [*Enters.*] What's the matter, Tom?

Policeman. I caught the kid that's been breaking the windows in all them vacant houses.

Judge. Take him down to the jail, Tom. There will be a session of Court at four this afternoon.

[*Club member, Mr. Paine, enters.*]

Paine. Just a minute, Judge, before you take this boy—
you probably know that we fellows for several years have
been acting as big brothers to some of the boys in this community. This one seems to have been overlooked. I'd like
to ask him a few questions if you don't mind.

Judge. Sure, Mr. Paine. Go right ahead!

Paine. What's your name, sonny?

Boy. Johnny Carter.

Paine. Where do you live?

Boy. 618 Southern Avenue.

Paine. How old are you?

Boy. Thirteen.

Paine. What do your folks do?

Boy. My dad's a night watchman at a factory. I ain't got
no mother.

Paine. Any brothers and sisters?

Boy. No.

Paine. Why did you break those windows?

Boy. It didn't make no difference! There ain't nobody
lives in them houses.

Paine. Why aren't you in school, Johnny?

Boy. I don't go! I don't like school!

Paine. Does your father know you don't go to school?

Boy. Sure! He don't care so long as I leave him alone.

Paine. Johnny, I know a man in our Club who would be
glad to have a boy like you for a younger brother. Would you
like that?

Boy. Sure! I'd like to have a big brother.

Paine. Judge, if you'll turn Johnny over to me instead of
taking him to Court, I'll be responsible for him, and I believe we can work out a lot of things that might be to our
benefit.

Judge. That suits me fine, Mr. Paine. You're getting me

out of an awkward position. I have no choice but to send such a boy to the reform school, or to send him back to the streets. Either would be fatal to him. He needs the helping hand of a big brother.

Paine. Thanks, Judge! I want to show you what results can come from our program of Personal Service to Boys in the course of three years. Let's go, Johnny!

Act II

[*Crash of breaking glass off stage. Second small boy saunters on—looks around to see if he is observed— then pulls flip from pocket, fits stone, and aims it at window. First boy, grown taller, enters and grasps his hand.*]

First Boy. Don't do that, buddy! You know better than that!

Second Boy. What of it? Nobody lives there!

First. That doesn't make any difference! Somebody has to pay for every window that's broken. Suppose you had a house and went away for the summer and found your windows smashed when you came back. How would you feel?

Second. Who do you think you are, anyhow?

First. It doesn't make any difference who I am. You've got no more right to break windows than I have to break your flip. This is a free country, but that doesn't give you any right to break windows. Free means that you can own things and that no one else has a right to break them, or take them from you. [*Second boy looks at him in wonderment as he continues after a brief pause.*] I used to have a flip like this. I used to go around town and break windows just the way you are doing. I guess I didn't have anything else to do. But I got into trouble, lots of it, and once I got arrested. A man happened to be there and he got me out of the jam, and we've been brothers ever since. He sent me to school, showed me all about his business, watched my school work, took me on trips. He is the grandest guy I ever met, and he belongs to a local civic club. He called what he did for me Personal Service. [*Pause.*] Say, did you ever play baseball?

Second. Yes; a few times.

First. I've got a baseball team and we're having a game tonight. If you want, you can come. We could use another boy.

Second. I'd sure like that!

First. O. K. Let's go!

SECTION II

Banquet Stunts

BANQUET STUNTS

It is the custom of many organizations to have an annual banquet. The writer knows of a Church School class that has had an annual banquet each year for the past twenty-five years. Persons who have been members of the class in past years and have left the city are invited to return for the banquet. In many young people's conferences and camps there is always a banquet during the camping period. At this time the young people put on their best dress clothing and partake of better than usual food, and arrange a special program for the banquet table. Many civic clubs have at least an annual banquet, and some have them oftener than annually.

INSTALLATION BANQUET

A suitable time to have a banquet is when the new officers are to be installed. Make this installation banquet a time to express appreciation to the officers who have served during the past year and a time to install the officers for the coming year. Have the program committee arrange a special program of music and stunts, and plan for a good speaker.

Decorations and Printed Programs

Decorations appropriate to the season of the year or to the selected theme of the banquet should be arranged. For example, the tables may be decorated to represent each month of the year, or there may be four tables decorated to represent the four seasons of the year. Many groups build their programs around some country, as, for example, a mission field. In a year when Africa was the subject of study by mission groups, many banquets were arranged with an African motif, both by adult and youth groups. For a jungle

145

atmosphere, brown and green strips of crepe paper were braided into thick vines and draped over ceiling, windows, and doorways. Leaves made of paper were attached at intervals on the vines. A large map of Africa was placed behind the speaker's table, and large cutouts of animals were placed at strategic spots on the wall. This is but an example, and many other themes or subjects could be treated in like manner. Much can be done with the printed program to create atmosphere. Many times these programs may be cleverly stenciled, as, for example, a banquet held near Christmas might have the programs printed in the shape of a bell, or a banquet near Valentine's Day might have the programs stenciled in the shape of a heart. Programs for more formal banquets should be printed and should give the menu, the program, and perhaps some songs to be sung by the group.

Naming Courses on the Menu for Members

A CLEVER stunt is to name the courses on the menu after members of the group. If this is done, it will be necessary to contact the caterer who is serving the banquet and ascertain what the menu will be. Given below is an example of the naming of the courses for members of the group, the name of the member being in quotation marks.

MENU

"MAA'S" COOKING

"PAINE" SHRIMP COCKTAIL

"KING" OLIVES   "CHRISTIE" CELERY

"GEORGIE" ROAST TURKEY A LA "DOVE"

WITH "RIDDLE" DRESSING

"HATFIELD" BEANS   "FLURRY" POTATOES

AS "PERRY" "GUS" TIPS SALAD

"GOODIE" "NEWBERRY" PIE   "THARP" KNIFE USE FORK

"BREWER" COFFEE   "WHITMAN" MINTS

"KATZ" NIP TEA   "BOWEN" MILK

"BLACKBURN" "BAKER" ROLLS   "ATWELL" WATER

"BERNHART?" - "FEARS?" - "BELLIN" PILLS CAN BE
OBTAINED FROM "BUTLER"
IF YOU DON'T LIKE THE FOOD, "DUTEL" "JACK."
WE HOPE YOU HAVE A "MARY TOOHEY" TIME

SEES ALL—KNOWS ALL

HAVE one of your members disguised with whiskers, let him wear a turban, and have him announced as the man who "sees all, knows all." Prepare in advance, or have him prepare, a list of funny questions which he is to answer. These questions are purported to have been asked by members of the club. In order to put this ruse over, have two boxes, just alike, with a hole cut in the top of each of them. Circulate slips of paper similar in size and shape to those on which the questions have been prepared in advance, and ask the members to write out questions for the man of mystery to answer. After each one has written a question and deposited it in the box, the assistant, before turning the box over to the man of mystery, changes the boxes and gives him the one prepared in advance. After the man of mystery has answered nearly all of the questions, he may state that time does not permit him to finish. In this way the members will be led to believe that all the questions have been answered except their own. This stunt will go over well if the ruse is carried out smoothly.

THE SUM OF THE NUMBERS

THE leader of any group may create much interest and teach a good lesson in mathematics by posing the following problem to the group: "Calculate the sums of fifty pairs of numbers from 1 to 100, or 1 to 1,000." If he has someone in the group who is an accountant, he might tip him off to hold up his hand and give the answer immediately while the others fumble around and figure and, in all probability, conclude that such a problem is impossible without too much

figuring. The solution is very simple, however. All one has
to do is to group the numbers as follows: 1 and 100, which
add up to 101. The same will be true of all the other numbers,
as 2 and 99, 3 and 98, 4 and 97. It will thus be apparent that
there are in 100 exactly 50 pairs of numbers each totaling
101, the sum of all the numbers will be 50x101, or a total of
5,050. In 1,000 the same would be true with an increased
number of pairs. For 1,000 it would be 500 pairs of numbers
each totaling 1,001. When you multiply 1,001x500, you have
the total of 500,500.

HOW TO TELL AGE AND BIRTH MONTH

HERE is a simple trick that will get a person to tell you
his age and the month in which he was born. Ask any person
or group of persons to write down the number of the month
in the year in which they were born, as: January, 1; February,
2; October, 10. Below is given an example of how this will
work out and the strange results to be obtained.

Number of birth month	10	(October)
Multiply this number by 2	20	
Add 5	5	
	25	
Multiply the answer by 50	50	
	1,250	
Add your age (the person was 32) ..	32	
	1,282	
Subtract 250	250	
	1,032	

When the person has finished, you ask for the total. In the
case given above, the first two numbers indicate the birth

month, the tenth month, which is October. The last two
figures indicate the age, which is thirty-two.

In a result with only two numbers, as for example twenty-
nine, this would mean that this person was born in February
and was nine years old. In a three-figure number, such as
319, this would indicate that this person was born in March
and is nineteen years old.

The results will be the same with any age or birth month,
and the leader can always tell from the final number both
the birth month and the age. Whenever the month is one
digit and the age is also one digit, the middle zero of the
final number must be disregarded.

A TOAST TO THE BANQUET

THE following poem may be read in unison at the banquet, or printed on the front of the program:

We may live without poetry, music, and art;
We may live without conscience, and live without heart;
We may live without friends; we may live without books;
But civilized man cannot live without cooks.
We may live without books—what is knowledge but grieving?
We may live without hope—what is hope but deceiving?
We may live without love—what is passion but pining?
But where is the man that can live without dining?
                                        —*Owen Meredith.*

DRAWING FOR THE BABY

SEVERAL years ago a very clever stunt was put on by a
Tennessee club. It was a Ladies' Night banquet and one
member was primed to make a speech telling the club about
a baby that had been left an orphan with no one whatever
to take care of it. He also told the club that it was a fine
baby and was worthy of a good home. He really made an
appealing speech and tried to touch the hearts of those who
were listening. At the conclusion of his speech, another mem-

ber was primed to get up and make a motion that the club adopt this baby and that they prepare attendance slips and the member whose name should be first drawn would be asked to take the baby and raise it, the club to pay that member the cost of taking care of the baby. Enough members should be in on this, especially the ones who have the most influence in the club, to put this motion through. Of course the one who is to receive the baby has been picked out in advance; the most bashful member in the club or some bachelor member should be the one whose name is drawn to receive the baby.

Of course, there is no such baby, but in the case of the Tennessee club they used a little goat or kid, and when it came time to bring the baby in, a woman dressed as a nurse brought in the little goat wrapped in a blanket, and put it in the arms of the member whose name was drawn.

TRUTH OR CONSEQUENCES

TAKING the radio program of the same name as a pattern, work up some stunts and questions. The penalty for not being able to answer the question would be to do the stunt. Such stunts as drinking a bottle of Coca Cola through a baby-bottle nipple, or eating crackers and then whistling a tune, might be used. The questions should be very difficult to answer, such as, "How many square miles in the state of California?" Or, "Which is farther south, Rome or New York?" Two or three who answer incorrectly might do one of the stunts, and another group of two or three would do another stunt.

THE ALARM

WE saw a very clever stunt worked at a Ladies' Night not very long ago, in which an alarm clock was set to go off in about two minutes. Flowers were given out to the ladies

at this table and lemons were given out to the men. They
were told that anyone who held a flower or a lemon when
the alarm sounded would have to pay a fine. The rule was
that if a lemon or flower was presented to you, you had to
take it; or if it was dropped, the person who touched it
last had to pay the fine. It would be a good plan to have
all the ladies who held the flowers to do a stunt, such as
singing a song, and after this is over present each one with
a corsage. Think of some crazy stunt for the men who held
the lemons and give each one of them a corsage of onion tops.

EXTRA! EXTRA!

At a Civic Club convention banquet the speaker was a
past president of the international organization. Someone
in advance had got hold of his subject and the gist of his
speech, together with his picture; in this case it was a large
newspaper cut. After the final edition of the afternoon
paper had been printed, the arrangements had been made
to change the "streamers" on the front page and some of
the set-up, making a streamer out of the subject of the
past president's speech, giving the gist of his speech, and
printing his picture in the center of the front page.

As soon as the speech was concluded, a group of news-
boys ran in shouting "Extra! Extra!" The papers were
given away in this case, not sold. It was quite a surprise
to the speaker, as well as to those in attendance, to read the
gist of the speech from the newspaper immediately upon
its conclusion.

LADIES IN CHARGE

A good stunt for a banquet would be to have the ladies
take charge of the program and conduct it as it should be
conducted. Let them start out with the introduction and let
each woman introduce herself by her first name, and her

husband by the name by which she calls him. The one who presides and others who take part in the meeting are required to do as the men do and call each other by their first names. If the speaker or any other person taking part on the program addresses any man, she must not call him Mister, but must call him by his first name or nickname. This will create a lot of good fun.

FAVORS

It is always a good plan to have favors at a banquet. Any local bookstore will assist the committee in getting in touch with a supply house and favors can be ordered at a very small cost. Paper hats for the men and ladies are always good; also there should be some noise-making toys like horns and whistles that make a noise if you blow in them; jumping frogs, etc. (Information on how to secure such favors may be obtained from a sporting goods store, costume shop, or department store.)

BREAK THE CAMERA

A good stunt to pull at a Ladies' Night banquet is to have someone come for the purpose of taking a picture of the group. Have a camera improvised out of some kind of stained glass and fasten this to a tripod. It does not make much difference about the construction of the camera, just so it will make a lot of noise when it is turned over. It can be covered with a black cloth so that guests will not know that it is a fake. After the photographer has succeeded in getting everyone to pose and is ready for the flashlight picture, someone very awkwardly turns over the camera and breaks it all to pieces. Perhaps by this time everyone will catch on that it is a joke.

BALLOONS

WE were present at a Ladies' Night banquet at which the chairman of the Program Committee released a large number of gas balloons. These immediately ascended to the ceiling. Each of these had a number attached to it, some of them lucky numbers, and prizes were given to those who got the lucky numbers. The idea is to give the ladies the task of bringing down the balloons without the assistance of the men. They may use any means, and it does not matter if they burst the balloons, just so they bring them down. The men will get a great deal of enjoyment watching the ladies bring down the balloons. The ladies will have a lot of fun out of it themselves.

THE VENTRILOQUIST

HAVE one of the large men of your club to act as the ventriloquist, and pick two smaller members and paint them up to act as dolls or dummies. These two are seated on the knees of the large man. He has prepared in advance some questions to ask them. He might get some ideas for these questions from the conundrums in the last chapter in this book, or he may work them out somewhat after the order of a minstrel show and crack jokes on different members. Three clever members could work this up into a very interesting stunt.

BEDROOM SUITE

AT a local civic club banquet, the chairman of the Program Committee was the manager of a furniture store. It had been announced in advance that as an attendance prize a bedroom suite would be given away. Before this occasion, the furniture store manager brought over a beautiful bedroom suite and had it on display. There was much excitement at the time of the drawing for the attendance prize. It was announced that the fifth name drawn would receive the prize and the names were called one at a time until the fifth name was called. This member was very much delighted, thinking he was going to receive the bedroom suite, which was in all probability worth hundreds of dollars; but instead of receiving a gift of a bedroom suite he was presented with a pair of pajamas and was told that that was the bedroom suit.

PRESENTING THE GRAND PIANO

As a reward for her services as a pianist of the club, it was announced at the "Ladies' Night" banquet that she was to be presented with a handsome present and that the committee, after thinking it over, had decided to present her with a baby grand piano. Six or eight members were sent to bring in the piano, and when they returned they carried a small toy piano from a toy store. The chairman explained that this was the baby grand piano. If the group really desires to make a presentation to the pianist, have the real gift presented following this stunt.

ENTERTAINING THE AMBASSADOR

A VERY clever stunt was worked out by the Entertainment Committee and put over at a banquet in the following manner. The chairman of the Program Committee, during the business session, read some correspondence from the secretary of a man who was supposed to be the Ambassador from Spain. Any other country would do just as well, as China, Japan, Czechoslovakia, or Cuba. The chairman of the program committee states that he has had some correspondence with this man's secretary and that he plans to be in our city in the near future and would like to appear on our program. Several of the members who are in on the stunt make a motion that we entertain this Ambassador.

Later on in the meeting a telegraph boy comes in bringing a telegram reported to be from this Ambassador's secretary, stating that on account of change of plans he will be in the city that evening, and as he has heard that the club is having a banquet he will come to the banquet instead of to the luncheon to which he had been invited.

After a while a bell boy comes in and announces that the Ambassador has arrived and one of the members, disguised with whiskers or in some other manner, comes in with another person disguised as the secretary. They are given a place at the speaker's table. All stand as they enter. The orchestra should play the national air of the country that they are supposed to represent, and finally the Ambassador arises to make a speech. By this time someone will perhaps recognize his voice; and if not, the chairman of the program committee should arise and accuse him of being a sham and jerk off his whiskers. This stunt will bring down the house.

WHERE DID YOU MEET HIM?

A GOOD stunt to pull on Ladies' Night is to call on each one of the ladies present to tell in thirty seconds where, how, and under what circumstances she met her husband. Be sure to limit the time or otherwise it may be too long drawn out.

BACKWARD PROGRAM

TRY running your program backward. The speaker rises and begins to speak at the opening of the meeting. After the speaker has finished, have the chairman introduce the speaker; then have the president introduce the chairman. Then have the introduction of members and guests. Have the song leader lead two or three songs, singing the last verse first and the first verse last, and close with the serving of the meal and the singing of an opening song.

ADVERTISING FAVORS

Ask different members of your club to volunteer to bring some advertising favors to the club each week to place at the plate of each member. Some suggestions: A candy manufacturer might bring to the luncheon a box of a special brand of candy and place one piece at the plate of each member. One of the local dealers in dairy products might bring for each member a pint of milk or a cup of ice cream. Some of the business firms might supply calendars, and a printing company might supply office pads. Manufacturers of different articles might supply samples of their products. In a club of a hundred members you would be able to find fifteen or twenty individuals or firms who would be glad to supply these advertising favors.

EXCHANGING WHITE ELEPHANTS

Nearly everyone has some articles that he no longer uses or cares for, which perhaps some other person would like to have. He may have a book that he has read, or perhaps some article that he has kept in his store until it has become shopworn, or any other article. Arrange a white elephant exchange, and ask each member to bring some such article with him to the luncheon. Put these on a large table, and let each member select the article he desires.

IMPROMPTU STUNTS

This would be a good stunt to put on at a civic club meeting or a party for which no program has been arranged, or in case the program fails to materialize. Pass around slips of paper to all present, and ask each one to write down some stunt that he knows. Where there are as many as fifty, there would be sure to be as many as a dozen good ideas for stunts given. When all have been written, have them placed on a table with the writing turned down. The committee in charge then takes these stunt suggestions, places them in envelopes, and seals them. They are then passed to the guests, and starting with the head table, each man is to do the stunt suggested in his envelope. This will make a good impromptu program.

FATHER TIME REVIEWS THE ACCOMPLISH-MENTS OF THE PAST PRESIDENTS

HAVE a member dressed as Father Time. He should have a bald head (natural or made up), should be dressed in a draped sheet with bare legs and sandals, have a long gray beard, and carry a scythe and scroll.

He enters slowly, and when he reaches the speaker's table he is addressed by the presiding officer, who says: "We are glad to see you, Father Time; will you tell us for what purpose you have come today?"

Father Time says: "My purpose in coming here to-day is to draw back the curtain of the past and let you see some of the important things that have taken place under the leadership of and during the administration of our past presidents. If you will kindly have them brought to me one by one, I shall refresh your memories as to the work accomplished under their leadership."

The past presidents are brought one by one and Father Time gives a brief résumé of the work accomplished during the administration of that president. In order to make it entertaining as well, there should be at least one humorous incident related that transpired during the administration of each one. Start with the oldest past president—that is, the one who was president the longest time ago—and come down to the immediate past president.

If this is used as an installation stunt, the new president could then be introduced and Father Time could make the following prediction: "To you, our President Elect, I extend the heartiest congratulations of one who is passing away never to return. My history is made and my record is forever sealed. But you have a year of accomplishments before you. I predict that under your leadership the club will make great progress and that your accomplishments will be manifold."

If this installation takes place at New Year's time, have a baby dressed as the New Year, with the date printed on a sash and wrapped over its shoulder and around its body, and as Father Time retires this baby is brought in and placed in the arms of the President Elect.

The success of this stunt will depend largely on the ingenuity of the one who writes up the history. By all means do not get a long-winded person, or one who cannot put some humor into it. Do not let it be too long drawn out.

SECTION III

Luncheon Stunts

A TALK ON ATHLETICS

THE meeting for which this stunt was planned was an athletic meeting, and the chairman of the committee had been asked by the other members of the committee to make a speech. He did it in a very unique manner. He went to a cartoonist, or rather an amateur artist, and had him draw several pictures representing the different phases of athletics. This could be done with colored chalk as well as with colors. These pictures he had on an easel, and he turned them as he talked about different athletic games.

The first picture had to do with tennis and was a sketch of one member of the club making a stroke behind his back with his left hand and breaking the strings of his racket in so doing. The ball had eyes, a nose, and a mouth drawn on it, and the mouth was saying, "Ouch!" The lettering on the picture said: "John Carroll, tennis champeen, burst his racket with a left-handed backstroke."

The next picture was of a member of the club who was interested in bowling. The lettering on the cartoon said: "Fred Martin, champion bowler, couldn't pull his finger at a critical moment, and he takes a trip down the alley." The picture showed a bowler following the ball down the alley.

The third picture was of a softball player whistling a merry tune. This effect was made with the notes proceeding from his mouth. He had a bat in his hand and was stepping high. The lettering on the cartoon said: "Lloyd Smith eventually gets a hit." This was pulled on someone who had gone several games without getting a hit.

The next picture represented the batter who had made the highest batting average in the club. He was pictured with a bat in his hand and a crown on his head. There was a picture

161

of a thermometer which had gone up past 500. The lettering said: "King White's Batting Average."

The next picture was of a member of the club with a cane and a crutch, and with bandages around his legs and arms. A bottle of arnica was seen in the background. The lettering said: "Jimmy Brown and His Charley Horses."

The next picture represented a golf course and a player missing a twelve-inch putt into an eight-inch bucket and breaking his putter. In a nearby tree sat a bird that was saying: "What a Shot!" A frog was in the hole with his fingers on his nose. The ball was shown rolling on past the green. The lettering said: "C. W. Misses a Twelve-inch Putt."

As these pictures were turned, the speaker related humorous things that had taken place in connection with the different atheltic games during the year. He also spoke of the facilities provided for lovers of tennis, and of the tennis courts and clubs in the city. He spoke of the plans for softball for the coming season, and of the golf courses and golfers' plans for the coming summer. Anyone who is clever can make a speech with the aid of pictures such as these.

GIVING AWAY AN AUTOMOBILE

A very clever stunt was worked out by an automobile dealer who announced that he was going to present one of his cars at the meeting. He announced that there would be no strings tied to it, and that the one who drew the lucky number would receive the car. All drew for the number, and by prearrangement the mayor received the lucky number. He was told that the car was out in front, and as it was time for the meeting to adjourn, the members would all adjourn to the front of the hotel, where the winner would be presented with the car. It was found that the car to be presented was the oldest and most dilapidated model that could be secured, and the mayor was told it would be necessary for

him to drive the car down the main street. This he did, much
to the amusement of the other members. Of course, the car
was not given away at all, but it was a good joke.

TEN BEANS

GIVE each member of the club ten beans. It would be better
to start this about ten or fifteen minutes before time comes
for the meal, or hold up the meal for a few moments until
this is completed. Any person must forfeit one of his beans
to anyone who speaks to him if he cannot immediately recall
the speaker's name and nickname. After ten minutes, sound
the bell and give a prize to the one who has the largest number of beans. Have the one who has the smallest number
make a two-minute talk on the importance of getting acquainted with all the members of the club.

RECREATION FUND LUNCHEON

THE members arrive at the luncheon to find that only
crackers and water have been prepared for the meal. The
speaker announces that the Board of Directors has decided
that for this day they will have a recreation fund luncheon and
give 95 per cent of the usual cost of their meal to this fund.
He makes a speech calling attention to the dire need of the
fund. He might say that it was brought to the attention of
the directors that many members are overeating and that
doing without one meal will not hurt any of them. After this
has been going on for about ten minutes, have the waiters
march in with the food.

CHANGED NAMES

HAVE the names of members written on cards; or, if you
have identification badges, give these badges out promiscuously. Be sure that no member gets his own badge. During
the meeting every man must answer to the name he has

drawn. The president calls for a report of a committee of which Bill Smith is chairman; Bill Smith must sit quietly while the one who has on his badge makes the report. It should be arranged in advance that the call for such reports as this will be given, and have these reports made by one who knows nothing about the work of that committee. A lot of funny situations can be worked out.

HURLY-BURLY

GIVE each one an envelope which contains written instructions as to what he is to do as soon as the signal is given. A large room would be a good place to pull a stunt like this. The instructions contained in the envelopes should be such as the following: Get up on a chair; jump over a chair; stand on your head; hop around the room; run on all fours, three times around the table; bark like a dog; mew like a cat; bray like a donkey; play like you are a dog chasing a cat; do a tap dance; turn three cartwheels; pose as an Egyptian dancer. This will create quite a hurly-burly when everyone has started doing what he is instructed to do.

PEANUTS AND MILK BOTTLES

DIVIDE your club into two or more sides. Give each member ten peanuts. It will be better to use raw peanuts so that members will not eat them; and, too, this will be cheaper. Each group passes by a milk bottle which is on the floor, and in his turn each member, standing erect and holding the peanut on a level with the nose, tries to drop the nut into the bottle. The group getting the largest number of peanuts in the bottle is declared the winner.

TALL-STORY CLUB

HAVE the stunt committee arrange a prize, say a loving cup, to be given to the one who tells the best story. This may run over an entire year, with a meeting set aside every month,

or two months, for four or five stories. The one who tells
the best story at this meeting gets to keep the cup until the
next meeting, and may compete for it again.

There should be some rules for the stories. A good rule
should be that they are not to be obscene or profane. As there
are usually ladies present, it would be a good rule that nothing
should be told which could not be told in the presence of
ladies. It would be a good plan to let the one who won the
cup at the previous meeting tell a story first; and if none
better is told, he may retain the cup for another month.

SUGGESTED STORIES

1. *Two Chances*. My friend told me that the other day he
met a young man who seemed very blue. He asked the young
man what he was worrying about. He replied that he was
worrying about being drafted into the army. My friend said
to him, "If I were you, I wouldn't worry. You've got two
chances. You may be drafted, and you may not. Even if
you are drafted, you've got two chances—you may pass the
medical examinations, and you may not. If you do pass the
medical examinations, you've got two chances—you may get
sent into battle, and you may get a nice desk job. Even if
you do get sent into battle, you've got two chances—you may
get killed, and you may not. And even if you do get killed,
you've still got two chances!"

2. *The Go-getter*. When a very wide-awake young man became a member of the church, he went to the minister and
said, "I am not a very good church worker in the usual sense.
I do not know enough about the Bible to be a teacher. I have
never tried to pray or lead a meeting. I do not have a good
enough voice to sing in the choir. However, if you will let
me serve on the finance committee, I think I can do some
effective work there. I suggest that you turn over to me a list

of those who are behind with their pledges and let me see what I can do with them." The preacher took him up on this and gave him a list of delinquent members. Pretty soon money began to come in, most of it mailed in by check. Then there was a check and a letter from one of the members which read like this: "Please find enclosed a check for thirty dollars for my delinquent pledge. By the way, that young fellow that is working on the finance committee is certainly a go-getter. But he is a poor speller. He spells "lousy" with a *z* and "skunk" with a *c*."

3. *Forgot the Key.* There were three brothers whom we shall call Tom, Dick, and Harry, who had been so successful in the mercantile business that they owned and operated a very fine department store in a small Midwestern city. They decided to take a trip to New York and really see the big city. They decided that they would not be too particular about the cost, as they could well afford such a trip. They took a suite of rooms on the thirty-sixth floor of one of the downtown hotels. The suite cost them fifty dollars per day. All day long they went sight-seeing, and in the evening they came back to the hotel, dressed in their evening clothes, and went to one of the swell restaurants for an expensive dinner. Then they went to the theater. But when they returned to the hotel at about 2 A.M., they found that the elevator was out of order, and they were given the choice of walking up to their rooms or sleeping on cots in the lobby. They decided that inasmuch as they had paid fifty dollars for the room, they would walk up. Tom, the oldest of the group, said to the brothers: "As we walk up the steps, let's tell stories. As we go up the first twelve flights of stairs, I will tell a funny story. As we go up the second twelve flights of stairs, Dick can tell an adventure story. As we go up the last twelve flights of stairs, Harry can tell a sad story, for we will be getting awfully tired by that

time." So they started up. As they climbed the first twelve
flights of stairs, Tom told a very funny story; as they climbed
the second twelve flights of stairs, Dick told an adventure
story; but when they got up to floors 25, 26, 27, Harry had
not said anything. Tom said, "Harry, why don't you tell
your sad story?" Harry said, "I'll tell you the saddest one
I know first of all: We forgot to get the *key*."

SPELLING BEE

A STUNT that always goes over good at a luncheon club is
a spelling bee. Do it as it used to be done in the schools in
the country. Select two pronouncers and divide the two sides
by numbering, one and two. Line up against the wall and
mark tally every time a member crosses over. Have a spell-
down at the conclusion and see who can remain up the
longest.

SPELLING TEST

ANOTHER way of putting on a good stunt with spelling is
to have someone pronounce eighteen words and ask certain
members, who have been provided with paper and pencil, to
spell them and turn in their papers. Some words suggested
for use are:

picnicking	chivalrous
asafetida	menagerie
mnemonics	chinquapin
ichthyology	cherubim
Milwaukee	omniscience
inconceivable	sorghum
pneumonia	xylophone
contumacious	cadaverous
vociferous	sauerkraut

The average person will do well to make a grade of fifty
per cent. Have the committee grade the papers and announce
the winner.

THE COW

A CONTINUAL source of good fun will result from securing a noise-maker from a novelty store that sounds like the bawling of a cow or calf. The members of the stunt committee should always have this in their possession and every time anyone pulls a wise-crack or tells a story that is supposed to be funny, turn this instrument upside down and let it bawl. This will always bring a good laugh. I have seen this worked hundreds of times at the same club and always attain good results.

GREASED PIG

IF you want to start something that will be really hilarious, have your stunt committee get hold of a small pig, grease him, and after announcing to the members of the club that you are going to give a prize to the one who catches him, turn him loose in the dining room. You will find that you have started something.

SLANG

GIVE slips of paper and pencil to members of your club and tell them that you are going to give the prize to the one that can write the largest number of slang expressions. After the papers have been collected, the prize should be given to the one who wrote the fewest number. In presenting the prize the speaker should say that the club encourages the use of language devoid of slang, therefore the one who knew the fewest wins the prize.

BIRTHDAY FLOWERS

WE were present at the meeting of a Jacksonville civic club when a member was presented with a bouquet of flowers. We were informed that it was the custom of the club to give such a bouquet to every member whose birthday happened to fall on the meeting day. To do this with a club of a hundred members would require less than a dozen bouquets of flowers through the year.

YARDSTICK BALANCE

SECURE from a furniture, paint, or hardware store a large number of yardsticks. Merchants will be glad to give them away for advertising purposes. Divide your club into two sides and let them try balancing these yardsticks on their noses. Have an elimination contest. Pick out the first three from each side who succeed in keeping the yardstick balanced for ten seconds, then match the three from one side against the three from the other side and give a prize to the one who can keep the yardstick balanced the longest.

BADGE PLACE CARDS

IN nearly every civic club the members have been provided with badges with their names on them. In order to mix up the members and break up sitting cliques, have the reception committee use these badges as place cards for the tables.

BABY SPOON

WE know another club that has a habit of presenting to the newest father a baby spoon for the new baby. This spoon contains the club's emblem. It is always presented to the recent father by the one who received it last and a humorous speech is usually made.

HIDDEN ANIMAL CRACKERS

IF you want to mix up the members of your club and have a good ice-breaker, hide animal crackers all over the dining room and announce that a prize will be given to the one who finds the largest number.

FAKE BROADCAST

HAVE certain members prepare talks in advance and have

special musical numbers arranged for a broadcast at the weekly luncheon. Tell the members of the club that you will be on the air at a certain time, tell speakers that they must speak in loud or subdued tones, and tell the club members that they must not make any unnecessary noise. After the program has been completed, inform the performers and the members that it is all a fake. You will have had a good program and some good laughs as well.

EGG AND MILK BOTTLE STUNT

HERE is one which you will have to try in order to convince yourself that it will work. You will need a hard-boiled egg and a quart milk bottle. If you try to put the egg into the milk bottle, you will find that this will be impossible. If, however, you light a piece of newspaper and drop the burning paper into the milk bottle and immediately place the small end of the egg in the neck of the bottle, you will be surprised to see the egg go down the neck of the bottle and into the bottle. Now it will seem impossible to get the egg out in one piece, but this may be done easily as well. Turn the bottle to a slightly inverted position so that the egg in the bottle will have the small end toward the neck of the bottle; and holding it in this position, with the egg resting against the neck of the bottle, blow into the bottle with all your might, and then completely invert the bottle. Out the egg will come in good enough condition to be served at the next meal.

TURN GLASS OF WATER INTO A BOY

THIS is done by taking the glass of water and getting a boy to drink it. This is turning a glass of water into a boy, is it not?

PIE-EATING CONTEST

SELECT four members of your club and state that they are the lions. Select four others and call them the unicorns,

Seat the lions at one table and the unicorns at another and inform them that they are to have a pie-eating contest. Have the waiter bring in a quarter of a pie for each one and place it before them. The leader tells them that they are not to eat until the signal is given and then all begin at once. While the pies appear to be perfectly good blueberry pies, they have been prepared by the cook and a quantity of Methelyn Blue has been placed in them. This is harmless but not tasteless, as anyone who takes a bite will soon learn. This will create a lot of good fun.

ARE YOU FROM THE COUNTRY?

ASK all members of your club who were reared in the country to indicate it by raising the hand. Select a half dozen, line them up in front of the speaker's table, and ask them to prove that they are from the country by doing some of the following things: (1) Crow like a rooster. (2) Show how you used to plow corn. (3) Bawl like a calf. (4) Moo like a cow. (5) Show how to milk a cow. (6) Bleat like a sheep. (7) Gobble like a turkey gobbler. (8) Imitate a hog when you had just poured in a bucket of slop. (9) Tell why you left the farm. (10) Do you wish you were back?

EMPTY POCKETS

WITHOUT telling anyone about this in advance, offer a prize to the one who can produce the largest number of articles from his pockets. Ask each one to spread the articles on the table in front of him and have two or three judges look over the collections and give a list of the articles produced by the prize winner.

REMOVING A SHIRT

WE saw this stunt pulled, much to the wonderment of the other members of the club. One member announced that he was going to take off another member's shirt without asking him to remove his coat or vest, and, to the amazement of all present, he did. He was able to do this because it had been prearranged; and while the collar and a couple of the top buttons only were fastened, his arms were not in the sleeves and the sleeves were folded down his back. When the collar and the top button were unfastened and the tie removed it was only necessary to pull the shirt, up from behind his back. It will always bring a good laugh.

COLLECTING MAGAZINES

WE know of one club that has a regular custom of having its members bring magazines which they have read and these are distributed by the Good Cheer Committee to the jails, old people's homes, and almshouses.

SPEAKING FROM NOTES

SOME member of the committee is asked to make a speech on some subject and to arrange a large stack of notes. While he is only to speak about five minutes, yet he leaves the impression, from his notes, that he has only started his speech. Have him remove only one sheet of his notes each minute of his speech. If there are as many as seventy-five or eighty sheets in his pile it will leave the impression that he is going to speak a long time.

SUIT CASE RACE

THE Stunt Committee fills two suit cases with women's clothing. Two members are selected for this race. They are told that they are to run up to the table on which the suit cases are placed, each one unfasten a suit case, take out the clothing and put it on, run twice around the table, take the clothing off, replace it and then fasten the suit case, then the one who finished first is declared the winner.

FOLDING CHAIR RACE

SELECT about five members for each side and have a relay race in the following manner. The person on the front of each line is given a folding chair, a bucket in which has been placed a whistle, and an umbrella. When the bell is tapped or the signal given, each one has to run to a given goal, unfold the chair and sit in it, raise the umbrella, open the bucket, take out the whistle and blow it; then put the whistle back and close the bucket, close the umbrella, fold up the chair and run back to give the articles to the one at the head of the line. The group finishing first wins.

PILLOW FIGHT

SELECT two of your members who are athletically inclined to have a pillow fight on a pole. Get a round pole about twelve feet long and support it on some objects about four feet from the floor. Set the two members astride the pole and give them each a pillow. The object is for one member to knock the other off the pole with the pillow.

BLINDFOLD BOXING

PICK up two hefty boys and bring them to the luncheon for this stunt. When the time comes, put boxing gloves on them, blindfold them, and tell them that they are to have a boxing match. The members of the committee add to the fun by bumping into the boys and making them think that it is the other boy.

The above stunt may be pulled by using your own members. Blindfold two of them for the boxing match and have other members of the committee act as "teasers."

PASSING THE BUCK

THIS stunt will always go over big. A committee has been appointed to handle the program, let us say a committee of five men. When the time comes for the program, the president calls on the chairman of the committee and he arises and says, "As I was very busy this week with a case which I had in court, I have asked Bill Smith to look after the program for today." Then Bill Smith arises and says, "Yes, Tom did call me about this program the first of the week, but I was tied up doing some estimating and so I asked Frank Jones to look after the program." The other member of the committee arises and says that the program had been all planned, but unfortunately the speaker had not yet arrived and the entertainment numbers did not materialize. After this passing the buck has gone the rounds, the chairman arises and takes charge of the program

FLOATING NEEDLE

To make a needle float on the surface of water, take a small piece of tissue paper and place it on the surface of the water and gently lay the needle on the paper. Pretty soon the tissue will become saturated and sink, and the needle will float.

NEW BOOK ON PSYCHOLOGY

HERE is a stunt that will always go over big. Get some clever woman who is not known to the members of the club and have her introduced as Madame Sofski. State that she has written a new book on Psychology which is going to revolutionize the thinking of a great number of people. The chairman of the committee states that he has read the book and became so interested he thought it advisable to let the other members of the club in on some of its contents.

This lady, holding a book in her hand, rises to make a speech. She says that she has only been allowed five minutes and that it will be impossible for her to tell very much of the contents of the book, but that she feels sure that it would be of great benefit to anyone to read it. She then states that she is taking orders for the book, which may be purchased for the sum of three dollars, and says that she would like to take the names of any who would be interested in buying the book. About this time a member, who has been tipped off in advance, arises and very rudely interrupts the speaker and says that it is not the policy of the club to allow anyone to come to it making solicitations or trying to sell anything. The chairman of the program take exception to this and answers back. About three members on each side—that is, three taking the part of the woman and three taking the part of the one who spoke against her—make speeches. It will be found that by this time other members of the club, who were not in on it, will be having something to say. It would be well for the chairman to explain, after this goes on for about fifteen minutes, that it is all a joke and have the lady who helped with the stunt properly introduced.

STRANGE DIVISION

It is interesting to take the number 987654312 and divide it by 8. The strange result will be 123456789. Note in the first number given above, the digits are in order, with the exception of the last two, which are reversed.

ARRANGE THE NUMBERS

The problem is to arrange the numbers from 1 to 9 so that they will add up to 100. There are a number of possible combinations, of which the following is an example: $57+32=89+1+4+6=100$. Another example would be $32+65=97-4-1+8=100$. Check these numbers and you will find that all the numbers 123456789 are used to make the total. *

KIDDIE CAR RACE

Procure three or four kiddie cars from a toy store. Select three or four of the most bashful members of your club and stage a kiddie car race, making them ride the kiddie cars. This will create a lot of good fun.

TELEGRAMS

GIVE each member of the club a telegraph blank, on which have been written the following letters: h, h, m, h, a, a, a, t, o, r, i, c. They are to write telegrams beginning each word with these letters consecutively. Some of the telegrams that may be written are: "Have Henry Miller handle all assets, and take out reasonable insurance coverage." "Hurry home. Mary had automobile accident and the old rooster is crowing." Have a committee select the ten most humorous and read them to the club.

CHINESE AUCTION

A GOOD way to raise some money in your club, and at the same time have some fun, is to have a Chinese auction. Bring some sort of fowl to the luncheon in a coop. This could be used near Thanksgiving, and a turkey auctioned off. A hen or rooster would do, however. We have also seen this plan used by a young people's Sunday school class, and they auctioned off dessert after a Chinese chop-suey dinner. It works in this way. Have an auctioneer and three or four collectors. In case of the turkey or chicken, have someone primed in advance to start the bidding at fifty cents or a dollar, and when they make this bid they must pay this money to the collector. Suppose the first bid is a dollar, the next one bids a dollar and twenty-five cents; he must pay the twenty-five cents to make the sum one dollar and twenty-five cents. The next one bids a dollar and fifty cents. He must pay another twenty-five cents to the collector. The next one bids two dollars, and he must pay fifty cents; and so the bid continues until someone rings a bell. It would be better to have a bell wired up so that the one ringing the bell would be outside the room. Whoever makes the last bid before the ringing of the bell gets the turkey or chicken. It will not be a difficult matter, with a club of a hundred members, to raise twenty-five or thirty dollars, each one contributing twenty-five or thirty cents.

In the case mentioned of the young people's party auctioning off the dessert, the biding was done mostly with pennies. A piece of pie was started at one or two cents and when it got up to ten or fifteen cents the bell was rung. The bell had been hooked up from the kitchen, so that the one ringing it could hear the bidding.

A DUTCH AUCTION

A DUTCH auction is just like the Chinese auction, except that it goes the other way. The first bidder has been primed in advance to bid twenty-five dollars. The committee may even give him the twenty-five dollars to pay his bid, or if the donations are for some worthy cause perhaps some member would be willing to make such a donation. The next one bids twenty-four dollars and fifty cents, and he pays the fifty cents to bring it down to twenty-four dollars and fifty cents. The next one bids twenty-four dollars and he pays fifty cents, and so on until it comes down to nothing, or the bell may ring as in the Chinese auction, and the last bidder before the ringing of the bell gets the prize or the article which is being auctioned off.

GIVING OUT DIMES

A GOOD get-acquainted stunt is to give out a dime each to the five most bashful and most reticent members of your club. Announce that the fifteenth person to shake hands with each of the members holding the dimes, giving his name, nickname, and business, will be awarded the dime. After this has been going on for ten or fifteen minutes, tap a bell and ask the holders of the dimes to announce the winners.

BIRTHDAY GREETINGS

IT has long been the custom of some clubs to have all members have charge of the program at one of the club meetings during the month in which their birthdays occur. The third week in the month is set aside for the birthday program. In case it becomes necessary to change, it can be held during the fourth week. The plan is that these members, born in this month, will match themselves off against other members born in the same month and each give a brief life history of the other. This has proved very interesting, and is also a good method of getting members of the club better acquainted, because all those born in the month must come together for a meeting to plan the program, and that naturally makes them better acquainted.

INTRODUCTION BY TABLES

THIS is a good get-acquainted stunt. The president announces that in ten minutes he is going to call on one man at each table to introduce every other person at his table, give his name, nickname, and business or profession. If anyone at that table does not know every other one, he will proceed immediately to get acquainted.

INTRODUCING MEMBERS AT OTHER TABLES

THE above idea may be extended by the president calling on someone to introduce every person at another table. Of course there may be some that he will not know, and yet it will give him an opportunity to become acquainted with members that he had not met before.

ORATORICAL CONTEST

ASSIGN four or more members who are late the task of making a speech. Bring them up to the speaker's table and line them up. Tell them that they each have to make a speech as a penalty for being late, but that owing to lack of time they will all have to make their speeches at the same time. The result is quite ludicrous.

TALK ON BUSINESS OR PROFESSION

SELECT about twelve or fourteen men from your club that you think would be willing, and ask them to make a three-minute talk at the club meeting on their business or profession. Let this run for about three months, having a different business or profession at each meeting. This will prove very interesting.

TALK ON HOBBIES

SELECT several members who have hobbies. Perhaps it might be flying, boating, cabinet-making, stamp-collecting, art-collecting, or any other hobby. Ask each of these members to make a short talk on his hobby. This will prove very interesting and beneficial.

TALKS ON TRAVEL

IN a club of a hundred members there will always be a number of men or women who have had interesting travel experiences. Ask such members to give short talks on their travels. Trips to Yellowstone Park, to Cuba, or to Europe would form a good basis for interesting talks.

PRESIDENTS' MEETING

IN almost every large civic club you will find that there are a number of presidents of different organizations, such as the Chamber of Commerce, the Red Cross, Boy Scout Council, Ministerial Association, Bar Association, the Commander of the American Legion, etc. Set aside one meeting as the presidents' meeting, and have each one of these presidents make a two- or three-minute talk about the object and accomplishments of his organization.

V.E. OR V.J. DAY

A VERY interesting program was put over by a civic club when all of its members who were World War II veterans were asked to make talks on what they did on V.E. Day or V.J. Day. As many of the boys were in distant parts of the world then, it proved very interesting and was enjoyed by all.

BACKWARD LUNCHEON

FOR a change and a surprise serve a luncheon backward. Turn the chairs with their backs toward the table, so that the members will have to sit astride of the chair to face the table. Serve the ice cream first and the soup last. This will create a lot of good fun.

A SPEAKING MARATHON

GET a five-pound block of ice for this stunt; call two men, preferably two who are fluent speakers, up to the speaker's table. Give the ice to one of them and tell him that he must hold it in his right hand while the other one is speaking. When the hand gets so cold that he can no longer hold the ice, he must then give the ice to the speaker and continue the speech himself. Let each one speak about three times.

ART CONTEST

GIVE out slips of paper and pencils to the members of the club and tell them that each one is to draw the picture of the member to his left. When they have finished, each one writes the name of his victim and his own name on the paper and turns it in to the judges. The judges pick out the ten best pictures and display them.

CHRISTMAS TOYS

PIN on the back of each member the name of some toy. This would be a good stunt for a Christmas program. Use the names of toys, such as the jumping jack, electric train, doll, woolly dog, etc. Each member tries to learn what is on his back by asking questions. All questions must be answered correctly. One may ask, "Am I a jumping jack?" or any other question. When one has learned what toy he represents, he may take the name from his back, pin it in front, and retire from the game.

ANIMAL HUNT

PIN on the back of each member present the name of some animal. Give out slips of paper and announce that each member is to try to find and write down the names of the animals the others represent and at the same time try to conceal the name that is on his own back. Give a prize to the person who gets the largest list.

WATER RUNS UPHILL

WILL water run uphill? Yes, in a sponge. It will also run uphill if you try the following experiment. Place a short lighted candle in a saucer full of water, so that the water surrounds the candle. Turn a water glass gently over the lighted candle so that the rim of the glass is under the water which is in the saucer. The candle will go out slowly as the air is burned out of the glass, but the water in the saucer will be drawn up into the glass.

A ROOSTER RACE

WE saw the following stunt pulled at a club in the West. Four members were selected to stage a rooster race. Four roosters were brought in with heavy ribbon tied around their legs—ribbon about eight feet long. These members held the roosters on the starting line, and the prize was to be given to the one who first drove his rooster across the goal line. This created a lot of funny situations, particularly when one of the rooters flew up on top of a table and turned some dishes over and another flew into a lady's lap. These members chased the roosters all over the dining room before they got them across the goal line.

ATHLETIC MEETING

THIS would be a good stunt for the Athletic Committee to pull when they have charge of a meeting. Have these events in which the members participate: (1) Cross-country Run; select four members and have them run a race with their legs crossed. (2) Standing Broad Grin; with a tape-measure you measure the mouths of different members while they are grinning. Give a prize to the one who can make the broadest grin. (3) Shooting Things; give each member a half dozen air rifle shots. Have them form a circle about five feet from a half gallon fruit jar and try to throw the shots, one at a time, into the jar. The club may be divided into sides and have two circles and two jars. (4) Track Meet; pick out the men with the largest feet and draw the print of their shoes on pieces of paper. Give a prize to the one making the largest track. (5) Discus Throw; select four members for this stunt and give each one a paper plate. Give a prize to the one who can throw the plate the farthest. (6) High Jump; give a prize to the one who can sing a song the highest. Such a song as "Old Black Joe" would be a good one to try them on. (7) Low Hurdle; place on the floor a number of objects, such as a folding chair, an umbrella, a stool, etc. Select four members, let them see these articles strewn on the floor, then blindfold them and tell them that they are to race to the other side of the room and not step on any of the articles. After they are blind-folded the objects are noiselessly removed. It will be amusing to watch them run, imagining that the objects are still on the floor.

SENSE OF SMELL

BLINDFOLD five or six members who are late and ask them to identify these objects by the sense of smell. Use an apple, an onion, castor oil, Vick's salve, ammonia, Limburger cheese, etc. Give a prize to the one who can identify the largest number.

SENSE OF SIGHT

PASS around a tray on which have been placed a number of objects—as many as twenty. It doesn't make any difference what these objects are, but they should be varied. Give a prize to the one who can write down the names of the largest number of objects on the tray.

SENSE OF HEARING

BLINDFOLD different members and test their sense of hearing by dropping certain objects, which have previously been displayed to them. As each article is dropped let the persons blindfolded guess what it was. Use a ball, book, bean bag, sponge, pencil, knife, coin, shoe, etc.

SUCKERS

SENTENCE four members who were late to come up to the front and give each one a baby's bottle filled with milk. Let them have a contest in sucking the milk, and give a prize to the one who empties his bottle first. This will create a lot of good fun.

JIG-SAW SENTENCES

WRITE out sentences, cut them up, place them in envelopes and pass them out to members of the club or guests at the party. If the group are members of a Spanish or French club or any other foreign or ancient language club, the sentences may be written in that langauge. Such a sentence as the following may be used: "He who first reads this sentence displays his aptness for folly thereby." This may be cut into words or even the words may be cut in two.

Such a sentence may be used in a civic club to impress a truth, as "Sad but true, dues are due." Such a sentence as the following may be used to impress the importance of attendance: "If a member misses four consecutive meetings or 40 per cent of the meetings in either half of the year, he is automatically suspended from the club," or "Members may make up their attendance at another club within six days before or six days after they miss a meeting of the local club."

A TRICK WITH NUTS

GET from the five- and ten-cent store a rubber English walnut. Then get ten or twelve real walnuts. On the rubber one paint a red spot and on the real ones paint white spots. To do a trick with them, lay them all out on the table, displaying the spots on them, and tell the members that you are going to put them all in a hat which will be held so high that you cannot see in it and that you are going to pick out the one that has the red spot on it. This can be easily done by the sense of touch, the rubber one, of course, feeling soft.

THE INTELLIGENCE TEST

THE person tested is blindfolded. Then he is given several objects and asked to identify them and give all their uses. Finally an egg—or lemon—is presented. After the victim has given all possible uses the question is asked, "Are these the only uses for the egg" (or lemon)? (If it is a lemon, do not question too severely.) The victim answers "Yes." Then the egg is broken against the head—a dunce cap having been donned for protection—and the examiner remarks: "Remember that the egg makes a very fine shampoo"—which remark may be adapted to the lemon if one is used. Both stunts here given should be modified to fit localities and personalities, since there are always some in a group who don't mind anything for fun and others who might be worried by such treatment.

THE SUBMARINE CLUB

You must have a group who are in on the know. After the stunt has been worked once those who know it keep the secret by common consent. Some tradition or reason should be worked out adapted to each locality where the stunt is pulled. For instance, suppose at Daytona the leader arises some night and says, "Being so near to the ocean, our ancestors at this conference long ago decided that we should be familiar and conversant with all things nautical; therefore for many years we have had a Submarine Club. We now call for members, and all those who wish to join will please make the fact known." He then points to faculty members and students and has them testify to the salubrious and inspiring effects of the Submarine Club. Nearly always some new people will volunteer. The candidates are then removed to a place secure from observation and brought forward one at a time. When a candidate is presented to the initiating officer, he says: "You will now be tested as to whether you can distinguish a command from a request. If you think anything I say is a command, you should say, 'Aye, aye, sir.' If the remarks do not appear to you to be commands, keep silence." After this a series of questions, proverbs, etc., are hurled at the candidate. He will make some laughable blunders. At the close of this stage, however, the initiating officer says: "Comrades,—— has shown himself [herself] to be competent in distinguishing commands, in spite of some few errors. He [she] has qualified for membership in so far as this test is concerned." The group of spectators heartily agree and congratulate the candidate. The initiator now says "——, you are now to be further tested as to your competency as a submarine officer." At this point an old slicker is brought and placed over the candidate's head and shoulders in such a way that one of the armholes is directly over his head. The initiating officer says: "Now, imagine yourself in the control cabin of a submarine. The sleeve is the periscope and I, the captain, am on deck." (A pause.) The officer continues: "Well, it's a fine day and a smooth sea. Remain on surface, full speed ahead." The candidate replies: "Aye, aye, sir." Officer: "There's a ship, I think a friendly ship. Steer for her and full speed ahead." The candidate answers as before. The captain: "Oh, oh, an enemy ship! Launch torpedo." Candidate answers as before. Captain: "It went wide; launch torpedo." Answer. Captain: "Missed! They're firing at us! We're sunk!!!" At this point a quantity of water is poured down the periscope, and when the slicker is removed the captain says to the audience: "I now pronounce —— a fullfledged member of the Submarine Club." A cap of some kind may be placed on the candidate or the quantity of water varied or shunted to one side, depending on the candidate. New members generally keep the secret, because they will enjoy witnessing other initiations.

A STRANGE NUMBER

THE number 142857 is a very strange number. When you multiply it by 7, notice what happens: $142857 \times 7 = 999999$. But you can take this number and rearrange some of the figures, as long as you keep them in the same sequence, and get additional strange results. For example, if you take the 142 from the left of the number and move it to the right, you will have 857142. When you multiply this number by 7, you will be surprised at the results: 857142×7=59999994. While you do not have the same row of nines, the sum of the first and last numbers is still nine. You may change again as follows: 428571×7 299997. You will notice that you have 9 all the way except for the first and last figures, and they total 9. It makes no difference where you begin as long as you keep the numbers in sequence, for the results will be the same. That is, you will have all nines except for the first and last numbers, and they will total 9.

NUMBERS

PIN a number on each member of your club. Then distribute to the members envelopes containing instructions such as the following:

1. Find numbers 7, 11, and 12. Form a quartet and sing a song.
2. Introduce yourself to 15, 19, and 23.
3. Find No. 10, and introduce yourself to No. 16.
4. Shake hands with 2, 4, and 6.
5. Ask No. 18 what time it is.
6. Talk to No. 9 about the weather.

MUM LUNCHEON

TRY this on your club and it will be long remembered and talked about by the members. At the beginning of the meeting the program chairman should make a brief statement, somewhat as follows: "I have heard a great many members say that there is too much talking in this club. Members will not even refrain from talking when a guest speaker is addressing the club or a guest artist is performing. Today for a period of 20 minutes (or any designated time) we are going to have a period when no one is allowed to talk. If anyone is caught talking, the sergeant at arms will collect a dime from you for breaking the rules. You may make signs if you wish to communicate with anyone else, or in case of extreme necessity you may write a note."

There will be a lot of amusement derived from watching the late arrivals. They will probably bustle in, hunt a seat, greet members cordially, and begin to ask what the trouble is. After a moment they will lapse into silence. When the talking ban has been removed, there will probably be a lively hubbub, as everyone begins to get everything off his chest that he thought of during the silent period.

FRIEND X

A GOOD time to start a stunt of this kind would be at the very beginning of the year. It should then run throughout the year. At the end of the year there should be a revelation party, at which it is revealed who each Friend X has been.

Have cards prepared with blanks for the following data on them: your name; address; wife's name; your birthday; your wife's birthday; wedding anniversary date. Pass these cards out and have the members fill them in. At a later meeting let members draw for them. It is better to wait for a later meeting, so that members who are absent can be contacted and sign cards. If any are absent when the drawing is done, keep the left-over cards to give them at a later meeting.

On the special occasions mentioned in the questionnaire, Friend X is supposed to remember his friend with an appropriate gift. Also on such occasions as Valentine day and Christmas a gift or card should be sent.

In order to make this worth while the committee should handle it and from time to time designate certain things that a member should do for his Friend X—such as buying a ticket for his Friend X for the charity football game; sending flowers to the wife of his Friend X, etc.

At the end of the year, or designated time, have a party and let each one reveal who his Friend X really is.

TELEGRAM FROM THE DISTRICT OFFICER

HAVE some clever person write up a telegram which is purported to have been received from the District Officer criticizing the club or its members. They may be criticized for failing to enter the district contest, or failing to keep up their attendance percentage, or failing to send in reports of their work, or any other thing that can be thought of. The telegram should be written in such a way that it will bawl out the club and its officers. The telegram may say also that "some of your members taken in are not up to the standards of the club. You should not let down the bars and admit riffraff." After the telegram has been read, there will possibly be some discussion of it, and some members may be rather angry about it. Then the committee chairman announces that it was all a joke.

HEN CLUB

THIS is the famous Hen Club. To belong to this club you have to be initiated by the other members. The new member is brought into the room and in the room are at least three old members. Two persons should be sitting in chairs, between which is another chair with a pillow on it to make it soft. The third person goes to meet the newcomer at the door. He is ushered in and told to sit on the empty chair. He is also told that he has to cackle three times. When this is done the third member takes him by the hand and he gets up. The third member tells him they are proud of him. He turns around and sees an egg, which he is supposed to have laid. The fact is that one of the other members placed it there when he arose. This game may be played by any number of people, both men and women.

FROM INCOME TAX REPORT LAST YEAR

THE following report gives some sidelights on some of our members, and makes us wonder if 60 per cent of their time is devoted to the business or profession under which they are classified.

Dairyman [*Use name of local dairyman*]. Straight income tax, $5; tax on water rights, $788.92.

Doctor [*Use name of local doctor or surgeon*]. Straight income tax, $2.87; tax on split fees from surgeon and pharmacists, $6,666.66.

Fire Insurance Man [*Use name of fire insurance agent*]. Straight income tax, $6.57; tax on commissions from successful fire sales, $2,546.62.

Druggist [*Use name of local druggist*]. Straight income tax, 23 cents; tax on profit from lunch counter and hardware department, $7,248.00.

Plumber [*Use name of local plumbing contractor*]. Straight income tax, $1.99; tax on rebates from men on overtime, $7,859.79.

Banker [*Use name of local banker*]. Straight income tax, $8.99; tax on money received in bonuses on certain loans, $10,497.58.

Distributor of Gas [*Use name of manager of gas company*]. Straight income tax, 98 cents; tax on money received by special arrangements with the gas company manager and gas meter readers, $17,867.88.

Distributor of Electricity [*Use name of manager of power company*]. Straight income tax, $15.47; tax on money received from special electric contract with the city for street lighting up to 1953, $20,499.89. (Change this to suit local conditions or fit any complaint against local utility company.)

Distributor of Water [*Use name of manager of water com-*

pany]. Straight income tax for water company, $12,478.98; special tax on service charges, $198,769.84.

Clergyman [*Use name of preacher who is member of club*]. Straight income tax on salary, 87 cents; tax on gifts from members who want to run the church and hope to do so by being in good grace with the preacher, $211.16.

GIGANTIC SNEEZE [1]

DIVIDE the company into three groups. One group is to shout "Ish," the second "Ash," and the third "Shoo" at a given signal. These conglomerate sounds resemble a gigantic sneeze.

MIRRORED NUTS

PLACE contestants one at a time in front of a mirror. The contestant is given a milk bottle and a spoon. He is told to place the milk bottle on his head and hold it there while he picks up twelve nuts one at a time with the spoon and drops them from a height of three inches above the mouth of the bottle into the bottle. Walnuts, pecans, or any nuts of this approximate size will do. Each nut landing in the bottle counts five points toward his score. While sixty would be a perfect score, there will be few who can make it.

REGISTERING THE EXPRESSION

CHOOSE a person who likes to be in the public eye, and seat him in front of the group. The leader prepares, and should write out so that his memory will not fail in the group, a number of facial expressions for this person to imitate. They may be something like the following: awe, enthusiasm, hate, grief, disappointment, contentment, joy, rage, scorn, surprise, conceit, pride, fear, excitement. Whisper the expres-

[1] From *Phunology*, by E. O. Harbin. Abingdon-Cokesbury. Used by permission.

sions that the victim is to imitate into his ear, and let the group guess what he is trying to express. Chances are that he and all the others will register hilarity most of the time!

BREAKING THE CHINA

THE custom was to present the pianist of the club with a gift each year in appreciation of her services. The committee selected some very beautiful pieces of china for this gift. But some other china was purchased at the five- and ten-cent store and placed in a case; and after the presentation speech had been made, a member of the committee was sent to bring the gift. Just as he approached the speaker's table, another member of the committee tripped him and he fell to the floor, breaking the china. Apologies were made, and the pianist said that, although the gift had been broken, she appreciated the spirit of the gift nevertheless. After this the real gift was then presented.

EATING GOLDFISH

THREE members are picked to eat the first course blindfolded. Actually only one is blindfolded. At his table he has noticed a bowl with one goldfish therein. Someone inquires of a waitress, who has been posted, concerning the first course, and she replies: "Oysters on the half-shell." As soon as the member is blindfolded, the lone goldfish is removed. After eating oysters, the bandage is removed, amid prolonged clapping, and he is declared the winner. He then discovers that he was the only one eating oysters. A few minutes later, someone calls attention to the fact that the goldfish is gone. Members ask him how the fish is behaving; is it swimming about, etc. After the fun has subsided, the goldfish is returned to bowl.

BALANCING EGG ON PENCIL

THE one who does this stunt says that he is going to show the club how to balance an egg on a pencil. He breaks two or three eggs in an attempt to balance them. When the others begin to kid him and wisecrack about being a rotten egg himself, he apparently gets mad and starts throwing the remainder of the eggs at them with all his power. The remaining eggs, however, have had a small hole punched in one end of the shell and the inside drained out of them. There will be a lot of dodging.

STAGING A FIGHT

THE following stunt would be a good initiation stunt for new members: Dress one as the head waiter, and have two others stage a fight. After the fight has gone on for a moment the head waiter comes up and throws them out. As they land, there should be a big crash, as the striking of a bass drum or turning over a table. This stunt will bring down the house if carried out as a surprise.

PRESENTING THE BOLONEY

A LOT of good fun was created at an American Legion meeting which I attended not very long ago, when a number of men were asked to select a present for the retiring Commander. The present was selected, all right, but before the real present was given a large flower box was brought in, a box such as is used for the delivery of flowers by a flower shop, and this was presented. The Commander was asked to open it, and upon opening it he found a large piece of bologna about two feet long. This he was told was his present—the members had had so much "boloney" from him during his administration that they wanted to give him some in return. After this stunt the real present was presented and an appropriate speech was made in which appreciation was expressed for the service he had rendered the Legion.

IDENTIFICATION BY A NOSE

Use a large piece of wrapping paper or a sheet. Cut a triangular hole in it about three inches on each side. Place this over a door and have the officers, directors, and distinguished members of your club stand behind it. Let the members identify them by their noses. Give a prize to the member who identifies the largest number. Three judges should be appointed in advance to decide who first identified each nose.

INTRODUCING MOTIONS

MANY times a newly elected officer will not know very much about parliamentary law, and a good stunt may be worked up by having someone introduce a motion and others introduce amendments, etc. This can be made very amusing if there are some lawyers who are familiar with parliamentary law to work it up. After the motion is made, have someone make an amendment. Then another to make an amendment to the amendment. Then have someone move to table the amendment but consider the motion. Then have someone make a substitute motion, a motion to limit debate, a motion to adjourn. Then there could be discussion as to whether a motion to adjourn is debatable or not. In a short time the presiding officer will be so confused that he will not know what it is all about.

TYING THEM UP

IF there are any ladies present, have them take part in this stunt. Tie a string around both wrists of three men. The string should be about two feet long. Then tie the ladies' wrists together, but pass the string through the string that has been tied around the man's wrist. This really ties them together. Have a contest to see which couple. can get loose first without untying the strings. It is really a very simple thing to do, as all that is necessary is for the man to make a loop in the girl's string, pass it under the cord tied around his wrist and up over his hand. This will completely free them. However, it will be found that they will not think of this and will twist themselves into all kinds of shapes trying to get loose. This will prove a very interesting stunt.

THE BAG RELAY

THERE are two lines of the same number of men. A pile of paper bags is placed about twenty feet in front of each line. At the signal those in front run up to the bags, blow up one each, pop them, and go to the back of the line. The line that finishes popping the bags first wins.

OVER THE SLIDE

WHAT to do with late members to impress upon them the importance of being on time is a problem in every club. One club we know procured a kiddy's slide and placed it near the doorway. Late members were required to come down the slide. It always created a lot of good fun and accomplished the desired results.

EXCUSES FOR BEING LATE

AT a club luncheon not very long ago, those who were late were required to give written excuses, stating why they were late. These excuses were written and turned in as they entered the dining room. They were then turned over to the club wit, and he made an effort to make them humorous. One excuse was: "I was chasing the depression around the corner." Another was (from a lawyer): "I was trying to collect a fee from a (female) client." A third was: "I thought I saw a prospective customer. Chased him about two blocks, but he finally got away. This delayed me somewhat." A dairyman: "Was ten miles in the country looking over farm land. Could not get here in time. Met up with one of my lost cows who had gone astray." From a preacher: "My wife was away and I had some telephone calls to make."

SINGING STUNT

ANOTHER thing to do with late members is to line them up in front of the speaker's table for a singing contest. Have a contest, and let them try, one at a time, to sing "My Country, 'Tis of Thee," singing two words and omitting two words. Give a prize to the one who does the best.

EATING RAW EGGS

A STUNT with eggs may be done in this manner. Prepare in advance four or five hard-boiled eggs, and have a raw egg carefully marked so that you will know which one it is. When you have the attention of the group, tell them that a doctor advised you some months ago that the best thing you could do for your health was to eat a raw egg before each meal. Tell how exhilarating it is, how stimulating, how it helps your wind, and gives you extra energy. Then say, "I am going to show you how it is done." Then break the egg, put it in a glass, sprinkle a little salt and pepper over it, and drink it. After you have done this pick up the hard-boiled eggs one at a time and start tossing them around the room, saying, "John, you try one; Bill, you try one." There will be a lot of dodging and a good laugh when they find that the eggs are hard-boiled.

LETTERFLY [2]

INTRODUCE your company one at a time to the Fly family. There are Mr. Housefly, Miss Butterfly, Mr. Horsefly, Miss Dragonfly, etc. The last to be introduced is Miss Letterfly, who has a wet cloth which she throws in the face of the person being introduced. The victim should not see the cloth until it hits him. All the "flies" stand with hands behind them, reaching out the right hand when introduced.

MEETING THE TRAIN

AT an American Legion meeting, several months ago, a stunt was pulled that might be adapted to a similar occasion. A member of the Legion arose on the floor and remarked that he had had inside information that the Secretary of State was coming to our city on Tuesday evening of the coming week, and to do honor to such a distinguished character he moved that the Drum and Bugle corps be on hand to meet the train and represent the Legion in doing honor to this great man. Another member had been primed in advance to get up and say that distinguished men of the Republican party (or vice versa) had visited our city and no special honor had been done them and that he did not feel right about having the Legion honor a Democrat in this way, when similar honor had not been accorded distinguished Republicans who had visited our city. There was much argument back and forth, and then the one who brought it up confessed that it was merely a joke.

LAST LINE CONTEST

HAVE sheets mimeographed or typewritten with carbon copies of the following familiar poems, leaving the last line blank. Guests are asked to fill in the last line:

[2] From *Phunology*, by E. O. Harbin. Abingdon-Cokesbury. Used by permission.

Be good, sweet maid, and let who will be clever;
 Do noble things, not dream them all day long;
And thus make life, death, and the vast forever,
 ONE GRAND SWEET SONG. (*Charles Kingsley.*)

Each morning sees some task begun,
 Each evening sees its close;
Something attempted, something done,
 HAS EARNED A NIGHT'S REPOSE.
 (*Longfellow.*)

The moving finger writes; and, having writ,
Moves on; nor all your Piety nor Wit
 Shall lure it back to cancel half a Line,
NOR ALL YOUR TEARS WASH OUT A WORD
 OF IT. (*Omar Khayyam.*)

Heaven is not reached at a single bound;
 But we build the ladder by which we rise
 From the lowly earth to the vaulted skies.
AND WE MOUNT TO ITS SUMMIT ROUND BY
 ROUND. (*J. G. Holland.*)

I held it truth, with him who sings
 To one clear harp in divers tones,
 That men may rise on stepping-stones
OF THEIR DEAD SELVES TO HIGHER THINGS.
 (*Tennyson.*)

To thine own self be true,
And it must follow, as night the day,
 THOU CANST NOT THEN BE FALSE TO ANY
 MAN. (*Shakespeare.*)

'Tis education forms the common mind;
JUST AS THE TWIG IS BENT, THE TREE'S IN-
 CLINED. (*Pope.*)

Half a league, half a league,
 Half a league onward,
All in the valley of death,
 RODE THE SIX HUNDRED. (*Tennyson.*)

There are pioneer souls that blaze their paths
  Where the highways never ran—
But let me live by the side of the road
  AND BE A FRIEND TO MAN. (*Sam Walter Foss.*)

The night has a thousand eyes,
  And the day but one;
Yet the light of the bright world dies
  WITH THE DYING SUN. (*Bourdillon.*)

In Flanders' field the poppies blow
Between the crosses, row on row,
  That mark our place; and in the sky
  The larks, still bravely singing, fly,
SCARCE HEARD AMID THE GUNS BELOW.
  (*Lieut-Col. John McCrae.*)

Under the sod and the dew,
  Waiting the judgment day;
Under the one the blue,
  UNDER THE OTHER THE GRAY. (*Francis Miles
  Finch.*)

Lord God of Hosts, be with us yet,
LEST WE FORGET, LEST WE FORGET. (*Kipling.*)

Laugh, and the world laughs with you;
  Weep, and you weep alone.
For this sad old earth must borrow its mirth,
  BUT HAS TROUBLES ENOUGH OF HER OWN.
  (*Ella Wheeler Wilcox.*)

The curfew tolls the knell of parting day,
  The lowing herd winds slowly o'er the lea,
The plowman homeward wends his weary way,
  AND LEAVES THE WORLD TO DARKNESS
  AND ME. (*Gray.*)

If you can fill the unforgiving minute
  With sixty seconds' worth of distance run,

Yours is the earth, and everything that's in it,
AND—WHICH IS MORE—YOU'LL BE A MAN,
MY SON. (*Kipling.*)

Breathes there the man with soul so dead
Who never to himself has said,
THIS IS MY OWN, MY NATIVE LAND? (*Scott.*)

Leave my loneliness unbroken—quit the bust above my
door.
Take thy beak from out my heart, and take thy form from
off my door.
QUOTH THE RAVEN, "NEVERMORE." (*Poe.*)

Lives of great men all remind us
We can make our lives sublime,
And, departing, leave behind us
FOOTPRINTS ON THE SANDS OF TIME. (*Long-
fellow.*)

'Twas the night before Christmas,
When all through the house
Not a creature was stirring,
NOT EVEN A MOUSE. (*Clement C. Moore.*)

THE REPORT OF THE STUNT COMMITTEE

THE president has asked all committees to report at a certain meeting. One committee, say the Stunt Committee, has
no report to make. They are called on, nevertheless, and the
chairman arises and says: "You will now hear the report of
the Stunt Committee." At this time someone fires a large
cannon cracker in or near the luncheon room.

SECTION IV

Introducing the Speaker

INTRODUCING THE SPEAKER

As a part of the program of almost every civic club, every church fellowship dinner, and every women's meeting, there is a speaker. This chapter is given over to a discussion of the speaker—his introduction, and the subject and content of his speech.

THE CIVIC CLUB SPEAKER

ANYONE who has listened to many speakers at civic clubs, Chamber of Commerce meetings, Boy Scout councils, church fellowship dinners, laymen's league meetings in the churches, and other groups, will have found that the speaker, if he is wise, will discuss some subject that pertains to the special interest of the group. At a Chamber of Commerce meeting, for example, an appropriate subject would be something like the following: "The Year's Program of the Chamber of Commerce," "The Need for New School Buildings," "What the Chamber of Commerce Is Doing to Make Our City a Convention City," or "Our Need for More Parks and Playground Facilities." Many of these subjects would also be appropriate for civic club luncheons. At church fellowship dinners and laymen's league meetings, such subjects as the following would be appropriate: "What the Men Can Do to Improve the Program of the Church" and "What I Learned by Attending a World Convention of Our Church." Speakers at a church fellowship dinner may be taken from a group who attended a state or district convention. They could be asked to give echoes from that convention. A missionary or an outstanding leader in the church could bring an interesting talk on foreign or home missions.

USING THE MONTH OF THE YEAR AS A SUBJECT

A SPEAKER once made a very interesting talk to a men's group on the subject, "These April Days." The speaker had selected a number of events in the history of the world that took place in the month of April, and he had built an interesting talk around these. This would be possible for each of the twelve months of the year.

THE OPENING THOUGHT OF AN AFTER-DINNER SPEECH

THE speaker will immediately get the attention of his audience if he can make some interesting or humorous observation at the beginning of his speech. I recall one speaker who began with this statement: "I have heard that if all after-dinner speakers were laid end to end—it would be a good thing." Another started with this statement: "An after-dinner speech is somewhat like the wheel of one of the early automobiles—the longer the spoke, the bigger the tire." Another speaker started with this remark: "I have heard that there are four rules for making a speech, and I am going to observe them today. They are: 'Stand up, speak up, shut up, sit down.'" "I have heard that an after-dinner speech is somewhat like a dog's tail, bound to occur. (Bound to a cur.) But perhaps the reason a dog has so many friends is that his tail wags instead of his tongue." "I have heard that whoever thinks by the inch and talks by the yard should be dealt with by the foot."

FORMAL INTRODUCTION OF THE SPEAKER

IN introducing a visiting speaker who is a man or woman of some prominence, it would be well to make the introduction formal, telling of the speaker's accomplishments, the positions of honor he has held, giving his degrees, or rank if he is in the armed services, etc. The introduction should always be brief.

HUMOROUS INTRODUCTION

THIS is a good way for one of the vice-presidents of a business firm to introduce the president and general manager of his firm. The vice-president starts in a rather halting voice reading his introduction as follows: "I have the signal honor today of being permitted to introduce to you our guest speaker. This man is unquestionably the greatest, the finest, most wonderful, most superb, most eloquent, most expert, most marvelous—" When he comes to the word "marvelous" he stops and holds the paper over to the speaker and says, "What is that word? I can't read your handwriting." Then he continues: "most pleasing, most enjoyable speaker in our city today. He is the most intelligent, the handsomest, most honorable human being on the face of the earth. He is also the greatest general manager a firm ever had. He is the most l-i-b-e-r-a-l (spells out) man I have ever known. He has been known to r-a-i-s-e (spells out) many important questions in the community. It is my pleasure to introduce to you Mr. Blank, the President and General Manager of my firm." As he leaves the speakers' stand, he is saying, "the finest, most capable, most intelligent, most superb, most excellent. . . ."

THE WALKOUT

WHEN one of the very popular members of a club was asked to speak, a large group of the members secretly plotted to get up and walk out as soon as the introduction was completed. After the walkout, the group returned to their seats and all enjoyed a hearty laugh, and the speaker proceeded.

NAME A HOUSEHOLD WORD

W HEN this introduction stunt was worked out, it brought a good laugh at the conclusion. The speaker for the day was a stranger to most members of the group, and so the chairman of the committee, when he arose to introduce him, said, "It is my pleasure to introduce to you today a man who, although perhaps you have never seen him before, is well-known to you by name. In fact, his name is a household word throughout the country. Not only is this true, but he is also well-known to our club because of the high positions he has held in it. It is my pleasure to introduce to you Mr. —.

At this point the chairman could not recall the speaker's name, and after an awkward pause he turned to the speaker and said, "I beg your pardon, but I cannot think of your name." Of course, this brought a hearty laugh, and after this the chairman made a serious introduction of the speaker.

SELF-INTRODUCTION

A CIVIC club used the following introduction stunt, letting the speaker introduce himself. A past-president of a club had been asked to be the speaker, and this fact was known only to the program committee. When the time came for the speech, the past-president arose as if to make an introduction speech. He told a lot of things about the speaker, some true and some the products of his imagination. He stated that he had known the speaker many years. He knew his accomplishments; in short, he knew the man so well that he was fully qualified to introduce him. He stated that he was better qualified to introduce the speaker than any other member. He then announced that he himself was the speaker and continued with his speech.

INTRODUCTION BY HIS WIFE

By arrangements made with his wife and unknown to him, have the wife of a speaker introduce her husband. She could tell some of his eccentricities, some of his pet peeves, a good joke on him, etc. The real success of this stunt will depend on the cleverness of the wife of the speaker; and if she does her part well, it will result in a good laugh and a fine bit of entertainment.

RESPONSE TO THE INTRODUCTION

When the speaker arises to make his speech, it is customary to make some reference to the introduction. Some such expression as "I wish my wife could have been present to hear all the nice things that the chairman has said about me" is appropriate. A speaker once remarked that he felt somewhat like the widow of a man whose funeral was being preached by a well-meaning preacher. So many fine things were said about the deceased that the widow got suspicious. She said to her small son, "Go up and take a peep in the coffin and see if that's your Paw in there."

The president of a large group of educators once made the following response to an introduction: He said that he was going to tell a story and if it proved to be humorous, this would be evidence of the fact that his audience had got the point. He then told about a farmer that was trying to get his calf to jump a ditch on the side of the road, but could not make the calf budge. A man drove up in a large automobile and asked the farmer if he could do anything to help. The farmer asked him to blow the horn of his automobile so that the calf might get scared and jump the ditch. But when the horn was blown, the calf got so scared that it jumped straight up and landed in the middle of the ditch and broke its neck. The man in the car said to the farmer, "I am sorry, but I did just what you asked me to do." The farmer replied, "Yes, you did, but don't you think that was a mighty big toot for such a little calf?" When the audience laughed at this story, the speaker then said, "I see that you got the point."

DEFINITION OF A BOY

THE following may be appropriately used at the time of the introduction of the Boy Scout Committee, or the Chairman of the Committee on Boys' Work, or any committee that has to do with boys. It might be used as a take-off on a member of your club who is the father of a new baby boy.

A boy is—
A piece of skin stretched over an appetite.
A noise covered with smudges.
He is called a tornado, because he comes at the most
    unexpected times, hits the most unexpected places, and
    leaves everything a wreck behind him.
He is part human, part angel, and part barbarian.
He is a growing animal of superlative promise, to be fed,
    watered, and kept warm.
A joy forever, a periodic nuisance, the problem of our times,
    the hope of the nation.
Every new boy born is evidence that God is not yet
    discouraged with man.—*Anonymous.*

READING THE NEWSPAPERS

NOT long ago at a civic club meeting the speaker was a former member of the club who had moved away and had been invited back to speak. Someone secured a number of old newspapers and divided them out by giving a double sheet to each member of the group. As soon as the speaker started his speech, each one of the members opened his newspaper and started to read. The speaker had a hard time getting their attention. After a good hearty laugh by everyone, including the speaker, the newspapers were removed, and the speaker continued his speech.

SECTION V

Attendance and Initiation Stunts

ATTENDANCE AND INITIATION STUNTS

WHILE the stunts included in this section are to be used at luncheon and banquets, we have segregated them, in order that they may be more accessible to the committee in charge of these particular features.

Every club should have an Attendance Committee, whose function is to provide, as near as possible, one hundred per cent attendance at the meetings. The first series in this section is designed to aid this committee.

When new members come into your club they should be initiated with proper ceremony. Many clubs, with which we are familiar, do this in the following manner: At the first meeting, which the new member attends after his election to membership, he is introduced to the club by the member who proposed him or sponsored him. At another meeting, later on, he is formally welcomed and initiated. This feature is usually handled by the club's Education Committee. This committee usually waits until there are two or three new members and initiates them all at the same time. On this day the new members are rolled in, in wheelbarrows, or required to go through some fake ceremony, and then the chairman of the Education Committee, or one of its members, makes a serious talk to them about their duties and obligations.

ATTENDANCE PRIZE

MANY luncheon clubs have a weekly attendance prize. The rule in some clubs is, that the person who last received the prize is to provide for the following meeting. It does not have to be anything expensive and its selection should be left to the judgment of the individual member. In drawing for the prize, all the attendance slips are collected and someone draws, one at a time, until the fifth one is drawn. The fifth one receives the prize if he is present. The attendance prize will always, to a certain extent, promote attendance.

MATCHING THEM OFF

DIVIDE your club into two sections and make each half of the members responsible for the attendance of the other half. In other words, John Smith would be responsible for the attendance of Bill Jones and *vice versa*. If either one of these members is absent from a meeting, it is the duty of the other one to ascertain the reason why and see that he gets to the next meeting. This is about the best attendance promoter we know.

ATTENDANCE COMMITTEE

THE best way for the Attendance Committee to promote attendance is to have the chairman get from the secretary, each week, a list of the absentees. These should be contacted immediately, and arrange for those who have missed a meeting to attend a meeting of a near-by club later in the week. It is the rule of most civic clubs, that a member has the privilege of making up his attendance at another club, six days before or six days after he misses a meeting in his own club. The Attendance Committee will probably consist of as many as five members, and each of these members could arrange to take a number of absentees to a near-by city once every five weeks. They could in this way bring up the attendance average of the club.

ATTENDANCE LETTERS

ANOTHER good way for the Attendance Committee to promote attendance is to write a personal letter to everyone who misses a meeting, and urge him to come to the following meeting and, if possible, to make up his attendance at another club before the next meeting. After a man has gotten one or two of these letters, it will begin to get on his conscience and he will come the next week.

ROUND TABLE LUNCHEON

WHILE we have not seen any ruling on the question of
Round Table Luncheons, and have heard the rumor that
they were not strictly legal, yet we know many clubs that
make a practice of having Round Table Luncheons when,
for any reason, the regular meeting date has been changed.
After an inter-club meeting, or a meeting held on a near-by
farm or a Ladies' Night, or any other meeting not held at
the regular meeting time, a special luncheon is arranged and
the attendance committee calls all who were absent from the
last meeting and tells them that they have the privilege of
making up their attendance at this Round Table Luncheon.
The secretary attends the luncheon and gives them credit
for regular attendance. While this may not be strictly according to the rules, yet we know it is done by nearly all clubs
that have a high attendance average.

NAMES IN THE BULLETIN

ANOTHER way to promote attendance is to have the secretary print in the club's weekly bulletin the names of those
who missed the last meeting. A member will not like to see
his name printed in the bulletin in this way and will be more
careful about his attendance.

TALKS ON ATTENDANCE

OCCASIONALLY the chairman of the Attendance Committee should have an opportunity to make a talk to the club
about attendance. Many members of the club do not understand that if they go on a trip to New York, Chicago, At-
lantic City, etc., they are not only welcome to attend the
luncheons in those cities but they are expected to attend
them, and that they must attend in order to have a perfect
attendance at the local club; this should be made clear to the
members. Also they should be familiar with the attendance

rules. In most civic clubs if a member misses four consecutive meetings he is automatically dropped from the club roll, or if he misses forty per cent of the meetings during either half of the club year, he is dropped. The chairman should also familiarize the members with the dates and places of meeting of near-by clubs and urge those members who are compelled to miss, to attend the meeting at another club.

ATTENDANCE CONTEST

ANOTHER good way to promote attendance in your club is to challenge some other club to a contest. Let this run for three months. The club that maintains the highest attendance average would win and should be entertained at a banquet by the losing club.

ATTENDANCE CHART COMMITTEE

HAVE the Attendance Committee make up a chart and place all the names of the members on it. Draw perpendicular lines and also vertical lines. Write the names of the twelve months of the year at the top of every five lines and keep every member's attendance record by the use of pins with large heads. These can be bought in different colors. Use a pin with a large red head to indicate present and one with a black head to indicate absent. If this chart is drawn on beaver-board and put in a frame, so that it will set out an inch from the wall, these pins can be pushed right through and will constitute a record which can be seen and read by all members at all times.

CHART COMMITTEE REPORT

IT would be a good thing to ask the Chart Committee to make a report each week upon the attendance; announce the number absent and the attendance percentage for the preceding week. This will keep the matter of attendance constantly before the club.

SPECIAL RECOGNITION

LEARN who has the longest perfect attendance record, and also find others who have not missed a meeting for some time. It would be a good thing to do them some special honor. One club we know has the custom of reading the names of all members who have one hundred per cent attendance for the year at the installation banquet. At this time, also, members who have not missed for three years or more are recognized, and the length of their perfect attendance record given.

CARD SERIES

HAVE a series of four cards printed to send to absentees. Enough of these cards should be printed to take care of probable absentees for several months. The first card is printed in white and merely calls attention to the absence of the member. The second card says, "Caution; we missed you again." This card is printed with a green border. The third card says, "Danger, beware," and is printed with a red border. The fourth card is printed in black, which indicates that on account of missing four meetings the member has been dropped.

THE BABIES

USE large baby diapers and pin them on the new members with large safety pins in baby fashion, and march them in. Seat them in improvised high chairs, and give them milk in baby bottles. Have rattles and other toys on the table. When the regular meal is served, make them eat with baby spoons.

FAKE INITIATION

WE saw this fake initiation worked with good results at a club meeting recently. The new members were lined up in front of the speaker's table, and the chairman of the committee asked them to raise their right hands to take the obligation. After they had all raised their hands, he started looking around among some papers and in the secretary's brief case, and then he called the secretary and asked him where the ritual was. The secretary left the dining room as if he were looking for the ritual. In the meantime, the new members were all standing with their right hands raised. The secretary did not come back for some time, and, of course, did not bring the ritual, as no civic club possesses such a thing, and so the hands began to drop one by one and the club had a good laugh at the expense of the new members.

THE ORDEAL

THE chairman has arranged some five-gallon paint cans. The tops have been removed and a piece of wrapping paper tied over the top.

The chairman announces that the new members will be tried by ordeal. In ancient times, in a trial by ordeal, persons were required to stick their hands in boiling water; but the new members will be required to stick their hands in a bucket of paint. The chairman has provided plenty of towels, with which to wipe the paint off. At the sound of the bell, all new members are to thrust their hands in the paint cans at the same time. Of course, there is no paint in any of the cans. This will get a good laugh.

ROLLING THE WHEELBARROW

SOME years ago five millionaires in our city were initiated as honorary members of our club. When the time came for the initiation, five members rolled them in, in five wheel-barrows. The funny thing about it was that the honorary members themselves got so much kick out of it.

THE BABY BOTTLE

FOR the same five members, wheeled in, in the wheelbar-rows, the committee had placed on the table a large five-gallon jar of water colored white like milk. This may be colored with a small quantity of milk or with chalk. There were five rubber tubes running from the large bottle, and the new members were told that they were baby Kiwanians and so must drink milk.

HOW'S YOUR MEMORY?

TELL the new members that they have to pass a mental test that is required of all new members to see if they are of sound mind. Take a large piece of cardboard about two by three feet and cut out of some magazines a number of advertisements of popular products. Paste these ads, about twenty or twenty-five of them, on the cardboard. Display this card to the new members for about thirty seconds. Then remove it and ask them to write the names of all the ads they remember. Give a small prize to the one who gets the largest number and a booby prize to the one who gets the smallest number.

KNOW YOUR MEMBERS

NEW members who come into a group or club usually know several of those who are already members. In order to better acquaint them with the membership and to acquaint the membership with one another, prepare a group of ques-tions and ask the new members to answer them. In the end supply the answers to the questions so that all the members will know them. Such questions as the following would be apropos: What member is a Court of Appeals judge? What member is a mortician? What member is a pediatrician? What member is a college professor? These are but samples. At the conclusion of the stunt when the new members have given their answers, introduce all those about whom the questions have been asked. This will give all members an opportunity to know each other better.

LEAVES FROM A MEMBER'S DIARY

IN initiating a new member who is getting well up in years, the initiator may say that he has found some leaves from this member's diary which were written recently. He then reads the following:

"Everything is farther than it used to be; it's twice as far from my place to the bus now, and they've added hills that I've just noticed. The buses leave sooner too, but I've given up running for them, because they go faster than they used to.

"You can't even believe the time tables any more, and why ask the conductor? I'll bet I ask him a dozen times if the next stop is where I get off, and he always says it isn't. I gather up my packages anyway just so I won't go by the right stop. Once in a while I make double sure by getting off at the block ahead.

"Seems to me they are making steps steeper than in the old days; the risers are higher and there are more of them, because I've noticed it's harder for me to make them two at a time; it's all one can do to make one step at a time.

"Have you noticed the small print they are setting lately? Newspapers are getting farther away when I hold them, and I have to squint to make out the news. Now, it's ridiculous to suggest that a person my age needs glasses, but it's the only way I can find out what's going on without someone reading aloud to me, and that is not much help because everyone seems to speak in such a low voice that I can scarcely hear them.

"Times sure are changing. The material in my clothes, I notice, shrinks in certain places (you know, like around the waist or in the seat). Shoe laces are so short that they are next to impossible to reach.

"Even the weather is changing. It's colder in the winter and the summers are hotter than in the good old days. Snow is much heavier, too, when I attempt to shovel it, and rain is so much wetter that I have to wear rubbers. I guess the way they build windows makes drafts more severe.

"People are changing too. For one thing, they are younger than they used to be when I was their age. On the other hand, people my age are so much older than I am. I realize my generation is approaching middle age, but there is no reason for my friends tottering into senility.

"I ran into a friend the other night, and she had changed so much that she didn't recognize me. 'You've put on a little weight,' I said. 'It's this modern food,' she replied. 'It seems to be more fattening.'

"I got to thinking about her this morning while I was dressing; I looked at my own reflection in the mirror; it seems they don't use the same kind of glass in mirrors any more."—*Anonymous.*

UPSIDE DOWN

THE new members are taken behind a screen which is just low enough for their heads to be seen when they are standing, and they are seated in chairs. They are asked to take off their shoes and place them on their hands. When they are ready, the initiator tells the group that he is asking the new members to sing. If there are four, he may say that he has formed a quartet. Have them sing the first verse of a familiar song. After this a scuffle is started, and there is quite a bit of moving about behind the screen. Finally the feet—actually their shoes on their hands—of all the men appear over the top of the screen, and they sing the second verse of the song apparently upside down. The stunt will be more effective if the men put socks on their hands so that their wrists will resemble their ankles. A good laugh will result if the screen or curtain is removed and the men are shown squatting and holding their shoes on their hands.

RENDERING A MUSICAL SELECTION

THIS stunt may be used to introduce new members to the club or group. It would be better to use it with one, two, or four new members who are being initiated. After the formal introduction has been finished, the leader announces that he has learned that the new members have musical talent and that they are going to render a selection. Have a record player concealed behind a curtain, and select a solo, duet, or quartet record that will fit the situation. While the new members fake singing by moving their lips and making gestures, the record machine gives forth the sound. Of course this will require a rehearsal and other advance preparation.

GIVING THEM THE SACK

GIVE each of the new members a paper sack large enough to draw over their heads. Ask them to cut out eyes, nose, and mouth, and provide scissors for this. Have them take crayon and do some art work on their paper sack, such as painting eyebrows, color in cheeks, and perhaps a moustache. When all the sacks are on, each man is given a colored crayon, and he starts greeting other members of the club. Every one of the members he identifies is asked to take the crayon and make a cross somewhere on the paper bag. At the end of five minutes give a prize to the one who has the most crosses on his bag.

SECTION VI

Group Action Stunts and Songs

GROUP ACTION STUNTS AND SONGS

THE stunts and songs found in this section are designed to be carried out by a group in unison. A leader is essential in the stunts and in the songs, and the group must follow his leadership. The best leader will be one who can not only lead in the actions but who is able to lead the music as well.

THE LION HUNT

THE writer first heard a missionary from India tell this story and lead a group in the actions as they rode in a chartered bus from a convention. This is but one of the many versions, however, and there is no end to the ramifications that one can go into by using his own imagination a little. Sometimes it is a native of India who is the hunter. Sometimes it is an African chief who is the hunter. Sometimes it is a tiger and not a lion. But in any case the actions are approximately the same.

The following version is adapted by permission from *The End of Your Stunt Hunt,* by Helen and Larry Eisenberg. In this case the hunter is an African Chief. The teller of the story may use his own words and may ad-lib other words at will. He leads in the actions, and the others follow his lead and make the same motions.

"Once there was an African village that was menaced by a ferocious lion. The lion was stealing the livestock of the villagers and scaring the wits out of them. It was necessary for someone to go and hunt the lion and kill it so that the village could again be safe.

"So the Chief called a council of his people by beating the drums, and they assembled. The name of the Chief was O-o-o-o." (This is said by the leader in a deep voice; and

223

as he says it, he beats on his chest while all others follow his lead.) "The name of the Chief's wife was Ah-h-h-h-h." (This is spoken in a high-pitched voice and with the action of beating on the chest. Each time the Leader speaks the name of O-o-o-o or of Ah-h-h-h-h, the group shouts the name, and each one beats on his chest.)

"The Chief O-o-o-o called for volunteers to go in search of the lion, but no one volunteered. He turned to his wife and said, 'I guess I will have to go myself, Ah-h-h-h-h.'

"On the morning that O-o-o-o was to start on the lion hunt, all the people were out to see him off. All the people said, 'Our Chief, O-o-o-o, is a brave man; he is going to kill the lion.' Ah-h-h-h-h said, 'Be careful, O-o-o-o, and don't let that lion get you.' The village people made a great hubbub, all of them talking at once." (All the female voices say, 'The bear went over the mountain,' and the male voices say, 'A jay bird died with the whooping cough.') After the people had said 'Au Revoir' to O-o-o-o and after Ah-h-h-h-h had taken a last long, lingering look (put hands up to eyes and look) at the Chief, O-o-o-o started on his perilous journey. The villagers opened the gate (the gate is opened by putting hands together and then parting them to represent the opening of the gate), and after O-o-o-o had passed through, they closed the gate (close gate by bringing hands back together again).

" 'This is the most beautiful day of the year,' O-o-o-o thought as he walked along. (Leader indicates walking by alternately slapping his left and his right thigh with his hand. All the group joins in this action.) As O-o-o-o walked along, he looked to the right. (Shades eyes and looks to the right, as group imitates his action.) He looked to the left (similar action from the group), and he sniffed the fresh morning air. (Throw head back and sniff, while the group follows the action.) But O-o-o-o saw no lion.

"So O-o-o-o continued to walk leisurely. (Slap thighs with hands more slowly.) Before long he came to a swinging bridge. (Action should change to a swaying motion back and forth, and as he sways, the leader continues to slap his thighs with his hands.) After he had crossed the bridge, he looked to the left (shades eyes with hand while group follows action), but still there was no sign of the lion.

"He continued to walk along until he came to a fork in the trail. 'Which way shall I go?' O-o-o-o said. (All scratch heads.) 'I'll try the right fork,' he said. (Slap thighs slowly, at the same time leaning toward right.) This trail didn't seem right, so he decided to go back to the fork. (They walk backward by patting the hands higher and higher up their thighs.) Then he walked up the trail to the left. (Pat on thighs with hands and lean to left.) This left trail seemed to be better, so he decided to go on. (Continue to slap thighs and straighten the body, ceasing to lean to left.)

"It was not long before he came to a small river. It looked to O-o-o-o like he would be able to jump over the river, so he backed up (patting higher on thighs) to get a running start. He ran toward the river with the intention of jumping (pat thighs faster), but he suddenly stopped. He decided he couldn't make it. (All stop patting momentarily.) O-o-o-o backed up and tried again (others follow action), but again he stopped. (All stop.) O-o-o-o scratched his head. He said to himself, 'I'm going to try it this time even if I have to swim.' Again he went back to get a running start (group imitates action), but when he got to the bank he decided he would have to swim after all. (Puts one hand out in front as if to part water for a dive while holding his nose with the other. Group imitates action.) And he swam the river. (Makes swimming motions, which group imitates.) When he climbed up on the bank, he shook himself (imitate a wet dog shaking himself) and started looking for the ferocious lion. (Shade eyes and look to right and left.)

"O-o-o-o started walking once more looking to the right and to the left (group follows actions) and sniffing the air, but still he saw no sign of the lion.

"Finally he came to a long steep hill (walk more slowly); and when he started down, he stopped and looked to the right and to the left. (Group follows action.) He started walking faster on the downward trail. Very soon he came to some tall grass. He had to part the grass with his hands to find the trail. (Make swishing motion with hands and arms as if parting tall grass, while the group imitates.)

"Finally he came to the very edge of the grass, and he looked to the right (action), and he looked to the left (action), but still no lion. He looked straight ahead (action) (Roar)—there was the lion!

"O-o-o-o made the world's record for the 100 yard dash— he made it in a second and three quarters—with the lion in hot pursuit. (Pat thighs very fast.) He ran through the tall grass (swishing motion with hands); he ran up the hill (more slowly) and down the hill (faster motions). He dived into the river and swam across. (Actions by the group.) He came to the forks of the road but did not stop running. As he glanced back over his shoulder, he saw the lion in hot pursuit. (All look over shoulder.) He went right down the home stretch at something like seventy-five miles an hour. The tribe had gathered expecting the return of their chief, and as they waited, they made a hubbub (as at the beginning of the story). When they saw him coming, they opened the village gate. (Motion of putting hands together and then separating them.) After the Chief was through, they closed the gate. (Motions.) The lion was coming so fast that he could not stop, so he ran into the closed gate and broke his neck. O-o-o-o fell into the waiting arms of

A-h-h-h-h, his wife, and was welcomed by the whole tribe as a conquering hero."

JOHN BROWN'S BABY

ALTHOUGH this is an old one, it is always good for a stunt song. The group sings "John Brown's Baby" and makes the actions by omitting words of the song and substituting appropriate actions as follows:

JOHN BROWN'S BABY

John Brown's Baby had a cold upon his chest,
John Brown's Baby had a cold upon his chest,
John Brown's Baby had a cold upon his chest,
So they rubbed it with camphorated oil.

The verse is sung the first time without any actions. When the verse is sung the second time, the word "Baby" is omitted, and all persons in the group follow the leader's actions of clasping hands together and swinging them back and forth to imitate the motions of rocking a baby. In the singing of the verse for the third time the word "cold" is omitted, and a little cough is given where the word is omitted. This must be done in addition to omitting the word "Baby" as in the first stanza. The stunt is to eliminate many of the words, an additional one for each verse, until most of them have been omitted and only actions remain in their place. Other actions are as follows: When the verse is sung the fourth time, omit the word "chest," and tap on chest with open hand. In the singing of the verse for the fifth time, omit the word "rubbed" and substitute a rubbing movement with the right hand on the chest. When the verse is sung the sixth time, the words "camphorated oil" are omitted, and a little sniff is substituted.

MY HERO

THE best way to do this stunt is with paper table napkins, and for this reason it would fit into an after-dinner period best of all. The leader takes a napkin from the table and presses it into the shape of a bow tie or a hair ribbon as the case may be, for it is to be used in this case for either.

The leader places the napkin on the right side of his head and at the same time tilts his head to the left and says, "I can't pay the rent, I can't pay the rent, I can't pay the rent." All persons in the group imitate his actions and repeat the words. These words should be spoken in a pleading feminine voice. The leader next places the napkin in the position of a moustache and says in a stern voice, "You must pay the rent, You must pay the rent, You must pay the rent." All repeat his words and follow his actions. The action of the leader should now be repeated, with the "I can't pay the rent" and the "You must pay the rent," each repeated by the group.

The leader then leads the group in the stamping of feet to indicate the approach of a horse, and after this has gone on for a moment, the leader cries, "Whoa, whoa," and pulls as if pulling on the reins of a horse's bridle. The leader places the napkin in the position of a bow tie and says in a manly fashion, "I'll pay the rent." The leader then places the napkin on the right side of his head, leans the head toward the left and says in a sweet feminine voice, "My Hero." The leader then places the napkin in the position of a moustache and says, "Curses, foiled again."

THE GRAND OLD DUKE OF YORK

WHILE this stunt is often used following a fellowship dinner, it can be used at any time with any group. The words are sung to the tune of "The Farmer in the Dell," while the leader indicates the actions in which all are to participate.

> The grand ol' Duke of York
> He had ten thousand men.
> He marched them up the hill and then
> He marched them down again.
>
> And when you're up, you're up,
> And when you're down, you're down,
> And when you're only halfway up,
> You're neither up nor down.

When the words "He marched them up the hill" are sung, all persons stand. On the words "He marched them down again," all are seated. On the words "And when you're up," all arise, and on the words "And when you're down," all are seated. On the words, "And when you're only halfway up," all stand in a stooped position, or halfway up position. On the words "You're neither up," all stand. And on the words "nor down," all are seated. This song should be repeated with the actions three or four times, getting faster each time. Don't try this if your heart is bad!

I DON'T WANT TO MARCH WITH THE INFANTRY

SING the following words to the tune of "The Old Gray Mare, She Ain't What She Used to Be," putting in the actions as indicated below:

> I don't want to march with the infantry,
> Ride with the cavalry, shoot with artillery,
> I don't want to fly over enemies,
> I want to be friendly!
> I want to be friendly!
> I want to be friendly!
> I don't want to march with the infantry,
> Ride with the cavalry, shoot with artillery,
> I don't want to fly over enemies,
> I want to be friendly.

The words "March with the infantry" are accompanied by a stamping of marching feet. The words "ride with the cavalry" are accompanied by motions as if riding a horse. The words "shoot with artillery" are accompanied by the pointing of the index finger and the cocking of the thumb to represent shooting. The words "I don't want to fly over enemies" are accompanied by the waving of the hands as if flying. The words "I want to be friendly" are accompanied by the motion of clasping the hands together and raising them to about the level of the left shoulder and moving them back and forth. Another action that may be used here is to have each one reach across the table or to the one in front or behind him and shake hands. These actions are repeated as the words are repeated. Sing the words about three times, each time getting a little faster with the words and actions.

ONE FINGER KEEPS MOVING

THIS is a motion song. If it is sung with a musical instrument, the accompanist must know to add the extra notes with each verse. The leader should indicate the actions and lead them.

1. One finger, one thumb, one hand, one arm, keep moving;
   One finger, one thumb, one hand, one arm, keep moving;
   One finger, one thumb, one hand, one arm, keep moving—
   And we'll all be happy again,
   And we'll all be happy again.
2. One finger, one thumb, one hand, one arm, two arms,
   keep moving, etc.

3. One finger, one thumb, one hand, one arm, two arms, one
   foot, keep moving.
4. One finger, one thumb, one hand, one arm, two arms, one
   foot, two feet, keep moving, etc.
5. . . . two feet, stand up and sit down and keep moving, etc.
6. . . . two feet, stand up, run around the table and sit down,
   keep moving—
   And we'll all be happy again.
   And we'll all be happy again.

YOU CAN'T GO TO HEAVEN

THIS is a refrain song. The leader sings the first line, "You can't go to Heaven," and the group sings these words back as a refrain. The leader then sings, "In a rocking-chair," and the group sings the refrain. He then sings, "You'll rock right by," which is sung back as a refrain. Then the leader finishes the verse, "That golden stair." After the group has echoed this refrain all join together in the chorus:

Ain't goin' to grieve my Lo'd no mo'
Ain't goin' to grieve my Lo'd no mo'
Ain't goin' to grieve my Lo'd no mo'.

After the verses here are sung, or as soon as anyone can think of the words to another verse, he should raise his hand and lead it. The object is to see how long it can go without stopping. A group of a hundred young people between the ages of sixteen and twenty-four kept it going for almost a half hour.

You can't go to Heaven
   In a rocking-chair
You will rock right by
   That golden stair.

Chorus

Ain't goin' to grieve my Lo'd no mo',
Ain't goin' to grieve my Lo'd no mo',
Ain't goin' to grieve my Lo'd no mo'.

You can't go to Heaven
   On a roller skate;
You'll skate right by
   That golden gate.

You can't go to Heaven
   In an air-o-plane;
You'll sail right by
   That heavenly lane.

You can't go to Heaven
   On three point two;
They'll smell your breath,
   Won't let you through.

You can't go to Heaven
   In a jinriksha;
It don't know gee,
   And it don't know haw.

You can't go to Heaven
   If your name is Jack;
They'll look you over
   And send you back.

You can't go to Heaven
   In a Chevrolet;
For if you do
   You'll lose your way.

You can't go to Heaven
   In a Cadillac;
It'll take you there
   And bring you back.

You can't go to Heaven
  On a rubber check;
They'd throw you down
  And break your neck.

You can't go to Heaven
  On a dancing floor
You'll dance right by
  That open door.

You can't go to Heaven
  On a battleship;
In the lake of fire
  You'll take a dip.

If you get to Heaven
  Before I do,
Just bore a hole
  And pull me through.

You can't go to Heaven
  In a Ford sedan;
You'll bump right by
  That promised land.

Get down on your knees
  And say a prayer;
You can't go to Heaven
  In a rocking-chair.

You can't go to Heaven
  If your name is Ken;
St. Peter will send
  You back again.

JACOB'S LADDER

"JACOB'S LADDER" is a very beautiful spiritual which is
more often used by young people as a devotional hymn than

for any other purpose. Young people frequently sing it as they leave the dining room after the evening meal and walk to the evening vesper hour. It is also used after the recreational period to change the attitude of young people and turn their thoughts toward the closing worship of the friendship circle or similar service.

Jacob's Ladder[1]

Negro Spiritual
Harmonized by Lawrence Curry

1. We are climb-ing Ja-cob's lad-der, We are climb-ing Ja-cob's
2. Ev-ery round goes high-er, high-er, Ev-ery round goes high-er,
3. Sin-ner, do you love my Je-sus? Sin-ner, do you love my
4. If you love Him, why not serve Him? If you love Him, why not
5. Do you think I'd make a sol-dier? Do you think I'd make a

lad - der, We are climb-ing Ja-cob's lad-der, Sol-dier of the cross.
high - er, Ev-ery round goes high-er, high-er, Sol-dier of the cross.
Je - sus? Sin-ner, do you love my Je-sus? Sol-dier of the cross.
serve Him? If you love Him, why not serve Him? Sol-dier of the cross.
sol - dier? Do you think I'd make a sol-dier? Sol-dier of the cross.

6. Rise, shine, give God glory,
   Soldier of the cross.

7. We are climbing higher, higher,
   Soldier of the cross.

[1] Music copyright, 1941, by Presbyterian Board of Christian Education. Used by permission.

HOKEY-POKEY

The Hokey-Pokey is a stunt which is usually required by the group of some prominent person for some infraction of the rules or of etiquette. This person is required to stand up and do the hokey-pokey while the group sings the words to the tune of "Looby Loo." When this person comes to the words, "You do the hokey-pokey and turn yourself around" he holds up both hands with the two index fingers pointing upward, turns his head to one side, as if to be cute, and turns himself around to the rhythm of the music. A whole group may be required to do this together, such as the members of a committee, or the faculty of a Young People's conference. Below are given the words of the song and the music to "Looby Loo," to which they are sung.[2]

You put your right hand in,
Take your right hand out,
You put your right hand in
And shake it all about.

[2] From *The Fun Encyclopedia* by E. O. Harbin. Abingdon-Cokesbury. Used by permission.

You do the Hokey-Pokey and
Turn yourself around.
That's what it is all about.
Hey!

Other verses start as follows:

You put your left hand in, etc.
You put your right foot in, etc.

Continue with "left foot," "right shoulder," "left shoulder," "right hip," "left hip," and conclude with, "You put your whole self in."

DO YOUR EARS HANG LOW?

Tune: "Turkey in the Straw"

Do your ears hang low?
Do they wobble to and fro?
Can you tie them in a knot?
Can you tie them in a bow?
Can you throw them 'cross your shoulder
Like a Continental soldier?
Do your ears hang low?

Actions: On "Do your ears hang low?" wave hands with fingers together under ears. On "Do they wobble to and fro?" shake head and wobble ears. On "Can you tie them in a knot? Can you tie them in a bow?" make motions with hands as if tying a bow. On "Can you throw them 'cross your shoulder like a Continental soldier?" make motion as if throwing something across shoulder. On "Do your ears hang low?" make the same motions as for the first line. This song should be repeated several times, getting faster each time.

TAPS

A NICE way for a group to say "Goodnight" when in camp or conference is to use the following words to the tune of "Taps":

Day is done. Gone the sun,
From the lake, from the hill,
    from the sky.
All is well.
Safely rest
God is nigh.

On the words "From the lake" raise hands palm down to
waist level. On the words "from the hill" raise hands and
arms to shoulder level, and on the words "from the sky"
reach hands and arms high above head. On the words "All
is well" drop hands to shoulder level, and on the words
"Safely rest, God is nigh" drop hands to side.

WE'RE GLAD THIS WEEK HAS COME

Tune: "Auld Lang Syne"

We're glad this week has come around,
    For friends like you and me
Are closer drawn, and ties made dear
    That ne'er forgot shall be;
So here we are, so sing our praise,
    Our hearts are filled with cheer,
Let's make each day a time like this
    Throughout the whole long year.

EVERYBODY LIKES HIM

Tune: "John Brown Had a Little Indian"

Everybody, everybody, everybody likes him,
Everybody, everybody, everybody likes him,
Everybody, everybody, everybody likes him,
Everybody likes ———.

SMILE A SMILE, EVERYBODY

Tune: "How Do You Do"

Smile a smile, everybody, smile a smile,
Smile a smile, everybody, smile a smile,
    Part your lips an even mile,
    Turn the corners up a while,
Smile a smile, everybody, smile a smile.

HERE'S TO THE BANQUET
Tune: "The Old Oaken Bucket"

Here's to the Banquet,
The cooks that prepared it,
The waiters that served it—
They sure made a hit.

I'M AS HAPPY AS A DONKEY
Tune: "Battle Hymn of the Republic"

I'm as happy as a donkey that's just had a bale of hay,
I'm as happy as a donkey that's just had a bale of hay,
I'm as happy as a donkey that's just had a bale of hay,
Hee-haw! Hee-haw! Hee-haw!
(Put hands to side of head and flap like donkey's ears.)

"JINGLE BELLS" PARODY
Tune: "Jingle Bells"

Mr. ——, Mr. ——,
 Listen while we sing;
You are good at all your work,
 Great at everything.
Here's to you, here's to you,
 Here's to you to-day,
Here's to you in future years—
 May good things come your way.

ALL YOU ET
Tune: "Alouette"

All you et a,
Think of all you et,
All you et a,
Think of all you et,
Think of all the soup you et   [*leader*],
Think of all the soup you et   [*group*],
Soup you et   [*leader*],
Soup you et   [*group*],
All you et   [*leader*],
All you et   [*group*],
Oh—all you et a,

Think of all you et.
Think of all the meat you et [*leader*],
Think of all the meat you et [*group*],
Meat you et   [*leader*],
Meat you et   [*group*],
Soup you et   [*leader*],
Soup you et   [*group*],
All you et   [*leader*],
All you et   [*group*],
Oh—all you et a,
Think of all you et.

The leader may continue naming all the dishes, as fish, bread, pie, coffee, and may end up with "Think of all you could of et."

SING-A-LING-A-LING

Dear Miss Smith, we'll sing-a-ling-a-ling
We'll sing-a-ling-a-ling for you.

Is there any-thing-a-ling-a-ling
That we can do for you?
Winter, Summer, Spring a-ling-a-ling
And all the whole year through
We'll sing-a-ling-a-ling
And jing-a-ling-a-ling
And ting-a-ling-a-ling for you.

(The singing should be to the accompaniment of the jingling of knives or forks on the water glasses.)

A GOOD ROUND

Little Tommy Tinker

Little Tommy Tinker sat on a clinker,
Then he began to cry,
Oh, ma-a, Oh, ma-a!
Poor little innocent guy.

Little Polly Flinder sat on a cinder,
Then she began to yell,
Oh, ma-a, Oh, ma-a!
Poor little innocent belle.

(After the whole group has sung through one time and learned the song, then have them all rise up when they come to the words "Oh, ma-a, Oh, ma-a." Then divide the crowd into two or more sections and start one section off and when it has sung the first two lines then start the second section. By doing this you will have one section rising at one time and another at another time.)

MEDLEY

Good-Night Medley

The old oaken bucket, the iron-bound bucket,
The moss covered bucket, that hung in the—

Evening by the moonlight.
You can hear those darkies singing
In the evening by the moonlight;
You can hear those banjos ringing—
How the old folks would enjoy it.
They would sit all night and listen
As we sang one song for my old Kentucky home—
Good-night, ladies, good-night, ladies,
Good-night, ladies,
We're going to leave you now—
Merrily we row along, row along, row along,
Merrily we'll row along, o'er the deep blue sea.

BIRDS IN THE WILDERNESS

Tune: "The Old Gray Mare"

Here we sit like birds in the wilderness,
Birds in the wilderness,
Birds in the wilderness—
Here we sit like birds in the wilderness,
Waiting for the food to come.
(Repeat and keep on repeating.)

MAGIC CARPET

A LARGE rug is placed on the floor in a position where persons walking around the room must pass over it. Men and women line up single file and march around the room to lively march music played on a piano. When the music stops, all persons who are touching the carpet are out of the game. Continue until most of the guests have been eliminated. When the number has been reduced to three or four, it will be hard to catch anyone on the carpet.

CONVERSATION CHANGEABLE

A PERSON to play march music on the piano or other musical instrument is the first essential. The girls line up on one side of the room and the boys on the other. When the signal is given, all move toward one end of the room and form couples as they happen to come in the line. They march down the center of the room until all have their partners. If there should be more boys than girls or vice versa, some girls may have to play the part of boys or the other way around. When all the partnerships have been formed, the leader stops the marching for a moment by having the music stopped and announces a topic of conversation on which all are to converse for one minute. The music is then resumed, and all march and converse. After a minute the music stops, and each boy steps forward and takes the next girl for the next minute, and the leader announces a new topic of conversation. Some suggested topics of conversation are: What I did last Christmas; Are permanent waves permanent? How hard it is to get up in the morning; What I like for breakfast; How to reduce; What I did on my last vacation; My home town; My favorite kind of cake; Blind dates; College life; etc.

O CHESTER, HAVE YOU HEARD ABOUT HARRY?

THE words to "O Chester, Have You Heard About Harry?" are sung to the tune of "Yankee Doodle," and the motions are put in as indicated. The leader indicates the motions, and the group follows his leadership.

> O Chester, have you heard about Harry?
> Chest got back from the Army.
> I ear he knows how to wear a rose,
> Hip, Hip, Hooray for the Army.

On the word "Chester," beat on chest. On the word "heard," put hand to ear. On the word "Harry," put hand on head. On the word "chest," which is a substitute for the word "just," put hands on chest. On the word "back," put hands on back. On the word "Army," fold the arms. On the words "I" and "ear," put hand on the eye and ear. On the words "wear a rose," put hands on left breast, at about the position a rose would be worn. On the words on "Hip, Hip, Hooray for the Army," shout the yell, and when you come to the word "Army," fold the arms.

This song should be repeated about three times, getting faster each time.

SMILE SONG
Tune: "Battle Hymn of the Republic"

It isn't any trouble just to S-M-I-L-E,
It isn't any trouble just to S-M-I-L-E,
So smile while you're in trouble,
It will vanish like a bubble
If you'll only take the trouble just to S-M-I-L-E.

(Change to L-A-U-G-H, G-R-I-N-GRIN, G-I-GIGGLE-EE, Ha-Ha-Ha-Ha-Ha.)

SECTION VII

Musical Stunts

THE HOUSE BY THE SIDE OF THE ROAD

THIS is a very impressive stunt, and would not be out
of place at any sort of church meeting. It would be very
suitable for a church youth group to give as a part of a
Sunday evening program.

There should be about six or seven who have good voices
to sing and one to read. The poem written by Sam Walter
Foss, "The House by the Side of the Road," is recited and
sung to the tune of "Perfect Day."

The singers stand in a semicircle around the reader, who
reads the first verse of the poem:

> There are hermit souls that live withdrawn
>   In the place of their self-content;
> There are souls like stars, that dwell apart,
>   In a fellowless firmament;
> There are pioneer souls that blaze their paths
>   Where highways never ran—
> But let me live by the side of the road
>   And be a friend to man.

The next verse is then sung to the tune of "Perfect Day":

> Let me live in my house by the side of the road
>   Where the race of men go by—
> The men who are good and the men who are bad,
>   As good and as bad as I.
> I would not sit in the scorner's seat
>   Or hurl the cynic's ban—
> Let me live in a house by the side of the road
>   And be a friend to man.

The next two verses should be given by the reader:

> I see from my house by the side of the road,
>   By the side of the highway of life,

247

The men who press with the ardor of hope,
  The men who are faint with the strife.
But I turn not away from their smiles nor their tears,
  Both part of an infinite plan—
Let me live in a house by the side of the road
  And be a friend to man.

I know there are brook-gladdened meadows ahead,
  And mountains of wearisome height;
That the road passes on through the long afternoon
  And stretches away to the night.
And still I rejoice when the travelers rejoice
  And weep with the strangers that moan,
Nor live in my house by the side of the road
  Like a man who dwells alone.

The last verse should be sung:

Let me live in my house by the side of the road,
  It's here the race of men go by—
They are good, they are bad, they are weak, they are strong,
  Wise, foolish—so am I.
Then why should I sit in the scorner's seat,
  Or hurl the cynic's ban?
Let me live in my house by the side of the road
  And be a friend to man.

FAKE CONCERT

This is a sit-down fake musical game. Players choose an instrument which they will fake, such as a drum, trombone, cornet, bass violin, violin, or some other. The leader stands in front of the orchestra or in the center of the circle of players. He also chooses an instrument, such as a harmonica. Either someone plays a tune on the piano or the leader announces a tune that all must fake. The rule is that no two persons may play the same instrument at the same time. If the leader changes from playing his harmonica and starts playing the violin, the player who is playing the violin must then start playing the harmonica or himself become the leader. The leader changes instruments until he catches someone not changing quickly enough.

CARRY ON THE SONG

SOMEONE who starts this stunt stands up and sings the first line of a familiar song. He then points to someone who must sing the second line. If this person responds, the one who is "It" must point to someone else to sing the third line, and so on until the verse is finished. The leader may then start another song or continue with the second verse of the same song. If anyone who is pointed out does not respond with his line, that person must take the place of the leader and start another song.

STOP THE MUSIC

THIS would be a good stunt for the music committee to use when it presents a program. Get someone who can play almost anything on the piano to play that instrument for the stunt. He should be able to play both popular and classical music. There should be some old as well as new tunes. The first member to name the tune stops the music. The one who stops the music the greatest number of times should be given a prize. This will create a lot of good fun and amusement.

THE YOWELL CLUB

THIS is a good stunt for a luncheon or party. Select a group of singers, eight or ten if the number of attendants is large, and have them come to the piano. Announce them as the Yowell Club and say that they will render a musical selection in the key of Q. In advance each man has been assigned a song to sing, such as "Tipperary," "When You and I Were Young, Maggie," "Over There," "There's a Long, Long Trail A-winding," etc. At a given signal they all start and sing their songs through. This will get a good laugh.

SWELL SOLO

PICK out a man soloist for this stunt and arrange for it in the following manner. Buy a large rubber bladder and attach to it a small bathroom hose about 2½ or 3 feet long. Attach to the end of this a rubber air pump such as that used on an atomizer. When the singer starts his solo he has this rubber bladder concealed under his sweater, which he is wearing, and the hose passed around behind his back. When he sings he stands with his hands behind him and keeps squeezing the pump and inflating the bladder. The audience will be surprised and astonished as his chest keeps getting larger and larger. When he concludes the solo he can relieve the curiosity of the audience by showing them the air pump.

UPSIDE-DOWN QUARTET

STRETCH a sheet across a double doorway, the top of it being about five and a half feet from the floor. Introduce the upside-down quartet. They have taken off their shoes and put them on their hands. They sit in chairs or stand behind the sheet and stick the toes of the shoes over the edge of the sheet and render a musical number. It appears that they are upside down.

TWO-FACED QUARTET

HAVE your quartet fix false faces on the back of their heads. As far as possible put their clothing on backwards. It would be better to have a rail on the stage with a curtain to hide their feet. They step sidewise on the stage and render a number with their backs to the audience and their false faces showing. For the encore they turn around and sing the same number with their own faces toward the audience. This may be arranged in such a way that they appear to be dressed on both sides. This must be worked out by the quartet itself.

COMIC QUARTET

HAVE your male quartet dressed in a comic manner for this stunt. We recall one quartet in which one member was dressed in a bathing suit with rubber boots and a high silk hat, another had on a lady's evening dress.

BABY QUARTET

SECURE four baby high-chairs and dress up four dummy babies by stuffing baby dresses and socks. Hang a sheet directly behind the four chairs, having a hole cut in the sheet large enough for the head of one member of the quartet above each chair. If it is not desirable to cut the sheet, arrange it so that two sheets can join together at this point. It should be arranged so that it will appear like each baby head is the head of a member of the quartet. Have the quartet render a musical number or two in this way.

FARMER QUARTET

DRESS your quartet up like farmers. Have one member to beat time and let them render musical numbers in this way.

BACHELOR'S QUARTET

PICK out four bachelors from your club and ask them to render a musical number. In all probability they will not have musical talent and will sound "terrible," but it will get a good laugh just the same. If there are not enough bachelors available, use "summer bachelors."

GUESSING MUSICAL NUMBERS

HAVE the pianist play a few bars of several selections of popular melodies or old-time Southern melodies. Give the members of the club slips of paper with numbers on them. Let them guess the name of the song and put it after the number in the order played. Give a prize to the one having the largest number correct.

SINGING CONTEST

DIVIDE the club into four groups by having them number 1, 2, 3, 4. Have three judges, selected in advance; let each group get together around the piano and sing a song. "I Been Workin' on the Railroad" would be a good number for this. Let the judges decide as to which is the best group.

FAKE CORNET SOLO

WE saw this put over in a very clever way at a luncheon. One of the members that no one knew had musical talent was announced as a cornet soloist, and to the surprise of all the members of the club he rendered a very brief number. For the encore, however, after he had played a few bars he took the instrument from his lips and the music continued. It was then discovered that the director of the municipal band was just behind the curtain and that he was doing the playing all the time.

HUMAN XYLOPHONE NO. 1

THIS stunt will require some little rehearsing. Pick out eight members of the club and stand them up in a line or semicircle. The director has a yardstick or other light stick in his hand, and he gently taps the "bars" of the "human xylophone" on their heads one at a time, indicating where they are to take up the song and continue. This makes a very funny stunt, although never a very musical one.

HUMAN XYLOPHONE NO. 2

GET a large sheet of sign cloth about ten feet long, and have a large musical scale drawn on it with eight notes with staffs. Cut out the notes, which should be large enough to admit the head of a woman. Select eight women or girls who can sing pretty well and another as the director and let them render a song in the same manner as "Human Xylophone" No. 1.

PAST PRESIDENTS' CHORUS

CALL all the Past Presidents around the piano and tell them that they are to render a musical number. Have them select a song and sing it. It might not sound very good or produce much music, but it will get a good laugh and produce some wise-cracks.

DISCORDANT ENCORE

HAVE a quartet sing a musical number, and when they are encored and start to sing it through the second time, one of them sings in one key, another in another key, and then have the pianist play the music in still another key. This will make a very "discordant encore" and create a good laugh.

SIAMESE SINGING

WRITE out the following song and assign a group of new members the task of singing it to the tune of America:

> O wat ta goo Siam,
> O wat ta goo Siam,
> O wat ta goos,
> O wat ta goo Siam,
> O wat ta goo Siam,
> O wat ta goo Siam,
> O wat ta goos.

They will perhaps discover that they have been singing "Oh

what a goose I am." Members of the club who have been tipped off in advance may then sing the following words to the tune of America:

> So say we all of us,
> Every last one of us,
> So say we all,
> So say we all of us,
> So say we all of us,
> Every last one of us,
> So say we all.

VICTROLA MUSICAL

ARRANGE a victrola behind a curtain or outside of a door; one with a radio loud speaker would be best. Use a quartet, duet, or soloist, depending upon the record to be played. The idea is to pick out members of the club, who are not known as good singers, and stand them up in front of the curtain or door and announce that they will sing, then turn on the victrola. Of course, they are to move their lips and act as though they were singing. The stunt will create a good laugh.

A LA "AL JOLSON"

As a punishment for some member of your club who is a good soloist, sentence him to sing "Sonny Boy" or "Mammy" *a la* Al Jolson. It would be better to tip him off in advance and have him prepare for it, and yet leave the impression with the members of the club that the stunt is impromptu.

MUSICAL COUNTS

THE players form a ring, join hands, and promenade about the room until the leader calls a number. Immediately the players must form smaller rings containing the same number of players that the leader has called. If the leader knows the number of persons that are playing, which he should, he will

call a number that will force some to be left over when the
smaller groups are formed. For example, if there are twenty-
three players and the leader calls the number five, there will
be three players left over after four groups of five have been
formed. After this has been done, the remaining players
should again join hands and promenade around the room,
and the leader will continue to call numbers until only a very
small group remains.

PASS THE FRUIT

THIS stunt may be done with the group seated in a ring
or around tables after a luncheon or dinner. The leader gives
an orange, lemon, or apple to someone in the group, or in
the case of groups at banquet tables there may be one piece
of fruit for each one of the long tables. While the music is
being played, the persons pass the fruit from one to another.
But when the music stops, the player unfortunate enough to
be holding the fruit has to drop out of the stunt. This continues until there are only two left in. The winner would be
the one who palms off the fruit on the other one as the last
note is played. If this stunt is done with table groups, instead
of having those holding the fruit drop out, have them do
some stunt or display their talent by such means as singing
a solo, leading a song, reciting a Mother Goose rhyme, or
something else that would amuse or entertain the group.

PIANO DUET

HAVE two people who can play a piano duet to pull the
following stunt. If they are girls, it would be nice to have
them dress up as boys: if they are men, dress them as
women; but if there is one boy and one girl, let the girl put
on boy's clothing. The chairman of the meeting announces
a piano solo; but instead of one person appearing to render
this solo, two appear. They have an argument about which

one has been asked to render the number and the chairman finally settles the argument by telling them that they can both play at the same time; one may have one end of the piano and the other the other end. They take their places at the piano and render a musical number.

SONGS IN TABLEAUX

HAVE singers dressed to represent the characters described in certain songs. A quartet, duet, or soloist may sing these songs in which the characters appear; or if enough singers of ability can be secured, the ones, who make up may sing the songs themselves. Some of the following songs may be used: "Old Black Joe," "Farmer in the Dell," "Spanish Cavalier," "Awearing of the Green," "There's Something About an Old-Fashioned Girl," "Bluebells of Scotland," "Mary Had a Little Lamb," "School Days," "Mother Machree," and ending with "The Star-Spangled Banner."

FINDING ASSOCIATES WITH A SONG

WRITE out the chorus of a number of familiar songs and cut them in two parts. Have half as many choruses arranged in this way as you have members of your club. Shuffle these up and give them out to the members before they enter the luncheon hall. Each member is expected to find the member who has the other half of this chorus and sit with him during that luncheon. This will enable members who have never known each other to get acquainted.

SINGING NURSERY RHYMES

DIVIDE the group into smaller groups of five or six, and number each of the smaller groups. Have each smaller group appoint a leader, and give each smaller group a number. Before the game really starts, have each group prepare a list of nursery rhymes that they can sing if called upon.

Now all is ready to start the game. The whole party sings through the letters of the alphabet to the tune of "Auld Lang Syne." At the end of the song the leader calls out the number of one of the groups, such as group 3, or group 5. At once the conductor of this group must start his group singing a nursery rhyme, also to the tune of "Auld Lang Syne." The number of another group is then called, and the game continues. No group is allowed to sing a rhyme that has already been sung. Should a group fail to start singing before ten can be counted, that group must drop out. The last group in is declared the winner.

WHISTLING TOURNEY

THE leader should have a stop watch or a regular watch for this stunt. Players stand back to back, and at a given signal they face each other and start whistling and continue for thirty seconds. At the leader's signal they stop. The group votes which of the two is the better whistler. In this way have an elimination contest and choose the best whistler of the group. Of course, it will be hard for anyone to whistle while everyone else is laughing hilariously.

WHISTLING FOR ENDURANCE

PICK five or six persons from the larger group and have a whistling endurance test. Start all of them whistling, and see which one can whistle the longest. The others may try to get the contestants to laugh and thus force them to drop out. Get a reproduction of the famous painting familiarly known as "Whistler's Mother," and give it for a prize to the one who stays in the longest.

MUSICAL MYSTERY MESSAGE

A PLAYER is sent from the room, and in his absence the group decides on some mysterious message he is to decipher on his return. It might be to take a girl's earring and put it on a boy's ear, or to untie a boy's tie and put it around a girl's neck. This may seem a difficult message for one to get, especially as he is required to get it merely by listening to the music. A good pianist plays the piano, and as the person who is trying to untangle the mystery gets closer to the place where he is to perform his task, the music grows louder. As he gets farther away, the music becomes softer. When he begins actually to perform the task agreed upon, the music becomes very loud. In this way he is guided about the room and to his task. Finally, when he has at last solved the mystery and performed the task assigned, the music gets very loud. You will be surprised at how difficult a problem can be solved in this way.

PLAYING THE FOOL

This is not really a musical stunt, but rather a fake musical stunt. The leader picks out about twelve persons from the larger group and sends them out of the room, telling them that they are to form two orchestras of six each and that when they return, they are to fake the playing of certain instruments while the judges determine what they are playing and decide which group is the better. While the orchestras are out, the judges are instructed to be wrong in each one of their judgments. One orchestra, the first one that says it is ready, comes in and begins playing, or rather begins faking. If a person is obviously faking the playing of the violin, the judges are to say that he is beating a drum. If one player is faking the playing of a saxophone, the judges might say that he is playing the piano. When the players begin to complain about the decision of the judges, the judges appeal to the group and ask, "What do you think they are playing?" The group answers in chorus, "The Fool." When the second orchestra is brought in, the first orchestra will get a keen enjoyment out of their performance.

MUSICAL BUMPS

PLAYERS move about the room to the music. When the music stops, all must bump down on the floor. The last one down is required to drop out. When the music starts again, all players pick themselves up and resume their march around the room. So the game continues until only one player is left.

HYDE PARK

THIS is an old English game somewhat like "Going to Jerusalem." Arrange the chairs in pairs about the room with one fewer pair than there are couples playing. All couples march around the room to the music, and as soon as the music stops, all make a mad scramble for the chairs. The couples must stay together until they are seated, and the couple that is left without chairs must drop out. A pair are deemed to have gained their chairs when one of them is safely seated in one of the chairs. Partners must stay together. After the first scramble, remove a pair of the chairs, and start again and continue until there are only four persons and two chairs. When one of these couples is eliminated, the game ends, and the last two seated are declared the winners.

MUSICAL BALANCE

PLAYERS march around the room to music, each balancing a book or small magazine on his head. When the music stops, the players kneel on the floor until the music resumes, at which time they continue their march. Should the book fall from his head or be touched by the hand, a player is disqualified. The game continues until only one player is left.

SECTION VIII

Stunts for Leaders

STUNTS FOR LEADERS

THESE stunts are designed for leaders to use in breaking the ice or livening up the party when there is a dull moment. These stunts consist of oddities with numbers, nonsense stories, fake intelligence tests, tricks, and stories, in which the leader directs the activity but encourages the group to participate.

FLICKER-FLICKER

THE story is told with the tongue curled back against the roof of the mouth through the entire story. Try to fit the expressions to the nonsense of the story. The group should be asked to follow the actions of the leader. When he blinks his eyes and opens and closes his hands at head level, all should do the same. All should try to register the proper expression. The story follows:

Once upon a time there was a handsome boy firefly. He thought himself really a "hot number." All the little girl fireflies agreed with him, for he knocked them off their wings. Whenever he would fly past them and flirt "Flicker-Flicker" [*blink eyes and open and close hands at head level*], all the little "bobby-soxer" fireflies would flutter and swoon. They all vied for his favor and did their utmost to appear attractive to him. One evening he was flying down Firefly Avenue, when he spotted a new little firefly girl coming in the opposite direction. She was cute, and the little boy firefly wanted to impress her. He spruced up, and looking very "sharp," gave his best "Flicker-Flicker" [*same gesture by all*]. She made no response. [*Register disgust and disappointment.*] He couldn't understand it. Although she had been some distance away, she could at least have given a little flutter. What was wrong? Always before he had "mowed 'em down" with no effort at all. Again he tried, "Flicker-Flicker." [*Same gestures by all.*] She didn't even give him a flash. She was getting very close now—This was his last chance. "Flicker-Flicker [*Gestures*] Flick—." "Oh, what rotten luck!" blurted the frustrated Romeo. *"What a time to blow a fuse!"*

THE BIGGER FAMILY

As the leader tells this nonsense story, let the group say which is the Bigger:

The Bigger family was made up of Father Bigger, Mother Bigger, Little Willie Bigger, and Uncle Jerry Bigger.

They all went to church. They sat in the pew in this order: Father Bigger, Mother Bigger, Little Willie, and Uncle Jerry. Which is the Bigger? [*Allow time for the group to respond, and then give the answer.*]

Mother Bigger, because she is by far the Bigger (by Father Bigger).

Little Willie and Mother Bigger went to the store. Mother Bigger was standing over by the sugar barrel, and Little Willie was standing by the candy counter. Which is the Bigger?

Mother Bigger, because she is "by a barrel Bigger."

Uncle Jerry went on a long journey. Which is the Bigger?

Uncle Jerry, because he is "way yonder Bigger."

Father Bigger died. Which is the Bigger?

Father Bigger, because he is "still Bigger."

Mother Bigger married Uncle Jerry. Which is the Bigger?

Mother Bigger, because she is "twice Bigger."

INDOOR SCAVENGER HUNT

THE leader has prepared for the Scavenger Hunt in advance of the party by placing around the room the articles to be found and providing papers and pencils for the use of the guests in listing the articles as they are found. The objects should be small and should be stuck to the furniture, window casings, and at other places where they cannot be readily seen. Use transparent tape to stick them in place. Some of the objects suggested are: A Band Aid, a stick of chewing gum, a toothpick, a match, a paper clip, a bobby pin, a nut, a postage stamp, a hairpin, a safety pin, a penny, a thimble, a pen point. Tell the guests that there are thirteen objects hidden, and a prize will be given to the one who finds the most articles. They may or may not be numbered, as guests will know when they have found them all. After two or more of the guests have found all thirteen of the objects, stop the game and have the first one who has found all of them to read his list. Give an appropriate prize to the winner and a consolation prize to the one finding the smallest number. This would work quite as well with couples working together, in which case the prizes would be given to the couples instead of individuals.

RAISE YOUR HAND

THE leader puts the following questions to the group and asks the one who knows the answer to raise his hand. The one first raising his hand gets the first try at the answer. If he does not answer it, let the next one who raised his hand have a try. Here are the questions:

1. What country reminds you of the first name of a famous composer of music? Franz.

2. What country reminds you of a famous holiday food? Turkey.

3. What country reminds you of a cold, shivery feeling? Chile.

4. What country reminds you of the discovery of a new territory? Newfoundland.

5. What country reminds you of a lot of microbes? Germany.

6. What country reminds you of a keen appetite? Hungary.

7. What country are you reminded of by what comes out of frying bacon? Greece.

8. What does a baby do when pricked by a pin? Wales.

9. What is a customary wedding gift? China.

KNOW YOUR NUMBERS

THE leader gives the group this problem and asks each one to take paper and pencil and work it out:

1. Take the number of Frenchmen that can't be wrong. (50,000,000)

2. Divide by the number of Solomon's wives (1,000): so far 50,000.

3. Divide by the number of birds in a bush that a bird in the hand is worth (2): so far 25,000.

4. If two is company, multiply by the number in a crowd (3): so far 75,000.

5. Multiply by the number of heads that are better than 1 (2): so far 150,000.

6. Divide by the number in "The Charge of the Light Brigade" that rode into the Valley of Death (600): so far 250.

7. Multiply by the number of stitches saved by a stitch in time (9): so far 2,250.

8. Divide by the number of lives a cat is supposed to have (9): so far 250.

9. Subtract the number of blackbirds baked in a pie plus 1 (24 plus 1 =25): so far 225.

10. Add the number that represents society's upper crust (400): so far 625.

11. Divide by the number of pennies in a quarter (25): so far 25.

12. Subtract the number of men on a dead man's chest (15): so far 10.

13. Multiply by the number of points possession is of the law (9) ; so far 90.

14. Add the number of gables in one of Hawthorne's stories (7) : answer 97.

THE SECRET NUMBER

THE leader writes a number on a piece of paper. It may be any number less than 99. Let's try 32. The leader folds the piece of paper and hands it to his friend and tells him to put it in his pocket without looking at it.

The leader's next step is to ask his friend to write down a number between 50 and 100 without letting the leader see it. Let us suppose that he writes 76.

The leader then subtracts the number he wrote on the paper and gave to his friend from 99. He does this mentally. (99-32=67.)

He tells his friend to add 67 to his number. (76 plus 67= 143.)

He then tells his friend to cross off the first number and add that digit to the result:

$$\cancel{1}43$$
$$\underline{1}$$
$$44$$

Now the leader tells him to subtract his result from the original number:

$$76$$
$$\underline{-44}$$
$$32$$

Now the leader tells him to take the paper out of his pocket and look at the number he (the leader) wrote on the paper. He will find that his last figure is the same as the one the leader wrote on the paper. Who wouldn't be mystified?

MYSTERIOUS ADDITION

THIS is very mysterious, because the leader can tell in advance the sum of five rows of figures of five figures each as soon as the first line of figures has been written. Proceed in the following manner: Ask someone in the group to write down a row of five figures. Any figures may be used except that the last figure on the right must not be either 0 or 1. Suppose that the row of figures written down is 37,486.

Now the leader can give the answer, which is 237,484. It is arrived at in the following manner: The first figure is always 2. The next four digits are the same as the first four digits in the original number. The last figure is obtained by subtracting 2 from the last digit on the right of the original number.

Now what about the other four lines? While the group may write the second and the fourth lines, the leader must reserve for himself the privilege of writing the third and fifth lines.

Let us suppose that the group, or a member of the group, writes down the second line:

Member of group writes	37,486
Another member writes	25,346
Leader writes	74,653
[*Leader's figures must each total 9 when added to number immediately above.*]	
Member of group writes	18,325
Leader writes	81,674
[*Again, leader's figures must each total 9 when added to number immediately above.*]	
Sum	237,484

This sum will be found to be the number the leader predicted at the beginning of the stunt.

SAFETY SPELLING

THIS stunt was used by a group to impress upon their members the importance of safety. Duplicate sets of letters of the alphabet are printed on 3x3 cardboards with colored crayons. These are given to the players. This stunt works better with a large group. If, however, the group is small, a number of letters which will not be used in the spelling of the words may be eliminated. Suppose you decide that you are going to spell *safety, auto, wreck, stop, look,* and *listen.* You can pick the letters that are in these words and not give out the others. When the letters have all been given out, place one group on one side of the room and the other group on the other side. Have some judges selected in advance to declare the winner. When the leader pronounces the word, those having the letters that go into the word arrange themselves from left to right with the one having the first letter standing at the left and others in the proper order. In case of a double letter in the word, the one holding this letter must run back and forth to fill both places. The group that gets itself arranged so that the word is spelled first wins.

THE MAGIC NUMBER

THE leader can make this really mysterious by taking a piece of wet soap and writing on his left arm the number 1089. This is done before the party starts. When the leader, who has planned this stunt in advance, appears before the group he asks each one to write down a number. The numbers must be below 10 and must be descending, as 864, 753, or any other combination of descending digits. While each one will write a different number, the result will be the same if the stunt is properly done. Let us take for example the combination 753. The leader asks the group to reverse the numbers and subtract the reversed numbers from the original number, as follows:

$$753$$
$$-357$$
$$396$$

To this number should be added a reverse of the second number as follows:

$$396$$
$$+693$$
$$1089$$

The leader now asks all persons to burn their numbers. This could be done by using a pan or skillet. The leader then takes the ashes and rubs them on his right arm. This will bring out the numbers previously written with soap so that they can be plainly read by all.

LEMON INK

THE leader writes out in advance a number of appropriate messages, using lemon ink and a new pen. These messages might be one of the following: "Merry Christmas," "Happy New Year," "Joyous Easter," "To my Valentine," or any other special holiday greeting. Also, any joke or gag or pun may be used. The answer to a riddle may be written in this way or the names of nominees submitted to the group by the committee on nominations. Although the paper will appear to be perfectly blank, the message will come out plainly when heat is applied. Use a hot iron, or hold a lighted candle under the message near enough to heat it but not near enough to burn it.

FIND PARTNER WITH A RING

FOR any game that requires partners or for the purpose of promoting acquaintance in a group the leader may prepare for the stunt of "Finding Partners with a Ring." Prepare in advance a number of sentences in which a word ending in "ring" occurs. Then cut off the first part of the sentence just before the syllable "ring" and give the first parts of the sentences to the girls and the second parts to the boys. Each boy tries to find his partner to match his ring. Some suggestions follow:

1. Joe went to the market and bought a her-
   ring for his dinner.

2. I saw the police car tea-
   ring down the road after a speeder.

3. They say that a Yankee is not content to merely b-
   ring home the bacon; he wants to bring home the whole hog.

4. We packed our things in the car and went tou-
   ring all over the western part of the United States.

5. Bob's girl friend has poor eyesight, is hard of hea-
   ring, but is a fine woman for the shape she's in.

6. His biggest job is to take the dog out for an ai-
   ring since he married the wealthy widow.

7. When a girl says that she has more than one st-
   ring to her bow, she means that she has more than one beau on her string.

8. One place not for "Officers Only" du-
   ring the war was the front lines.

9. Mary was greatly distressed because she lost her ear-
   ring just as she was ready to come to the party.

10. Many hardhearted persons are guilty of not ca-
    ring when others are cold or hungry or lonely.

11. The soldier was credited with a deed of great da-
    ring when he captured a machine gun nest single-handed.

12. There was a beautiful bevy of majorettes in the chee-
    ring section yelling, "Hold that line!"

RIDDLE REVIEW

THE leader poses the following riddles and asks members of the group to raise their hands if they think they know the answers.

1. Why are pianos noble characters? They are upright, square, and grand.

2. When is a lady's dress like a chair? When it's satin (sat-in).

3. Why is a wise man like a pin? He has a head and comes to the point.

4. Why do most carpenters believe that there is no such thing as stone? They never saw it.

5. What lives on its own substance and dies when it devours itself? Candle.

6. What is it that never asks any questions and yet requires many answers? Doorbell.

7. What is it that is seen three times in each week, twice in every day, and only once in a year? The letter E.

8. Why is a lame dog like a boy adding six and seven? He puts down three and carries one.

9. Why is a joke like a coconut? It's no good until it's cracked.

10. Why is a room full of married people empty? There is not a single person in it.

11. What does a poor man have, a rich man want, a miser spend, a spendthrift save, and all take with them when they die? Nothing.

12. What is always taken from you before you get it? Your picture.

13. If your uncle's sister is not your aunt, what relation is she? Your mother.

14. Which burns longer, a tallow candle or a wax candle? Neither. They both burn shorter.

15. What do we often return, but never borrow? Thanks.

SOPHISTICATED PROVERBS

THE leader reads the following proverbs, dressed up in somewhat stilted and sophisticated language, and asks the group to quote the proverbs in their common form:

1. Oxygen and hydrogen compounded in the proportion of two to one flow with profundity when placid.

   Still water runs deep.

2. A small steel instrument with a hole in one end used at the crucial moment rescues the square of three.

   A stitch in time saves nine.

3. A vessel under constant observation is hesitant in attaining a temperature of 212 degrees Fahrenheit.

   A watched pot never boils.

4. Always when the humidity attains the bursting point, the precipitation is profuse.

   It never rains but it pours.

5. Desirable mental tranquillity does not accompany the wearer of the usual symbol of regal power.

   Uneasy lies the head that wears the crown.

6. No one, when an *equus* is presented to him, should subject that quadruped to dental inspection.

   Never look a gift horse in the mouth.

7. A short vocal utterance to an individual possessing an unusual I. Q. is adequate to the occasion.

   A word to the wise is sufficient.

8. The species of canine that expresses its feelings vociferously refrains from using its bicuspids maliciously.

   A barking dog never bites.

9. The crook who surreptitiously filches my leather pouch will obtain nothing of great intrinsic value.

   He who steals my purse steals trash.

10. Extreme acceleration of execution is often accompanied by wanton squander.

Haste makes waste.

11. One feathered biped confined is of greater value than double the number at liberty.

A bird in the hand is worth two in the bush.

12. A group of people dwelling in a domicile of silica combined with oxides to form a substance which is usually transparent should never project small geological specimens.

People who live in glass houses should never throw stones.

NUT QUESTIONS

1. Why did the little moron take cream and sugar with him to the movies?

He heard there was going to be a serial.

2. Why did the little moron change his name to Vitamin?

He had heard: "Vitamin B 1."

3. "How Long" is a native of China?

So he is.

4. Under what part of a book do we sleep?

The cover.

5. How many school books can a student put in an empty school bag?

One. After the first, the bag will not be empty.

6. How many of you live on a trolley line? (Raise your hands.)

You had better get off. The trolley's coming.

7. If a peacock laid an egg in a neighboring yard, who would own the egg?

Pea*cocks* do not lay eggs.

8. Can you say taxation without representation?

Yes, taxation.

ADVERTISING JINGLES

THE leader starts this stunt by saying, "Suppose you are the editor of a small-town newspaper and you get the idea you can sell a page of small ads for different business firms in your town by writing an eight-line jingle on one of the following subjects: Automobiles, Bicycles, Toys, Turkey, Ham, Groceries, Sporting Goods, Travel by Train or Bus, or some other subject that suggests itself to you."

Here are two examples of jingles: The first for a Bank, and the second for a Coal Company.

Be prepared for another Christmas.
    Start a bank account.
Get your dollars all together,
    Though but small the first amount.
You will thus have formed a nucleus
    'Round which others will collect,
And next year you'll have a surplus,
    That today you'd scarce expect.

When you sit around the Christmas fire this year
    And your grate reflects the yuletide cheer,
You'll realize you have something rare
    If our good lump coal is burning there.
To insure this comfort, act today.
    Buy a ton, have it stored away.
You'll get a full 2,000 pounds for a ton,
    And the way it burns, "Ain't we got fun!"

Give recognition or a small prize to the one or the couple that writes the best jingle. This may also be used for any other season of the year such as Thanksgiving, Valentine Day, or Easter.

TELLING FORTUNES

USING lemon juice for ink and a new pen, write out enough clever fortunes or prognostications for each guest, and hand to each one what is apparently a blank piece of paper, for the writing will be invisible. Have the person who is to tell the fortunes seated in a booth lighted by a candle or by a strong light bulb so arranged that heat can be applied to the piece of paper. A small lamp with the shade removed and with a 100-watt bulb should not be as likely to burn the paper as would a candle. When heat is applied, the invisible lemon ink writing will be plainly discernible.

BIBLICAL QUIZ IN VERSE

THE following biblical quiz was written by the Rev. H. B. Patterson, Visalia, California, and was used with a group of young people in a Bible quiz. Members of the group are asked to number their papers with figures from 1 to 15 on the left-hand page of the paper and answer the questions by putting the answer after the corresponding number.

1. Who divided waves with a rod
    That to a serpent turned
   When Egypt's king upon his throne
    The Hebrew prophet spurned?

2. What Hebrew prophet cried aloud,
    "You'll die unless you turn;
   This nation shall to bondage go,
    But a remnant shall return"?

3. Who was a wise, much-married king
    Who built a temple great,
   But when the union he would save,
    God said, "It is too late"?

4. Who was the first of mighty kings
    That ruled fair Canaan's land,
   He disobeyed and met defeat,
    And died by his own hand?

5. Who was a prince of Judah's line,
   A king he longed to be;
   But death came to him while he hung,
   His hair caught in a tree?

6. Who was a ruddy, fair-haired boy,
   With a staff, a harp, a sling;
   But ere the sun of his life went down,
   He was Israel's greatest king?

7. Who was a son of the desert,
   Bold, fearless, determined, free;
   But he lost his head when a maiden
   Danced for a king to see?

8. Who was a strong man of ancient times
   Whose power no one could withstand;
   But when his head was shaven,
   He died in a foreign land?

9. Who of all men in this wide world
   Missed life's greatest joy?
   He was the only man on earth
   Who never was a boy.

10. Who sailed away o'er the mountain tops
    Before the days of the aeroplane;
    But was given a heavenly sign
    That 'twould never happen again?

11. Who, hidden beside a brook,
    Was fed by the birds unseen?
    He feared not the prophets of Baal,
    But fled for fear of the queen.

12. Who was the favorite of our Lord,
    Was with him on the mountain high,
    Was banished alone to Patmos' isle,
    'Twas said he should not soon die?

13. Who was a fisherman of Galilee,
    Who toiled while others slept,

But when the cock at morning crew
He bowed his head and wept?

14. Shipwrecked and beaten with many stripes,
    Hungry, and faint, and cold,
    He persecuted the Church in youth,
    But died for it when old.

15. Who was a Hebrew captive
    Who braved the great king's ire,
    But when they tried to roast him,
    He was unhurt by the fire?

ANSWERS

1. Moses. 2. Isaiah. 3. Solomon. 4. Saul. 5. Absalom. 6. David. 7. John the Baptist. 8. Samson. 9. Adam. 10. Noah. 11. Elijah. 12. John. 13. Peter. 14. Saul, or Paul. 15. Either Shadrach, Meshach, or Abednego.

SPELLING NUMBERS

TAKE thirteen 3x5 file cards and number them from 1 to 13. Place card number 3 on the table, with the numbered side showing. On top of it place the other cards so that the following order will be obtained: 3, 8, 7, 1, 11, 6, 4, 2, 12, 13, 10, 9, 5. Take up the pile of cards and turn them over—that is, with the numbers facing down—so that they cannot be seen. Take off the top card and start spelling the word ONE. Each time you take off a card, call a letter in the number and slip a card from the top to the bottom of the stack. After you have spelled ONE, take off the next card and turn it face up on the table. It will be found to be the card with 1 on it. Start spelling again, TWO—and when you have placed another three cards, one at a time, on the bottom of the stack, you then turn up the next card and it will be 2. You can spell out each number in this way until only the card numbered 13 remains.

This is not a "trick." It just works this way if the cards are properly arranged.

PINCHY-WINCHY!

THIS is a very amusing and laugh-provoking stunt. The leader chooses one to be the victim and places him on his left while all stand in a circle. They are told to be very serious. They are not to laugh, or grin, or show their teeth during the entire performance. This will prove to be impossible. The leader has put soot or lampblack on the thumb and forefinger of his right hand. When the game starts, he reaches over and pinches the victim on the cheek, saying, "Pinchy-Winchy on the right cheek." All persons in the circle are told to do as the leader does, and so this is passed around the circle. The leader then says, "Pinchy-Winchy on the left cheek," blacking the left cheek of the victim. Each time this action goes around the circle. Each time it gets funnier, as the victim does not know that the joke is on him. The leader continues with "Pinchy-Winchy on the chin," "Pinchy-Winchy on the nose," and "Pinchy-Winchy, look in the mirror." He passes the mirror around the circle, this time from left to right so that the victim will be the last to see it. When the victim looks in the mirror, he learns why the others were laughing so hilariously.

STAY ON THE NARROW WAY

THIS is a relay and may be done with the large group divided into any number of smaller groups. If there are not more than twenty players, divide into groups of approximately ten to a group. The leader gives the captain of each group a yardstick, a penny, and a toothpick. The group captain holds his yardstick at about the level of his chest with his hands, to form the "narrow way." Each player in his group must in turn push a penny with a toothpick from one end of the yardstick to the other. If the penny falls off, it must be picked up and replaced at the starting point. The group that finishes first is declared the winner.

AUTO RACE

MAKE the automobiles for this race by taking a piece of lightweight cardboard of about 8 x 10 inches. Fold the cardboard down the center, the long way, to crease it. Then take a paper clip and fasten two of the corners together, leaving the other end open. This will make your "auto" in the shape of half of a boat. Now take another paper clip to weight down the back of your "auto," and you are ready for the relay. Draw out a number of tracks on the floor—two, three, or four, depending upon the number of groups participating in the relay. These tracks may be made with chalk or with string, or, if the floor is made of wooden boards, certain boards may be indicated as the track. When the relay starts, the "auto" is placed on one end of the track, and the first player is given a palm-leaf fan or cardboard fan and is required to fan his "auto" to the goal and back to the starting place by using the fan to produce air to propel it. When one player in a group has returned, he gives the fan to the next one. If the "auto" turns over, it must be replaced right side up before the player continues. The group that finishes first is declared the winner.

STAY ON THE SIDEWALK

THIS is a race among four couples. Cut a regular-sized roll of crepe paper into four lengths, which will make each piece about five inches wide and ten feet long. Provide each couple with a pair of scissors. One person is to hold one end of the crepe paper while the other cuts through the length of it with the scissors. If a person cuts his paper in two, he and his partner are out and must stay at the curb until the race is over. The couple that finshes first is declared the winner.

STRETCHER RELAY

DIVIDE the players into four teams. Cut the figure of a man or woman out of cellophane, using a different color for each of the four teams. Use cardboard for stretchers. Each player must lay his team's cellophane figure on a piece of cardboard and race to a goal about twenty feet away and then return. If the figure flies off the cardboard stretcher, the runner must stop and pick it up and replace it. The open hand, instead of a piece of cardboard, may serve as the stretcher. The fleetest runner will not always win, as there is always the danger of the cellophane falling off the stretcher. The team that finishes first wins.

JACK BE NIMBLE

THE leader prepares for this stunt by taking about fifteen feet of clothesline and tying to it a beanbag, softball, or some other object of sufficient weight. The players stand in a circle about thirty feet in diameter, if there is room, while the leader stands in the center and swings the beanbag or ball. He should swing it about ankle high and should swing it inside the group for a time or two, gradually letting out more line until it becomes necessary to jump to avoid being hit. If a player is hit, he must become "It" and swing the beanbag. This will create a lot of fun and is an excellent game for "breaking the ice."

DOUBLETS

LEWIS CARROLL, the author of *Alice in Wonderland,* is credited with originating the game of Doublets. The object is to change one word into another of equal length by changing only one letter at a time. For example, to change "pig" to "sty," it would go somewhat as follows: pig, big, bag, sag, say, sty. This would be four changes, not counting the first word or the last.

But why not play this game with a group of persons, each of whom has been supplied with 3 x 3 cards on which the letters of the alphabet have been printed with colored crayons? It may be done as a contest with judges deciding which group finished first and with fewest changes, or it may be done by one group with no contest as to time. The leader suggests the words to be changed, or, rather, he gives the Doublets to the group. Given below are some Doublets with the number of links which may be considered "Par":

Change Hair to Comb .... Par 6
Change Fish to Hook .... Par 6
Change Sad to Fun .... Par 2
Change Wet to Dry .... Par 3
Change Wheat to Bread .... Par 6
Change Poor to Rich .... Par 5
Change Hate to Love .... Par 2
Change Lamb to Lion .... Par 2

PROVERBS IN CODE

THE code used in writing the following proverbs is that of substituting for each letter the one which follows it in the alphabet. This stunt may be used in two or more ways with a group.

1. Type or stencil the following proverbs, or others you may want to use, in code, and ask the group to decipher them:

BCTFODF NBLFT UIF IFBSU HSPX GPOEFS.
Absence   makes   the heart grow fonder.

CFUUFS CF TBGF UIBO TPSSZ.
Better   be safe than sorry.

DIBSJUZ CFHJOT BU IPNF.
Charity begins at home.

EJTDSFUJPO JT UIF CFUUFS QBSU PG WBMPS.
Discretion is the better part of valor.

FBTJFS TBJE UIBO EPOF.
Easier said than done.

GBJOU IFBSU OFWFS XPO GBJS MBEZ.
Faint heart never won fair lady.

FBSMZ UP CFE, FBSMZ UP SJTF, NBLFT B
Early to bed, early to rise, makes a
NBO IFBMUIZ, XFBMUIZ, BOE XJTF.
man healthy, wealthy, and wise.

2. Another way to use this stunt would be to read out
the proverbs, tell the group how to use the code, and ask
them to translate the proverbs into code.

QUOTATIONS

THE leader prepares in advance of the party a list of
famous quotations. These may be typed or stenciled. The
guests, working either separately or in couples, give the
name of each author. The leader may use this stunt in another way. He can read the quotation and ask anyone who
knows the answer to raise his hand. A prize may be given in
either case to the individual or couple who has the largest
number of correct answers. The list of quotations given
below may be supplemented by using any good book of
familiar quotations:
1. "Give me liberty, or give me death!" [Patrick Henry]
2. "Men may come and men may go,

But I go on for ever." [Alfred, Lord Tennsyon]
3. "Ill fares the land, to hastening ills a prey,
   Where wealth accumulates, and men decay." [Oliver Goldsmith]
4. "The gift without the giver is bare." [James Russell Lowell]
5. "He prayeth best who loveth best." [Samuel Taylor Coleridge]
6. "If Winter comes, can Spring be far behind?" [Percy B. Shelley]
7. "A man's a man for a' that." [Robert Burns]
8. "Only God can make a tree." [Joyce Kilmer]
9. "With malice toward none; with charity for all." [Abraham Lincoln]

TONGUE TWISTER

WE have all tried the old tongue twisters like "A sifter sifting sand thrust three thousand thistles through the thick of his thumb" and "Rubber baby buggy bumpers" and "Six long, slick, slim, slender saplings grew in the woods." How about trying these new ones? "A skunk sat on a stump. The skunk thunk the stump stunk, and the stump thunk the skunk stunk," or

A tutor who tooted a flute
Tried to teach two tooters to toot.
Said the two to the tutor,
"Is it harder to toot, or
To tutor two tooters to toot?"

THE I-KNOW CLUB

THE leader announces that he is going to organize an "I-Know Club" and that anyone who can answer properly one question may be admitted. Players may have another try if they do not answer correctly the first question. The leader can admit only those who answer with a word that does not contain the letter "I," for this is really a "No I" Club. The leader asks: "What do you know?" The player answers, "I know women." He is admitted. But the next one answers, "I know girls," and is rejected because he has used the letter "I," which is forbidden in this game. It may happen that a person is admitted on the first round of questions just by accident. He may have guessed a correct word. The leader may require all who do not answer correctly to sit on the floor, while Club members retain their seats. After half a dozen rounds it is best to tell the whole group the solution to the game.

CONVERSATION STARTERS

THIS is a good ice-breaking and get-acquainted stunt. The leader has a number pinned on each guest and prepares for each guest a list of the things he is to do. The list may be written on the back of the number card. Even numbers are for the women and odd numbers for the men. Two or three things are all that are necessary for each guest to do to thoroughly break the ice.

Here are some suggestions for instructions:

Men: 1. Introduce yourself to Number 9.

2. Find Number 6 and learn the color of her hair and eyes.

1. Find all the persons in the room whose names are Mary, Louise, Jane, or Ann.

2. Discuss your favorite sport with Number 5.

Women: 1. Find all the boys whose middle names begin with a vowel.

2. Tell Number 7 about the most interesting motion picture you have seen recently.

1. Find all the blue-eyed boys in the room.

2. Find Number 3 and tell him about your hobby.

These are but two suggestions for each. A good leader can make this into a very clever ice-breaker and party-starter.

SECTION IX

Party Stunts

HUMAN JIG-SAW

In these days of Jig-Saw puzzles, why not try a human one? This may be done in the following manner: Divide into two or more equal groups, leaving an extra person for each group to do the untangling. Suppose there are 26 in the party; divide into two groups of 12 each, leaving out two of the honor guests or officers to do the puzzle.

In the above case, with two groups of 12 each, members of each group join hands, taking a double wrist grip so that they will not break and form a circle. The leader of the party then tells them to tangle themselves up in the most difficult way they can without breaking hold on their hands. This is done by weaving in and out through the other side of the line and in some cases stepping over the arms of the persons in another part of the line. When the tangling has been going on for about a half minute, the leader's whistle blows and the players are told that they are not to move any more except on the command of the one who is working the puzzle, and that when they are moved to a certain position they must keep that position. In other words, they are not again to entangle themselves while someone is trying to untangle them. This will create a lot of good fun, is an excellent ice-breaker, and will consume from 10 to 15 minutes of time.

SILHOUETTE SHOW

A silhouette show is an amusing party stunt and would especially go over big with children from 8 to 12. It must be done at night or in a darkened room.

As the guests enter they are taken one at a time to a room to have their pictures drawn. Each one is asked to sit be-

tween a bright light and a cardboard on the wall, in such a
way that the shadow of the profile will be outlined on the
cardboard. Have someone who is clever at drawing trace
the outline of the profile with colored chalk or crayon. When
all have been traced, these are cut out with shears, leaving
enough of the cardboard to hold in the hand below the neck
and shoulders.

The ones who are doing the stunt then get ready for the
show by placing a piece of dark cloth or a heavy blanket over
the lower half of a large door. The upper half is covered
with a white sheet or other white cloth. The silhouettes
should have been drawn and cut to very near life-size. The
guests are assembled in a darkened room and the ones doing
the stunt stand on the other side of the curtained door, their
movements hidden by the dark cloth on the bottom half of
the door. A light is thrown on the sheet on the top half of
the door and the silhouettes that have been made are held up
so that they make a shadow on the sheet which can be plainly
seen by the guests in the darkened room.

This stunt can be made very amusing by having the different silhouettes bow as they enter, by putting hats on some,
ribbons on the girls' hair, hitting some over the head with
a baseball bat, having two kiss, putting a dunce cap on another, and any other things that can be imagined.

HOT DOGS

A GOOD stunt to pull at a benefit party is the following:
Have a hot dog stand with some hot dogs somewhere in
evidence. The man who sells them has his forefinger painted
with iodine or mercurochrome. The buns have been cut in
two, but instead of placing the hot dog in the sandwich he
places his finger in it and hands it to the purchaser as he takes
the nickel or dime. There will be a surprised look on the
purchaser's face when he finds that he hasn't received any

hot dog at all, and he will probably bring a friend around to get the same trick played on him.

PICTURE-TAKING

THIS is a good stunt to pull at a children's party. Improvise some sort of camera, and as the children come in they are taken in the photographer's room or gallery and pose for their pictures. In advance funny pictures of different sorts have been cut from magazines and the names of the children are written upon these. Later on in the party they are told that their pictures have been completed and these pictures are then distributed.

TRY YOUR BALANCE

SOME suggestions for balancing relays are: A hard-boiled egg on a yardstick, wet soap on a table knife, a yardstick balanced on the forefinger, a book balanced on the head, an orange speared on a pin, etc.

SAFETY SPOTS

DRAW a large number of circles on the floor with chalk. It would be better to have these in corners and inaccessible places about the room. The group of guests is divided into couples and they march about the room as long as the music continues. When the music stops they must jump for the safety spots. The partners should keep their arms linked together, and in order to be safe must have both feet of both partners in the safety spot. As the game continues erase some of the spots until only one spot remains. In the absence of a piano player, the leader may blow a whistle as the signal to jump.

NOISY PEANUT HUNT

A VERY hilarious and amusing game is a noisy peanut hunt.

Peanuts have been hidden all over the room before the game starts. The leader asks the group to divide into four smaller groups, which is done by counting off in fours; the one's form a group, the two's another, etc. The leader then gives to each group a signal. One group must bark like a dog, one crow like a rooster, another bray like a donkey, and another bleat like a sheep. Each group is asked to elect a captain, and they are all told that everyone may look for the peanuts, but only the captain may pick them up. When anyone finds a peanut he must stand with his finger on it and give the signal and stand there until the captain comes to pick it up. Give a prize to the group that finds the largest number.

FAKE PEANUT HUNT

A GOOD stunt to pull at an April fool party is to announce that there is a five-pound bag of peanuts hidden somewhere about the room. After the guests have searched for these peanuts for two or three minutes, blow a whistle and say "April fool."

PLACE THEM

Two or three couples go into an adjoining room to start this game and other couples are brought in, one couple at a time. Those in the room designate one couple to be placed and they tell the couple that has been brought in that the boy is to place the boy in any position he desires and the girl is to place the girl in any position she desires. After they have finished placing them in this position they are then told that they are required to take this position themselves. This couple is then permitted to enjoy seeing the other couples brought in, one at a time. This will create a lot of good fun.

CAPSULE REVELATION PARTY

IN your Sunday school class, young people's society, or club arrange the names of the men or boys in one lot of capsules and the names of the girls in the other. At a meeting of your group, shuffle these capsules and give the capsules containing the girls' names to the boys, and the capsules containing the boys' names to the girls. They are not to reveal who their capsule is. If your group has weekly meetings, designate what each one is supposed to do for your capsule, such as, send candy, flowers, postal cards, etc. At the end of a designated time have a revelation party, at which time each one reveals who his capsule has been.

CHECKERS

DRAW on the floor with chalk a large checkerboard, large enough to place chairs on the squares. Select two of your best checker players to play the game and set persons on these chairs for the men. They are moved about just like checker men, crowned kings, etc. This will prove very interesting.

If the group has been divided into sides, let one side play against the other. In this case one would be in charge and would be privileged to consult with all other members about what move to make.

BACKGAMMON

THE above stunt may be worked just as well with backgammon. Draw a backgammon board on the floor and play the game in the same manner.

THINK OF A NUMBER

THIS must be worked by two people who know the game. One leaves the room, after asking the group to decide on a number from one to five. When they have decided on the number the one outside is called back and tells the group that he is going to determine the number by feeling the heads of different ones, and he goes along pressing his fingers on the temples. When he comes to his confederate, the confederate indicates the number by the means of bites—that is, by tightening down on his teeth he makes the muscles in his temples tighten and the number of bites indicates the number decided on by the group. This is very easy to do.

SPOON PICTURES

ANNOUNCE that you are going to take the pictures of different individuals with a spoon. Your confederate leaves the room, and when he comes back he is supposed to shake hands with the one whose picture has been taken. Of course, he picks up the spoon and looks into it and acts as if he were trying to determine whose picture is in it, but in reality he determines whose picture was taken by his confederate inside of the room assuming the same position and doing the same thing as the person whose picture has been taken.

PUTTING BABY TO SLEEP

THE only material needed is a pillow. The guests are seated in a circle and one person is designated as "It" to start the game. He must take the pillow and go to some person in the circle and go through the motion of putting a baby to sleep. He may sing to it or pat it or anything else he cares to do, the object being to make the person before whom he pauses laugh. If he succeeds in making the person laugh, that person must then be "It" and put the pillow to sleep. If "It" does not succeed in getting a laugh, he must then go on to the next person.

LINE INTRODUCTION

A GOOD way to introduce a large number of guests to each other, is to have them all stand in line with the officers of the organization at the head of the line. When the introduction starts, the first person introduces himself to the second person, then to the third person, and on down the line until he comes to the foot, where he takes his place in line. The next person in line follows him, and so on until every person has been introduced to every other person.

THE COTTON FLIES

PLAYERS are seated in a circle with the leader standing in the center of the group. He has a small piece of cotton, or a bit of down, or even a piece of light paper. When the game starts, he blows this in any direction he chooses. The person toward whom the cotton is blown tries to keep it from lighting on him or hitting him, by blowing it away. If it does light on him or hit him, he must take the leader's place and be "It" until he succeeds in making the cotton land on another player. It would be very easy to blow the cotton and keep it from landing if it were not for the fact that it is hard to blow and laugh at the same time. A variation of this game—and one that would naturally follow it when the group tires of playing it in this manner—would be to throw the cotton into the air and require all players to laugh hilariously while it is in the air and to cease laughing or smiling as soon as it hits the floor. The person who continued laughing or smiling would have to take the leader's place and toss the cotton into the air.

FINDING PARTNERS WITH CONUNDRUMS

PICK out from the list of conundrums in this book, half as many as you have guests. Give the boy the conundrum and the girl the answer. At a given signal have them find their partners by the answers to the conundrums.

RABBIT

This would be a good stunt to pull on officers and committee chairmen. Let us suppose that the occasion is a Sunday school class party. The leader asks all the officers and committee chairmen to form a circle in the center of the room. He then announces that we are going to play "rabbit." He says, "Do as I do," and then gets down on his right knee and places his thumbs to his temples, making ears like a rabbit's ears with his hands. When they are all in this position he turns to the one on his left and says, "Do you know how to play?" That person asks the same question of the one on his left, and each will get the same answer, No. When the question has gone all the way around the circle the leader then says, "I do not know how to play rabbit either"; but he gives the person to his left a shove, causing him to lose his balance and in falling causes the next one to lose his balance and the whole line of players will find themselves tumbled onto the floor.

SCRAMBLED NAMES

A very good mixer to use at a party where some of the guests are not acquainted with the other guests is to get a list of all the names, by having each one write his on a card as they enter. Shuffle up the cards and give them out promiscuously and have each one find the person whose name is written upon his card.

DOUBLE SCRAMBLED NAMES

A variation of the above is to have all the guests write their names on cards and then have the committee scramble the letters in these names, and the cards are then shuffled and distributed. The guests first have to decipher the scrambled letters and then each finds the person whose name he has and pin the card on him.

ELECTRICITY

ALL join hands in a circle and have one in the center. The electricity is started by one person pressing his hand, and it must go around in rotation. The person in the center tires to find the electricity; and if he catches the one pressing someone's hand, then that person is to get in the center.

SPOONING CONTEST

PICK out three couples and tell them that they are to do a stunt, not letting them know what they are expected to do. Give to each of these couples two spoons tied together with a six-inch string and provide each with a dish of ice cream. Announce that they are to feed each other the ice cream. The couple finishing the ice cream first will be declared the winner.

SNOOTIE

ALL people sit in a circle about the room, except one, who stands in the middle of the room. This person is called the pointer. The pointer points to any one in the circle. While he is counting ten, that person must take his nose with his right hand and his right ear with his left hand. If the person in the circle fails to do this, he has to be pointer. If, on the other hand, the pointer points to a person and says nothing, and that person catches his nose and ear, or starts to, he has to be pointer.

HOT AND COLD

GET someone who can play the piano well for this stunt, and have someone leave the room. While he is out the group decides on some object which the person who left the room is to discover when he returns.

When he returns the piano player is to indicate to him by loud, lively music when he is very near the object. If he is far away from the object, the music is slow and low. In this way he is to find the object decided upon by the group.

DOMESTIC SCIENCE

THE girls of the group stand in a line or circle. Each one has been provided with paper or card and pencil. Each girl's partner stands in front of her. When the signal is given to start, each man writes down on his partner's card all the household articles he or she can think of, beginning with the letter A. It may be albums, alarm clock, alum, etc. When the whistle blows the men move to the left, and during the next minute or half minute write down all the articles they can think of which begin with B, and so they pass all the way around the line, writing articles beginning with different letters of the alphabet. If the game gets too long, it would be advisable not to allow more than thirty seconds for some of the letters.

WHICH BOOK?

FIVE books are laid out on a table, and while one player leaves the room, his confederate, who is in on the trick, asks the group to decide on one of the books. When the one outside the room returns, the confederate points to the books one at at time, saying "Is it this one?" "Is it this one?" and he is always able to identify the book decided upon by the group.

It is done very simply in this way. If the book decided on by the group is the third book, the confederate points to the third book on the third question, or if it is the second book he points to the second book on the second question. In other words, every time he points to a book that corresponds with the number of the question asked, that will be the right book. Suppose, for instance, the book decided on is the fourth book, the order would be as follows: The person staying in the room points to the second book and says "Is this it?" then to the first book, then to the fifth book, and then to the fourth book.

BUMPITY, BUMP, BUMP, BUMP

THE leader has the crowd gather in a circle. She then gets in the center and starts the game off. She walks up to some person unexpectedly and with her hands at her ears, flapping them like a donkey's, she says very rapidly, "Bumpity, bump, bump, bump." The person she does this to, is supposed to count to ten before she finishes. If he fails to, he takes her place in the center of the circle and she takes his place and the game continues.

SPINACH

THE group is arranged in a circle. One person starts counting, beginning at one. The person next to him says two, then three, etc. The person saying seven or any multiple of seven, such as 14 or 35, or as 17 or 37 must say "spinach" instead. If they fail to say "spinach" for seven or its multiple, they are required to sit in the middle of the floor. The last one remaining seated in a chair wins. Each time a person has to sit on the floor, the next person starts at one again, thus seeing how high the count can be taken.

HE CAN DO LITTLE

A LEADER, knowing the trick, starts by taking a walking cane and rapping it on the floor while repeating these words, "He can do little who can't do this." But before he says anything he clears his throat loudly. The cane is passed on to the next person. Each one has a turn until everyone catches on to the trick of clearing the throat before saying anything.

ACTING PROVERBS [1]

DIVIDE the crowd into groups. Let each group act out a proverb of its own selection, the rest endeavoring to guess what it is. You might have judges to decide which group makes the cleverest presentation.

Suggested proverbs are: "All is not gold that glitters," "A fool and his money are soon parted," "There's many slip 'twixt the cup and the lip," "All's well that ends well," "Two heads are better than one," "Birds of a feather flock together," "Every dog has his day."

The last one could be represented by persons standing on all fours in a row, each dog with a name and the name of a day of the week on a card hung about the neck. Thus there would stand "Carlo, Monday; Fido, Tuesday; Rover, Wednesday," etc. This will require some original thinking and produce some good laughs.

MURDER

ALL are given slips of paper. Two of these slips have writing on them; one has "Detective," the other has "Murderer." Each player has a slip of paper, but no one knows what the other has. The "Detective" leaves the room for five minutes. The lights are turned out—the "Murderer" pretends to murder someone. The "Detective" then comes back into the room and asks questions of anybody he likes, but he can only ask the question once, "Are you the

[1] From *Phunology,* by E. O. Harbin. Abingdon-Cokesbury. Used by permission.

'Murderer'?" The person he asks has to tell the truth. No one can lie except the "Murderer." If there is a large crowd, the "Detective" has three trials at guessing who the "Murderer" is. He loses the case if he does not guess the third time.

MYSTIC CIRCLE

SEAT the group in a circle with one person in the center. Everyone must be quiet, no moving, no talking. The person in the center of the circle says, with one hand raised overhead and making a circle, "Around and around the room moves the mystic circle. Does it move anyone to leave the room?" Those who know how to play watch and listen. The first person who moves or speaks or makes any kind of a noise is the victim. One who knows the game leaves the room. The one in the center shakes hands with the person who made the noise or spoke, and the one who left the room has to come in and shake hands with the same person. As soon as one who did not know the trick at the beginning thinks he has caught on, he may go out and come back and try shaking hands with the right person. Let the stunt continue until several have caught on, then tell them all the trick.

CHINESE WRITING

Two persons must know how to play the game. One goes out of the room; the other remains and asks the others to select some word. After the word is chosen the one who left the room is called back. The person who remained in the room says, "Can you follow me?" and makes lines and circles, as if writing letters on the floor with a pointer or stick. Since the writer said "Can you follow me?" the reader knows that the first letter of the word is "C." The vowels are A, E, I, O, U, and are written by 1-2-3-4-5 taps on the floor. The more mysterious the writing on the floor, the more deceptive. The writer continues using sentences beginning with consonants as they come in the word, and indicating the vowels with taps on the floor, until his confederate deciphers the word.

INDOOR ZOO

MATERIALS needed are: Pencils and slips of paper numbered to twelve. A naked doll, a necktie, a paper on which several numbers have been written and their sum found, a chain, a bottle of ink, a coin, two keys, a tie rack, a pillow, a pan, a tape measure. Have written on separate slips of paper, numbered to twelve, the following expressions: 1—ena; 3—ger; 4—opos; 6—m; 8—oon; 10—don; 11—ther; 12—ir. Assembling materials: Tie the expression "ena" to a light fixture; number it 1. Lay the following on a table: The naked doll, number it 2. Necktie and "ger," number it 3. "Opos" and the paper on which numbers have been added, number it 4. The chain, number it 5. "M" and the ink bottle, number it 6. The coin and a key, number it 7. "Con" and the tie rack, number it 8. Pillow, number it 9. "Don" and the key, number it 10. The pan and "ther," number 11. Tape measure and "ir," number 12. Conducting game: Give each guest a numbered paper and a pencil. Lead them to the table where the above articles are displayed and tell them that this group of objects represent animals found in a zoo. They are to identify the groups on their papers opposite the numbers of the objects. The person identifying the largest number should be presented a prize. The answer is:

1. Hyena	5. Lynx	9. Lion (lie on)
2. Bear	6. Mink	10. Donkey
3. Tiger	7. Monkey	11. Panther
4. Opossum	8. Raccon	12. Tapir

NURSERY RHYMES

ONE person goes out of the room and the remaining group selects some well-known nursery rhyme. Each person is given one word (an important one in the rhyme, if there are only a few players; otherwise both the telling words and the others may be used). When the person who is "It" returns he asks each individual a question and then the person must answer, using his selected word in the rhyme. "It" must find out what the rhyme is. One question at a time should be asked and "It" may ask in turn as many times as needed.

LUCKY CIRCLES

THIS game is similar to "Going to Jerusalem." Instead of having one chair less than the number of people playing, there is one less circle drawn on the floor. When the music stops everyone tries to get in a circle. After each stop, a circle is erased, until there is only one circle left. The last time the piano stops the one who gets the circle is the winner. This may be played by couples, also.

EMPTY CHAIR

FORM a circle of chairs, having enough chairs for everyone to have one, then have one of the persons vacate a chair and get inside the circle, leaving his chair in the circle vacant. Then the person sitting on the right of the empty chair moves over and sits in the chair of the person in the center. Each player in turn moves to the vacant chair, keeping the circle moving all the time. The one in the center tries to sit in the vacant chair. If he does happen to sit down in the vacant chair, the one on the right has to get up and get in the center and go through the same procedure as before.

CRAZY QUESTIONS AND ANSWERS

DIVIDE into two equal sides and give each person a piece

of paper and have players on one side write questions and players on the other side an answer to any question. Then have one person take up the questions, mix them up, pass them back out, and have another take up the answers and mix them up and pass them out again. The two sides face each other and the first in line asks his or her question and the one opposite answers it. You will be surprised sometimes how well the answers fit.

ONE-EYED THREADING-THE-NEEDLE CONTEST[2]

GET girls into one room and boys into another. The boys are called in two at a time and are told that they are to engage in a contest in threading a needle with one eye shut. Previous to their entrance two of the girls have gotten some soot on the palm of the right hand. The boys are requested to sit in two chairs; one young lady provides them with needle and thread, and the two designated ones hold the smutted palms over the closed eye to make sure the contestant doesn't cheat. You can imagine the effect. Each boy will wonder, when the contest is finished, if he looks like the other fellow. We heard of one young fellow who, after the girl had covered his right eye, complained that he could see better out of that eye and preferred that the left be covered. Of course he was accommodated.

CONSTANTINOPLE

BEGIN by writing the word "Constantinople" along the left margin of the paper. On the right side of the paper start at the bottom and write the same word. Players have to think of a word that begins with the letter on the left side and ends with the one on the right. The idea is to think of a

[2] From *Phunology,* by E. O. Harbin. Abingdon-Cokesbury. Used by permission.

word with the most letters, for each letter counts one. When players have finished they count up their score, and the one having the most points wins.

First Letter	Word	Last Letter
C	Conference	E
O	Optimistical	L
N	Non-Stop	P
S	Sombrero	O
T	Transubstantiation	N
A	Alibi	I
N	Neatsfoot	T
T	Temptation	N
I	Insomnia	A
N	Naturalist	T
O	Omnibus	S
P	Politician	N
L	Lasso	O
E	Emblematic	C

JIG-SAW PUZZLES

DIVIDE guests into four groups and give each group a jig-saw puzzle. It would be better to have these puzzles all alike, but it is not absolutely necessary if all are about equally difficult. The first group to complete the puzzle wins the prize.

CONTINUOUS STORY

A PENCIL and paper are handed to one person to begin a story. It is best if the story follows the theme of the party. He may write a short paragraph, or a sentence, and then pass the paper on to the next person. This is kept up until everyone has contributed to the story. The story may then be read aloud by the "leader" of the games. If the number of guests is large, it would be best to start two or three stories, in which case all would be read when completed.

GEOGRAPHY

GUESTS are supplied with papers and pencils. On the papers are written or typed the letters in the word G-e-o-g-r-a-p-h-y. These should be placed in a vertical position down the left side of the paper. When the leader gives the signal players start writing the names of countries after the letters in Geography; as, G-Germany, E-Egypt, etc. Give a prize to the one who finishes first or the one who gets the largest number in a given time.

PEANUT POLO

CONSTRUCT goal-posts five feet apart and about one foot from the wall, if you play indoors. The "peanut" is a three or four-inch stick, one-half inch thick and rounded at each end. There are eleven players on each side, each having a stick fifteen to eighteen inches long. The game is played like regular polo, each side having its guards, centers, and goal-keepers.

ENDING WORDS

PLAYERS sit in a circle. One player is asked to start spelling a word. He names a letter, having a completed word in mind. He may name the letter C, having in mind cat. The third player does not have to finish the word, but may use the letter L, having in mind calling. Also he may use the letter t, and declare that the word he has in mind is "Catholic." The one who finishes a word (that is, cannot name a word which he had in mind with additional letters in it) must do a stunt, suggested by the leader of the party.

CROSS-WORD PUZZLES

DIVIDE the guests into four groups and give each group a cross-word puzzle and a dictionary. These puzzles may be cut from any daily paper. It would be best to have them all alike. The group that completes its puzzle first wins. The leader may have the answers to these puzzles by using all old papers.

TRUTH OR CONSEQUENCES

THE success of this stunt depends largely upon the cleverness of the leader. As he approaches each player he says: "Truth or Consequences?" If the player says "Truth," he must then answer any question truthfully that is asked him by the leader. If he says "Consequences," he must do any stunt demanded by the leader.

DESCRIPTIONS

GUESTS are supplied with papers and pencils. They are asked to describe someone in the group. This description should be as humorous as possible. When the papers have been selected, some of the most humorous should be read.

ENDLESS THREAD[3]

HAVE a piece of white cotton thread sticking on the back of your coat. Naturally someone will attempt to remove it. Then the fun begins, for as the obliging person pulls the thread away from the coat it becomes longer and longer, while the joker walks away, finally turning around and appearing astonished and chagrined at what has happened. The trick is worked by putting a spool of thread in the inside pocket of the coat, after just enough of it has been threaded through a needle and passed through the back of the coat so that a bit of thread appears to be only sticking to the clothes. This would be a good stunt to work at an April Fool party.

[3] From *Phunology*, by E. O. Harbin. Abingdon-Cokesbury. Used by permission.

SECTION X

Stunts for Scouts and Camps

THE TABLE

CONSTRUCT a large table, with the posts buried in the ground, making the top of the table about 2½ feet high and about 4 feet wide and from 10 to 12 long. Two teams of equal number, from 6 to 12 boys on a side, may play. One group gets on the table and the other on the ground. When the leader's whistle blows, the fight is on. The object is for the boys on the ground to push those boys on the table off and climb up themselves. This is a rough and active game, but not too dangerous.

CIRCLE PASS

A GROUP of about 8 boys sit in a circle. One boy stands in the center, stiffens his body, and falls over against the extended hands of the boys in the circle. He is then passed around by a gentle push by each pair of hands. The boys in the circle have to sit "tailor fashion" so that there will be room for the boy in the center to stand. Play until every boy in the circle has had a round or two.

SINK THE SHIP

THIS game is played by two teams, from 6 to 10 on a side. One team forms the ship by the first boy getting on all fours, while the second one stops behind, puts his head between the first boy's legs, and grasps his thighs with his hands. The other boys continue to form the line in the same way. When the ship is formed in this way with all the boys in a stooping position with heads between the legs of the boy in front and hands on his thighs, the game is ready to start. The opposing team lines up about 30 feet back of the rear boy and the first player runs and springs as if he were playing leapfrog over the back of the last boy and remains where he lands. The next boy does the same thing. The object is for this team to pile up their men on part of the line and make it sink. If this object is accomplished, the same boys have to be the ship again. On the other hand, if the ship does not sink, the opposite men have to be the ship the next time; and so the game continues. It is always advisable to put the strongest men near the back of the line.

BEAN BAG SNATCH

About 16 boys, 8 on a side, play this game. Line them up and have them number from 1 to 8. They line up so that 8 is opposite to 1, 7 opposite to 2, etc., with a bean bag in the center, as:

```
1   2   3   4   5   6   7   8
        0 Bean Bag
8   7   6   5   4   3   2   1
```

The leader calls a number, as: "One." Those numbered "one" on each end of the line make a grab for the bag. The one who gets it scores five for his side. The first side to make 25 wins a game.

BEAN BAG GOLF

Using flower pots, pans, and kettles from the kitchen, and other vessels such as wastepaper baskets and vegetable hampers, lay out an 18-hole golf course. Make some score cards or get some from the country club. Pair the boys off in twosomes or foursomes and give each a bean bag. Of course the course has been laid off so that some of the vessels are difficult to get a bag into. There should be some "dog legs" or sand traps on the course. Each boy throws his bag at the vessel, which should be from 5 to 25 yards, varying the distance on different holes. Each player keeps his own score, marking down the number of throws it took him to hole out his bean bag. This may be worked into a tournament.

BEAN BAG GRAB

No camp will be complete without a number of bean bags. A couple of dozen will be enough for the average camp. Pile the bean bags in a heap and have the boys form a circle about forty feet in diameter. When the leader blows the whistle, all run and make a grab for the bean bags. The boy who gets the largest number should be given a prize. Bean candy makes a good prize.

BEAN BAG BASEBALL

DRAW out on the ground a baseball diamond. Divide this diamond into 9 squares. If the diamond is laid out three feet on a side, this will make the squares one foot each way. Players stand about ten feet from the home base and toss the bean bag at the diamond. In these squares write: 1-Out at 1st; 2-Struck out; 3-Base on balls; 4-Fly out; 5-Strike [In this case, when one throws he keeps count and is out on three strikes]; 6-One-base hit; 7-Two-base hit; 8-Three bagger; 9-Home run. Select two teams of 9 each and play 5 innings.

BEAN BAG BOARDS

USE pieces of beaver board about 2½ feet square. Cut 3 holes in each board about 6 inches in diameter. Mark one hole near the top "10," one about 6 inches below this "5," and one 6 inches below this "2." Make a braced frame of wood for this board and have players stand about 15 feet away and throw the bean bags. Each player should have 5 throws and the team first making 100 points is the winner.

BEAN BAG SHUFFLEBOARD

SHUFFLEBOARD may be played with bean bags, the player standing about 20 feet from the front of the court and throwing the bag. Any number of points may constitute a game. The court should be laid out as follows:

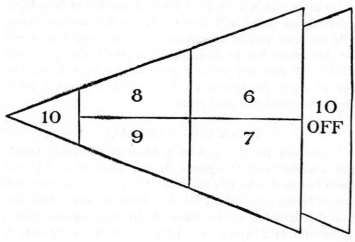

SHOT PUT

USE an inflated paper bag or inflated ballon. This is thrown for distance as though it were a shot.

HUNDRED-YARD DASH

TIE as many strings to the wall as there are contestants. These strings should be about 4½ feet from the floor and at least 2 feet apart, and from 10 to 12 feet in length. Each boy takes the string in his mouth on the starting line and when the whistle blows he starts chewing on the string. The boy who first, without the use of his hands, reaches the goal is declared the winner.

SPINNING ON A STICK

USE a stick about 3½ feet high. The boys are taken one at a time and asked to place the end of the stick on the ground and grasp the top end with both hands. The head is then placed on the hands at the top of the stick, the boy asked to close his eyes, and the leader then spins him around ten times. After this has been done he tries to touch a target with the end of the stick. This target should be about 5 feet high and about 25 feet from where the spinning was done.

DISCUS THROW

USE a paper plate and throw it for distance as though it were a discus.

BLOWING RACE

USE inflated paper bags or rubber ballons. Select five boys to compete. Place the bag or ballons on a starting line and when the whistle is blown each boy must blow his bag or balloon to a goal and back. The boy that gets back first wins.

NEWSPAPER ADVERTISEMENT RELAY

Two folded newspapers of the same kind and date are placed on tables about 30 feet in front of each of two lines of boys. There should be an equal number of boys in each line. The leader has made up a list of the advertisements that are to be cut from the paper and placed the list on the tables. For example: 1-Buick Auto Ad.; 2-Macy's Department Store; etc. When the whistle blows the first boy in line runs to the table, unfolds the paper, finds the ad, cuts it out, refolds the paper, and checks it off of the list. He then runs back to the line, touches the one in front, and takes his place at the back of the line. When every player has cut out an ad the game is finished, and the side that finished first is declared the winner.

NEWSPAPER RELAY

CHOOSE about 10 boys on each side for this relay race. Have them stand facing a goal about 30 feet away. Give each boy two newspapers, folded quarter size. When the whistle blows the front boy in each line races to the goal, but can only advance by stepping on the newspapers. He must run back the same way. The next boy then runs while the first takes his place at the back of the line. The side that finishes first wins.

NOSE AND POTATO RACE

FIVE boys compete in this race. Potatoes, one for each contestant, are placed on the ground about 25 feet from a goal. The boys are required to roll the potato to the goal using only the nose.

NAIL DRIVING

GIVE each boy a 20-penny nail, and the first one to try, a hammer. A large piece of wood at least 4 x 4 has been provided. See which boy can drive his nail with the fewest number of blows.

OBJECT HUNT

THE leader has written on slips of paper a list of three things that may be found near the camp. There are enough lists for each boy to have one, although there may be duplicate lists. Some of the things that may be on the lists are: A round stone, an oak leaf, a pine burr, an acorn, a wild flower, a tin can, and any other objects that may be found around the camp or in the woods. The boy who first returns with all three objects is the winner.

TEN NAILS

GIVE each boy ten 20-penny nails. Have about 5 contestants, selected from the best drivers in the above contest. See which boy can drive all ten with the fewest number of strokes.

STORK TAG

BOYS form a circle. One is chosen as the "It" and takes his place in the circle. When the whistle blows the "It" may tag anyone who is not holding his nose with one hand and his feet with the other and reciting a nursery rhyme. The one so tagged must be "It."

MUSICAL OBJECT HUNT

ONE boy leaves the group while the others decide on some object that he is to locate on his return. The object must be within the circle or room where the game is played. When the boy returns to the group and starts looking for the object the others sing or whistle. When he is a long way from the object the music is very low and as he gets nearer the music gets louder. In this way he can know when he is near the object.

COAT AND VEST RELAY

THE boys line up in two or more lines facing a goal about 30 feet away, and at this goal tables have been placed and on each table a coat and vest. The first boy, and in turn every boy, must run to the table, pick up the vest, put it on and button it up, then put on the coat and button it up, then take them both off, place them on the table, run back, touch off the next boy, and take his place at the back of the line.

CHANGING ATTIRE

SELECT five boys for this contest. Each boy must wear a coat. In case there are not enough coats, it may be done

with shirts. When the whistle blows each boy must take off
the coat or shirt, turn it wrong side outward, and put it back
on. He then must take it off, turn it back right, and put
it on again. The boy doing this first is declared the winner.

DRESSING RELAY

Secure two suitcases and fill them with old clothes. It
would be better to have women's clothes. Place the suitcases on tables or chairs and pick out two contestants. They
stand about 30 feet from the suitcases, and when the whistle blows they race to the suitcases, open them, and put on
all the clothing in them. They then are required to run
three times around the table, take off the clothing, pack it
back in the suitcases, and race back to the starting point.
The one who gets back first is declared the winner. This
may be made into a relay and four or five may be in each
team.

PEANUT RELAY

Line up in two or more groups facing a goal about 25
feet away. Give the boy on the front part of the line a table
knife, a spoon or a flat stick, and a peanut. He is to hold
the peanut on this flat object and race to the goal and back.
If the peanut drops, he is to stop and pick it up. As soon
as he returns the next boy starts. The group that finishes
first wins.

PEANUT PUNCH

Lay a dozen peanuts on the ground in front of each boy
who is competing and give each one of the boys an ice pick
or other pointed object, such as a hatpin. The leader calls
out, "Jab," and each boy stoops over and gives one punch at
a peanut. This must be done with one quick jab. See who
can get the largest number with 12 punches.

PEANUT THROW

DIVIDE into two or more groups. Give each boy in each group about 3 peanuts. Unroasted peanuts may be bought by the pound at most grocery stores at a very small price. Place a vegetable bowl in front of each line about ten feet away, each contestant in turn attempting to toss the peanuts into the bowl. Allow five points for every peanut that remains in the bowl.

ROOSTER FIGHT

SELECT a half dozen boys for the roosters. Each boy is given a stout stick about 18 inches long. This stick he places in the bend of his legs back of his knees and grasps it with both hands between his knees, bending the body in jackknife fashion. Draw a circle about 12 feet in diameter and start the fun, the "roosters" attempting to knock one another over. A round should last about 8 minutes. Five points are allowed for each boy knocked over, the one who knocked him over to receive the points. Allow ten points for each boy who stays on his feet throughout the round.

THREE-LEGGED RACE

A GOAL is marked off about 50 yards away. Two boys from each group make a team and have their inside legs strapped together and their arms around each other's waist. When the signal is given they race in this manner to the goal and back.

SHOE HUNT

GET a large box and have all the boys take off their shoes and place them in the box, then have them take their places in a circle with a radius of about 40 feet, and when the signal is given they race to the box and each tries to find his own shoes. In finding them he may throw the other shoes around in any manner desired. The first boy to present himself to the leader with his shoes on and tied is declared the winner.

CRACKER RELAY

DIVIDE the boys into two groups and have them stand in lines facing each other. Give each boy a cracker. Saltines are best. When the signal is given the first boy in each line eats his cracker, and as soon as he is able to whistle the next boy may start eating. There should be a judge for each line to determine when a boy has whistled and start the next boy off. The side that finishes first wins.

BANANA RELAY

LINE up the boys in two equal groups facing each other and give each boy a banana. He must place his right hand behind him and hold it there while eating the banana, which he is required to peel with his teeth. When the signal is given the first boy must peel and eat his banana, and when he is able to whistle the next one may begin.

PIE-EATING CONTEST (BOYS)

SELECT eight boys for the contest and have four blueberry pies ready. These should be cut in half and placed on the floor in pie pans. Each boy has his hands tied behind him and must eat the pie without the use of them. The first boy to eat his pie and pick up the pan with his teeth is the winner.

APPLE-EATING CONTEST

USING a large darning needle, thread a cord into it and run through half a dozen apples, allowing about 6 feet for each apple. Cut the string after each apple and tie a large button on to the end of each string. Suspend the apples from the ceiling so that they will be about six or eight inches below a boy's chin. At a given signal each boy is required to eat the apple without the use of his hands, which should be tied behind him. He is not allowed to press the apple against his shoulder or other part of his body, but must manage with his teeth and tongue.

CIRCLE ROPE JUMP

HAVE the players form a circle by joining hands. One stands in the center and has a rope longer than the radius of the circle with a weight tied on the end. This he swings around, about a foot from the ground. Players in the circle must jump the rope as it passes, and if a player fails to do so he must take his place in the center.

JUMPING THE ROPE

JUMPING the rope used to be a very common game in rural schools and is a lot of fun. Secure a large rope about 20 feet in length or get a grapevine about a half inch in diameter. Two players, one at each end, turn while the other jump. Those who jump should form a line and run in and out. Try running through as the rope turns without jumping at all. See which boy can jump the largest number of times without tripping. Try "hot pepper" and see if those who turn can turn too fast for another to jump. A little practice will develop some skillful jumpers, and a lot of antics will be invented.

CLOTHESLINE RELAY

A CLOTHESLINE, two dozen pins, and two dozen handkerchiefs, towels, or other pieces of laundry are needed for this contest. Pick two boys, tie the right hand of each behind his back, and require each boy to pin the clothes to the line with his left hand. The boy who finishes first is declared the winner.

PILLOWCASE RELAY

DIVIDE boys into two equal groups and have them stand facing each other. The first boy in each line is given a pillow in a case. When the signal is given the first boy in each line must remove the pillow from the case and replace it. He then passes it to the next boy, who does the same, and so on down the line. The side that gets the pillow to the end first wins.

SACK BOXING

PLACE two boys in potato or meat sacks and tie the sacks up under their arms; fasten boxing gloves on them and let them box. Each time a boy goes down his opponent should get 3 points. Change the contestants every 10 minutes.

RATTLE BOXING

BLINDFOLD two boys. Place a boxing glove on the right hand of each, and a tin baking powder can filled with pebbles in each left hand. The boxers must constantly rattle their cans and in this way disclose their positions.

ROPE BOXING

SELECT two boxers. Put the gloves on them and bring them together so that they can reach each other with the gloves. Tie a rope around the ankle of each, then tie the rope to some stationary object back of each boxer. After this has been done separate the boxers and blindfold them. While they are being blindfolded another boy puts on gloves, and someone ties a knot in each rope so that it will be impossible for the boys to reach each other. They are then told to shake hands. The boy who is not blindfolded and has on the gloves does the handshaking with each and acts as teaser while the blindfolded boxers strike frantically at him. This will create a lot of good fun.

SMUDGE BOXING

THIS is carried on like a regular boxing bout, with the exception that lampblack has been rubbed on the gloves and the winner is the one who can black his opponent up the worst.

DISTANCE BOXING

BOXING gloves are tied on poles about 8 feet long and the contestants stand on chairs or stools or barrels. The object is to dislodge the opponent.

HELLO, BILL

TWO boys have boxing gloves on their right hands. They lie face down on a wrestling mat or on blankets. They are then blindfolded and clasp each other's left hand. One says: "Hello, Bill, are you there?" The other answers: "Yes." He tries to move so that he will not be hit. It is then his turn to call out and take a lick. Let several boys try this.

BLINDFOLD RACE

CONTESTANTS are blindfolded and turned about several times. They have previously been shown a goal to which they are to run. The one who gets to the goal or nearest to it first is the winner. If this contest is held inside, have the contestants run to the opposite end of the room and back.

BAT KICKING FOR DISTANCE

CONTESTANTS take a baseball bat, place it on their right

toe, and hold the other end with the fingers of the right hand. Kicking it like a football, they try to get the longest distance.

JUG BALANCE

USE a large jug, bottle, or keg for this stunt. With the jug lying on its side the boy sits on it with his feet extended with one heel on the toe of the other foot. He is given a match and a candle, which he tries to light while in this position.

GREASED POLE CLIMB

GET a round pole or large pipe and bury one end in the ground, leaving about 12 feet above the ground. Grease or soap this pole and let the boys try to climb it.

WATCH YOUR STEP

SOME object which is easily tipped over, such as an Indian club, a soft drink bottle, or a piece of 2x4 about one foot long, stood on end, is placed on the ground, and the boys form a circle around it with hands joined. When a signal is given to start the game, the goal is to cause one of the boys to tip the object over. The boy who does this must drop out while the others continue the game. The game ends when only one boy is left. The game will work best with about seven boys. Several groups may do this simultaneously.

FUNNEL STUNT

ANOTHER good one to try on the fresh boy is to stick a penny on his forehead, then place a funnel in the top of his trousers and ask him to try to shake off the penny into the funnel. While he is busy trying to make the penny stick on his forehead, someone pours a cup of water down the funnel.

GREASED WATER POLE

CONSTRUCT a greased pole over the water at the swimming place, letting it extend out about 20 feet over the water. Place a small flag on the end. Boys try to get the flag before they fall into the water. This is a great fun producer.

WATER BALLOON RACE

SELECT contestants for this race and give each one an inflated balloon. They must swim to the other side of the pool and push the balloon along with them. Sometimes the balloon will not go as one wishes.

WATER BASEBALL

USE a rubber ball about 4 inches in diameter, a regular water ball. A float is anchored for second base if the game is played in a pool, the shallow part of the pool being near home plate; a designated spot on the side of the pool, first base; and on the other side, third base. Players must swim the bases and the fielders must swim for balls knocked into the deep water. Otherwise play like baseball.

WATER BASKETBALL

USE two tubs, one at the center of each end of the pool, for goals. Use a rubber ball about the size of a basketball for the ball. The game is played like basketball, except that the players must swim most of the time.

PLUNGING

PLUNGING for distance is a good competitive sport. Have the boys plunge one at a time and along the side of the pool so that the length of the plunge may be measured. After one springs from the end of the pool, he is not allowed to move another muscle, and the distance is taken at the ends of his fingers when he removes his head from under the water.

DIVING BETWEEN LEGS

IN water that is not more than 5 feet deep, or not above the shoulders of the boys, they stand in line with their feet apart and each with his hands on the shoulders of the boy in front. The boys in turn try to dive through the legs of all those in line. Some boys will be able to dive through the legs of 12 or 15. He can come up at any time. Boys enjoy playing this game.

SWIM UNDER WATER

HAVE contestants dive off the end of the pool and swim under water for distance.

DIVING FOR BRICK

THROW a red brick into water from 8 to 10 feet deep and let the boys dive for it. If you want to make it competitive, time them and give the prize to the one who comes up with it in the shortest length of time.

DIVING CONTEST

HAVE judges to decide as to the best dives. Try the swan, jackknife, and others. Give prizes to the best and the worst diver. Give a prize for the most humorous dive.

TURTLE RACE

As many boys as desire may compete. They all squat on the side of the pool, and when the whistle is blown swim across the pool and climb up on the other side. The judges eliminate the last five to touch the other side. If there is a large number, more may be eliminated. Those remaining in the contest squat on the side of the pool until the whistle is blown again and then swim back. Five more are eliminated, the last five to arrive. And so they swim back and forth until all are eliminated but the two. These two squat on the side of the pool, and when the whistle is blown swim for the other side. The first to arrive wins.

TUB RACE

SECURE some large washing tubs and have a tub race. Boys sit in the tubs and paddle with their hands.

THREE-LEGGED SWIMMING RACE

IF the camp is divided into groups or tribes, select two boys from each group for this event. Tie their inside legs together and have them hold hands with the inside hands. Contestants line up on the shallow side of the pool or swimming place, and when the signal is given swim to the opposite end.

LOGROLLING

GET a round log about ten feet long and place it in the water. Boys will have a lot of fun every day with the log. See who can stand on the log the longest with it turning rapidly. Put a boy on each end and have them face each other. Each boy attempts to turn the log to his right and dislodge the other boy. With a little practice the boys will become expert at the game of logrolling.

WATER CANDLE RACE

THIS may be done in two ways. Boys may be required to carry the candles in their teeth or in their left hands. At any rate, have them line up at the shallow end of the pool and give each one a lighted candle. They are to swim to the opposite side of the pool without extinguishing the candle. If the candle is put out, the holder is eliminated.

OLD CLOTHES ANTICS

DRESS one boy from each group or tribe in old clothes, including hat and necktie, shoes and socks. Have them race across the pool and on the way back remove the outer clothing down to their bathing suits. The boy who gets back first with the clothing all in a bundle is the winner.

TUG OF WAR

No boys' camp would be complete without a large rope to use for a tug of war. The rope should be about thirty or forty feet long and an inch in diameter. A knot is tied in the middle of the rope and a line drawn on the ground. Have an equal number of boys on each end, and at a given signal each side tries to pull the other over the line.

HUMAN TUG OF WAR

Two boys grasp each other's wrists in the center and over the line. Other boys line up behind, each boy locking his arms around the waist of the boy in front. At the signal one line tries to pull the other line across the mark.

LEAPFROG RACE

SELECT about ten boys from each group and let them have a leapfrog race. At the beginning they stand about 15 feet apart and in parallel lines. The goal should be about 500 yards away, or 250 up and 250 back. When the signal is given the man at the back of each line springs over all of the other men and then gets himself in position to offer his back to the others. Thus they continue until the first man in one of the lines reaches the goal and wins the race.

POISON INDIAN CLUB

Boys form a circle by catching each other's wrists. An Indian club or bottle is placed in the center, and near by an indoor ball or hollow rubber ball about 4 inches in diameter. As the circle rotates about the club in the center the object is to keep from knocking it over yourself, but to try to make the other fellow knock it over. As soon as it is knocked over the circle dissolves and all run. The person who knocked the club over grabs up the ball and throws it, trying to hit someone. If he succeeds, the person hit must retire from the game. If he misses, he must retire from the game himself. Continue until only two men remain.

DODGE BALL

One of the best beach or outdoor games ever invented is Dodge Ball. A soft rubber ball about 4 inches in diameter is used. Players divide into two equal teams of any number on a side, although from 15 to 25 should be about right. One team forms a circle with the others inside the circle. The team in the circle has the ball and throws it at members of the team inside the circle. As soon as a man is hit he must retire from the game. When all in the circle have been hit change sides. The winning team is the one that puts the other team out in the shortest time, consequently it is necessary to have a timekeeper.

WHIP TAG

Boys stand in a circle with hands behind them. One boy has a towel with a knot in the end of it. He runs around on the outside of the circle and places the towel in the hands of one of the boys. The boy thus given the towel chases the first boy, and if he gets near enough he has the privilege of whipping him with the towel until he gets back into the position vacated. This boy then places the towel in another boy's hand, and so the game continues.

WHEELBARROW RACE

SEVERAL teams of two boys run the race. One boy is the wheelbarrow and must propel himself by walking on his hands, while the other boy holds up his legs, grasping them by the ankles. The two boys that get to the goal first are the winners.

HOG TYING

ALL real boys like rough games. Here is one that will give every real boy a thrill. Select five boys from each of two groups and give each a rope about four feet in length. The game is finished when the legs of all five boys of one team are tied up. After a boy is tied he is then out of the game, and cannot untie himself. Try this for a thriller.

SKIN THE SNAKE

ANY number of boys can take part in this. The first boy stoops over and puts his right hand between his legs. Each boy behind him stoops over and places his right hand between his legs and grasps the right hand of the boy in front with his left hand. When all are ready the last man in line lies on his back and the line backs over him, the next boy then lying down, and so on until every boy in the group is lying on his back. The last man to lie down then rises to his feet and strides forward, each man in turn following until all are in their original positions.

BROOMSTICK TWIST

Boys like tests of strength. Try their grips on a broomstick. Two boys hold the broomstick as high as they can reach. They then lower the broomstick and the boy who does not let the stick turn in his hand is the winner.

LIFTING 150 POUNDS WITH FIVE FINGERS

TAKE a boy that weighs about 150 pounds and have him stand with his body stiff and his arms bent at the elbows. Two boys then place their right index fingers under his insteps, two others place their right index fingers under his elbows, and the fifth under his chin. When the signal is given all lift, and it is amazing how quickly he can be lifted from the floor.

PULL FINGERS APART

PLACE the ends of your fingers together in front of your body and ask the strongest boy to stand at arm's length and pull them apart, by pulling in a horizontal direction. If the hands are held about six inches below the chin and about six inches from the body, even the strongest will be unable to pull them apart.

PICK UP

Two boys hold the ends of a five-foot rope in one hand and each tries to pick up an Indian club placed six feet beyond his reach.

ALL FOURS RELAY

THE boys should be divided into two or more equal groups and these line up facing a goal about 40 or 50 yards away. When the signal is given the first boy in each line runs, on all fours, to the goal and back, touching off his next in line and taking his place at the rear of the line on his return. The group to finish first wins.

WEAVER'S RELAY

ONE of the finest of all relays is the Weaver's Relay. The boys are divided into two or more groups of equal number and these form circles by holding hands. One boy in each group is given some object to carry. This may be a flag if near the 4th of July, a hatchet if near Washington's birthday, a rose if in June, etc. When the signal is given the boy in each circle who holds the object starts weaving in and out between the others in his circle, going to his right. When he returns he gives the object he carries to the next person to the right of the place he started and that person weaves around the circle. The first circle to get all its players around is the winner.

ANGLEWORM RELAY

DIVIDE into two or more equal groups. Have all line up in parallel lines facing a goal about 50 feet away. All then squat and each man in line grasps the right ankle of the one in front of him with his right hand, the left ankle of the one back of him with his left hand. When the signal is given the whole line moves forward, and as each man reaches the goal he turns with the line and hops back. The first group to get every man over the starting line without breaking the line is the winner.

HEEL AND TOE RELAY

HAVING divided into two or more groups with an equal number in each group, try a Heel and Toe Relay. Players stand in parallel lines toeing a mark and facing a goal about 30 feet away. When the signal is given the first man in each line proceeds to run toward the goal and return, but at every step he must place his heel against the toe of the foot that is on the ground or floor. In other words, each step must be only the length of his foot.

BEAN-PASSING RELAY

THIS is a good rainy day relay. Place about 8 beans in a paper cup at the head of each line. If there are only two lines, they may stand facing each other. Each person in line has a paper cup and a straw, such as are used at soda fountains. When the signal is given the first man in line starts transferring the beans from his cup by placing the end of the straw against a bean and sucking on the straw, thus holding the bean on the end of the straw by suction. He must pass them one at a time in this manner. If a bean is dropped, it must be picked up and placed back in the cup. The side that gets all the beans to the other end of the line first is the winner.

CRAZY RELAY

Boys line up in two or more parallel lines facing a goal, there being an equal number in each line. The leader tells them that they are to run to a goal 50 feet away, which goal is a line on the ground or a chalk mark on the floor, and they must run two steps forwad and one step backward. No mincing of steps on the backward run is allowed. This will create a lot of good fun.

POP-BOTTLE RELAY

USE 6 or more pop bottles and place them in a circle about 18 inches in diameter. Two or more lines of boys face these circles, for there must be a circle and bottles for each line. When the signal is given the first one in line runs up to the bottles and sets them one at a time outside the circle. The next boy must place them back in the circle.

KANGAROO RELAY

Two or more lines of equal number face a goal about 40 feet away. The first boy on each line is given a basketball, football, or large rubber water ball. When the signal is given, the first boy in each line must hop to the goal and back holding the ball between his ankles. If he drops it, he must stop and pick it up.

PAUL REVERE RELAY

TEAMS are arranged in parallel columns, which are to stand about 10 feet apart. The first man in each line faces a goal about 30 feet away. The last man in each column is to be the rider, therefore a light man should be selected for this. When the signal is given, the rider mounts the next man in line and this man runs with him to the next man and the rider must then transfer to this man's back without touching the ground. When the rider has been transferred to the back of the man who stands at the front of the line, his man runs with him to the goal. The group that first gets the front man with the rider across the finish line is the winner.

BARREL-HOOP RELAY

DIVIDE into two or more groups and provide a barrel hoop for each group. This hoop should be placed about 40 feet in front of each line. When the signal is given the first player must run to the hoop, pass it over his head and down over his body, then run back and touch off the next player.

CHARIOT RACE

THIS is a bit rough and dangerous, but boys like it. Select four from your group to be the chariot. They stand at the starting line and form a hollow square with their backs, one facing east, another west, and the other two north and south, locking their arms at the elbows. This will mean that only one of the four will face the goal to which they must run. This goal should be about 40 feet away. When the signal is given, each chariot runs in this manner. The four to travel to the goal and back first are the winners.

MARSHMALLOW RACE

PLACE a marshmallow in the middle of a string six feet long. Two boys are given the ends of the string between their teeth. The one who, without the use of his hands, chews up the string and gets the marshmallow is the winner.

SILENT CONVERSATION

THE leader announces that for five minutes no one will be allowed to speak. Conversation may continue, but only by the use of signs. This will create a lot of good fun, and a lot of clever signs will be devised.

MAMMA AND BABY RELAY

Two boys are selected to represent each group. One of these is to be Mamma and the other the Baby. Two suit cases are placed on a table about 30 feet in front of the starting line, and when the signal is given the boys are to race to the suit cases and open them. In them they find clothing for Mamma and the Baby. Mamma puts on the dress, sunbonnet, shawl, etc., while Baby puts on the long dress, cap, and napkin. The Baby also gets a rattle. Then Mamma must carry Baby back to the starting line. The two boys who get the clothing all on and get back first win.

WHISTLING MARATHON

GIVE the boys a tune to whistle, such as "Old Black Joe" or "Way Down upon the Swanee River," and tell them that the boy who can whistle the longest will get a prize. Boys get a lot of kick out of this.

BLINDFOLD TEST

BLINDFOLD several boys and test their sense of smell by placing beneath their noses an onion, Vick's salve, castor oil, Limburger cheese, vinegar. Give a prize to the boy who identifies the largest number.

LIFTING SEVEN BOYS

THIS is a good frame-up on the smart boy. One boy boasts that he can lift seven other boys. The fresh boy would be the first one to challenge this. He demonstrates his ability to lift the seven men by lying on his back and asking six boys who are in on the stunt to sit on the ground and place their legs across his body. The smart boy is then asked to be the seventh man and to lie face down across the legs of the others with his head and shoulders near the head and shoulders of the boy below. When he has taken this position, the boy under him holds him down with his arms while the boys near his feet hold his feet down and two or three of the others administer a good paddling.

MEMORY TEST

PICK up, around the camp, about 20 articles and place them on a tray. A leaf, a stick, a spoon, a small stone, or anything will do. Pass the tray so that all may take a good look. See which boy can remember the largest number.

NAMES OF STATES

ASK the boys to see who can write the names of the 48 states in five minutes. You will have to extend the time, and it is doubtful if any will have the whole 48 in ten minutes.

INDOOR FIELD MEET

To this list of events may be added a lot more that may be thought of by the average boy.

1. *Track Meet.* Give a prize to the boy who can make the largest track. Trace his footprint on a piece of wrapping paper.

2. *Running Broad Grin.* Have the boys with the largest mouths try for this. As the boy smiles his mouth is measured with a tape. The one who can smile the broadest is the winner.

3. *Shot Put.* Throwing corn or beans into the mouth of a bottle or jug.

4. *Mile Run.* Add up a column of figures that have been arranged so that they will total 5280.

5. *Long Glum.* The boy is the winner who can go longest without smiling while the others are trying to make him smile.

SECTION XI

Mental Stunts and Brain Twisters

HUMAN CHECKERS

ARRANGE seven chairs in a row. Seat three women in the three chairs to the right and three men in the three chairs to the left, leaving one vacant chair in the middle. This is a good competitive game, and may be tried by two or more groups at a party or luncheon. The object is to jump the men and women like checkers and get them on opposite sides from which they were originally seated. The rule is, that if it is "messed up," they have to go back to the original starting point and start all over again.

Solution: This is done very easily if we keep the following rule in mind. Move one woman and two men, three women and three men, three women and two men, and one woman. But, in order to more fully explain, the men will be designated, from left to right, by 1, 2, and 3, and the women by a, b, and c. Move *a* into the vacant chair, jump *3* over *a* and move *2* to right. Jump *a* over *2*, *b* over *1*, and move *c* to left. Jump *3* over *c*, *2* over *b*, and *1* over *a*. Move *a* to left, jump *b* over *1*, *c* over *2*. Move *2* to the right, jump *1* over *c*, and move *c* to the left.

BOTTLE AND CORK

A BOTTLE and a cork cost $1.10, the bottle costing $1 more than the cork. Can you tell what the cost of each was?

Solution: The bottle cost $1.05 and the cork cost 5 cents.

WHAT COINS?

A MAN has $1.15 in 6 coins. He cannot change a dollar, a half dollar, a quarter, a dime, or a nickel. What coins did he have?

Solution: A half dollar, a quarter, and four dimes.

THE TWO FARMERS

FARMER A said to Farmer B, "If you will sell me seven acres of your farm, I will have twice as much land as you." But Farmer B said to Farmer A, "If you will sell me seven acres of your farm, I will have just as much land as you." How much land did each have?

Solution: A had 49 acres and B had 35 acres.

THE APPLES

Two boys are apple salesmen and each sells thirty apples a day. The first boy sells his apples two for a nickel and so receives for them seventy-five cents. The second boy sells his apples three for a nickel and receives for them fifty cents. The total received by both boys for the day's sales would be one dollar and twenty-five cents, as follows:

30 apples at 2 for 5 cents=$0.75

30 apples at 3 for 5 cents=   .50

One day, however, boy number one was sick and the other boy took his apples to sell for him. Instead of selling two apples for a nickel and three apples for another nickel, he put them all together and sold them five for a dime.

60 apples at 5 for 10 cents=$1.20

The problem is to find what became of the other nickel.

Solution: After ten sales have been made, all the three-for-a-nickel apples are sold. The boy continues to sell apples, which should be sold two for a nickel, at five for a dime.

THE CAMELS

AN Arab, who had three sons, willed his seventeen camels to them. The oldest son was to receive half of the camels, the next oldest a third, and the youngest one-ninth. After his death, the boys, finding it impossible to divide the camels this way, sought the advice of a neighbor and friend. He said: "I will help you out; I will just lend you one of my camels." The camel was loaned to the boys and the division made. The oldest boy received one-half of eighteen, which was nine. The next oldest received one-third, which was six; and the youngest one-ninth, which was two. When the oldest boy took his nine camels, the next oldest his six, and the youngest his two, which totaled seventeen, there was one camel left over, and so the neighbor took his camel back home.

Solution: These fractions do not total up to a whole.

DIFFERENCE BETWEEN SIX AND HALF A DOZEN

WHAT is the difference between six dozen dozen and half a dozen dozen?

Solution: Six dozen dozen would be 6 x 12 x 12 = 864; a half a dozen dozen would be 6 x 12 = 72.

SUBTRACTION

FROM 19 take 1 and leave 20.
Solution: From XIX take I and leave XX.

TWENTY-SIX SHEEP

A MAN had twenty six (sick) sheep and one died; how many did he have left?

Solution: Nineteen. (To say twenty *sick* sheep sounds very much like twenty *six* sheep.)

HUNDRED WITH SIX NINES

How would you write the number one hundred with six nines?

Solution: $99\dfrac{99}{99}$

THE FOX, GOOSE, AND CORN

A FARMER on his way to market with a fox, a goose, and a basket of corn, comes to a river. The boat will carry only the farmer and one of his charges. This presents a problem, for if he takes the corn and leaves the fox and the goose, the fox will eat the goose. If he takes the fox and leaves the goose and the corn, the goose will eat the corn. He must plan so that these combinations are not left together on the other side of the river as well. How does he do it?

Solution: He takes over the goose; returns and takes over the fox. He brings back the goose and leaves the goose while he takes over the corn. He returns for the goose.

INTERNATIONAL CATASTROPHE

WHAT catastrophes of international import are brought about by a waiter dropping a platter with a turkey upon it?

Solution: The fall of Turkey, the ruin of Greece, and the breaking up of China.

ORANGE TREES IN ROWS

A FLORIDA grower planted nineteen orange trees in nine rows with five in each row. How was this done?

Solution:

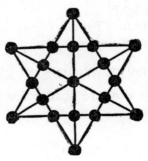

FROG IN THE WELL

A FROG at the bottom of a forty-foot well, every day jumps up three feet and at night falls back two. How many days will it take him to get out of the well?

Solution: Thirty-eight days. He jumps all the way out the last day.

100 HEAD $100

A TRADER buys 100 head of animals and pays $100 for them. He buys cows at $10, hogs at $5, and sheep at 50 cents. How many of each does he buy?

Solution: One cow, nine hogs, and ninety sheep.

HUNTER AND SQUIRREL

A MAN goes into the woods to hunt squirrels. He hears a squirrel barking on the limb of a large oak tree. In trying to get a shot at the squirrel, the man walks around the tree, but the squirrel keeps on the opposite side of the tree all the time by going around the tree and keeping the tree between himself and the hunter. Does the hunter go around the squirrel?

Solution: No. They both encircle the heart of the tree, and the hunter does not go around the squirrel.

HOW MANY COWS?

A BOY, driving some cows, was asked how many cows he had. He said, "When they are in line there are two cows ahead of a cow, two cows behind a cow, and one cow in the middle." How many cows had he?

Solution: Three.

MATHEMATICAL "IF"

IF a fourth of forty is six, what is a third of twenty?

Solution: Four. If a fourth of forty were six, a half of forty would be twelve and a third of twelve would be four.

HEAD AND FEET

A DROVE of sheep and turkeys have 99 heads and feet. How many are there of each, if there are twice as many turkeys as sheep?

Solution: Nine sheep and eighteen turkeys.

HOW LONG IS THE FISH?

A FISH's head is as long as its tail. The head, tail, and body are fifteen inches long. If the head were twice as long as it is, the head and tail together would be as long as the body. How long is each?

Solution: Body, nine inches, head, three inches; and tail, three inches.

CATS AND RATS

IF three cats can catch three rats in three minutes, how many cats could catch one hundred rats in one hundred minutes?

Solution: The same three cats.

STRANGE ANIMAL

WHAT animal is it which walks first on four legs, later on two, and in old age on three?

Solution: An infant crawls, a young person walks on two legs, and an old person uses a cane.

HENS AND EGGS

IF a hen and a half lays an egg and a half in a day and a half, how many eggs will six hens lay in six days?

Solution: Twenty-four. At this ratio, a hen will lay two-thirds of an egg a day. Six hens would lay four eggs a day and twenty-four in six days.

HOW FAR WOULD THE BEE FLY?

Two trains leave two towns fifty miles apart. They run toward each other. One of the trains runs thirty miles an hour and the other twenty. A bee, flying at the rate of fifty miles an hour, leaves as the fast train does and meets the slow train. It turns and comes back and meets the fast train; it turns again and in this way keeps on flying back and fourth between the trains until they meet. How far does the bee fly?

Solution: Fifty miles. As one runs twenty and the other thirty miles an hour, the trains would meet in one hour. The bee then flies only one hour, hence only fifty miles.

WATER UPHILL

Can water ever run uphill?
Solution: Yes, into a sponge.

CAN YOU READ THIS LETTER?

The following letter is said to have been written by President Washington? Can you read it?

STAND TAKE TO   TAKINGS AND STAND ME
  I   YOU THROW   MY   AWE THOSE WHO

Solution: I understand you undertake to overthrow my undertakings and overawe those who understand me.

CAN YOU NAME THE PRESIDENTS?

The following bit of patter will enable you, if you will memorize it, to remember the presidents in order:

WILL ALL JUDGE MY METHODS AND JUDICI-OUSLY VALUE HISTORICAL TRUTH; PAINT THE FUTURE PICTURESQUELY, BEAUTIFY LIFE'S JOURNEY, GIVE HONEST GRATITUDE, ARDENT

COMMENDATION, HEARTY CONGRATULATIONS; MAKE RIGHT, TRUTH, WISDOM, HONESTY, COURAGE, HAPPINESS, REALITIES THAT ENDURE. Thus we have the first letter in the names of the presidents in order by taking the first letter in each word as follows: Washington, (J.) Adams, Jefferson, Madison, Monroe, (J. Q.) Adams, Jackson, Van Buren, Harrison, Tyler, Polk, Taylor, Fillmore, Pierce, Buchanan, Lincoln, Johnson, son, Harding, Coolidge, Hoover, (F. D.) Roosevelt, Truman, Eisenhower.

DIVIDING THE FARM

A FARMER, who had originally owned a section of land one mile square, sold a quarter of it, one-half mile square. Upon his death, he willed the remainder of it to his four sons, decreeing that each should have a piece of ground of the same acreage and of the same size and shape. How was it divided this way?

Solution:

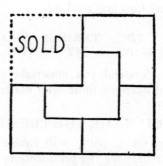

COST OF APPLES

IF an apple and a half cost a cent and a half, what would be the cost of a dozen and half apples?

Solution: Eighteen cents.

DIGIT PROBLEM

ARRANGE the digits 1, 2, 3, 4, 5, 6, 7, 8, 9, 0, so that they will equal 100.

Solution: 50½ and 49 38-76.

HOW MUCH GREATER?

How much greater than ¾ is 4-4?

Solution: Approximately 1-3 greater.

WHICH TRAVELS FASTEST?

THREE men stood on the bank of a river. Across the river a gun was fired. The first man on the other side of the river saw the smoke from the gun, the second saw the bullet strike the water at his feet, and the third heard the report. Which one first knew of the shot?

Solution: No. 1, who saw the smoke, knew of it first; No. 3, who heard the report, second; and No. 2, who saw the bullet strike the water, third. Light travels faster than sound and sound faster than a bullet.

TRICK WITH FIGURES

REQUEST the individuals in a group to write down a number of three figures. This should be written from numbers that will reverse and subtract; as 942, and from this take 249. If the number 249 is written first, it cannot have 942 taken from it. Ask them to start with a large number and then use smaller numbers. After they have written a number, and then reversed it and subtracted, you can tell them their answers if they will tell you the left-hand figure.

Solution: The middle number will always be nine and the last number will always be nine minus the first number. Example: 942 — 249 equals 693. You are told the first number, 6. The middle number is always nine. The last number is nine minus the first number, 6.

THREE TIMES SEVEN EQUALS TWENTY

How may three sevens be arranged so that they will equal twenty?

Solution: 7 plus 7 divided by .7.

GOLD OR FEATHERS?

Which weigh the most a pound of gold or a pound of feathers?

Solution: A pound of feathers weighs the most. Feathers, avoirdupois weight, weigh 7,000 grains to the pound; while gold, apothecaries' weight, has only 5,760 grains, the weight of a grain being equal in both cases. Of course, you would rather have a pound of feathers drop on your head.

HOW MUCH DID HE HAVE?

A man found a purse containing $2. He then had five times as much as he would have had, had he lost $2. How much had he?

Solution: He had $3.

UNLUCKY 1930

The year 1930, the year the depression began to be felt, was said to be an unlucky year, because the numbers in it added together total thirteen. In what year will this first occur again?

Solution: The year 2029.

THE BOOKWORM

There are three volumes of Mark Twain on a shelf, volumes 1, 2, and 3. There are three hundred pages in each volume and each volume is two inches thick. Without taking into account the thickness of the covers, if a bookworm starts at page 1 of volume 1, and eats through to page 300 of volume 3, how many inches does he travel?

Solution: Two inches. To convince yourself, examine three volumes on a shelf.

THEY TOTAL EIGHTY

WHAT four consecutive odd numbers, added together, total eighty?
Solution: 17, 19, 21, 23.

HOW OLD WAS BILL?

A MAN was asked, "How old are your boys, John and Bill?"
He replied, "John is 24 years old and Bill doesn't like to tell his age, but John is twice as old as Bill was when John was as old as Bill is now." What is Bill's age?
Solution: Bill was eighteen.

TOTAL TWENTY-SEVEN

WHAT are three consecutive numbers whose sum is 27?
Solution: 8, 9, and 10.

GRANDMOTHER'S PROBLEM

GRANDMOTHER desires to give three cents to each of her grandchildren. She finds that she lacks eight cents of having enough money. If she then gives them only two cents apiece, she will have three cents left? How many grandchildren had she, and how much money?
Solution: She has eleven grandchildren and twenty-five cents.

HOW OLD?

A MAN marries a woman half as old as himself. In ten years she is 3-5 as old as he; in twenty years she is 4-6 as old as he; in thirty years she is 5-7 as old as he. After another ten years, the man dies at the age of eighty. How old were they when they were married?
Solution: Twenty and forty years.

SEVEN THIRTEENS

A MAN told his friend that his salary was twenty-eight dollars a week and thirteen dollars a day. To prove it to him, he put down the figures as follows: First he divided twenty-eight by the seven days of the week in this manner:

$$7\overline{\smash{\big)}28}\ \underline{13}$$
7
—
21
21
—

Seven into 2 won't go, and 7 into 8 will go one time; put down the 1. Subtracting this, leaves 21, and 7 will go into 21 three times; hence 28 divided by 7 equals 13.

To further prove that 7 times 13 are 28, the man multiplied.

13
7
—
21
7
—
28

He said 7 times 3 are 21 and put down the 21. Then he said 7 times 1 are 7, and put down the 7. Adding these, it totaled 28.

But his friend was still not satisfied, so he put down 13 seven times, and added them up as follows:

13
13
13
13
13
13
13
—
21
7
—
28

Adding all the 3's in the right-hand column, they total 21, so he put down the 21. Then he added all the ones in the left-hand column, and they totaled 7, and these added together totaled 28.

Try this on your friends.

WHO WERE THEY?

"As I went over Heeple Steeple I met three people. They

were neither men, women, nor children. Who were they?
Solution: A man, a woman, and a child.

WHAT IS IT?

WHAT is the beginning of eternity,
    The end of time and space,
The beginning of every end,
    And the end of every race?
Solution: The letter E.

THE KING'S NAME

THE riddle is, to find the king's name.
    A king met a king in a right narrow lane.
    The king said to the king, "What is your name?"
    "Silk is my saddle, steel is my bow;
    I told you my name three times in a row."
Solution: The king's name is My.

WHAT IS IT THAT HAS?

WHAT is it that has:
    Marble walls as white as milk,
    Lined with skin as soft as silk?
    'Neath a fountain crystal clear,
    A golden apple doth appear.
    No doors are there to this stronghold,
    Yet thieves break through and steal the gold.
Solution: An egg.

RELATIONSHIP

A VISITOR in the penitentiary was asked what relation a
prisoner was to him. He replied, "Brothers and sisters have
I none, but this man's father was my father's son." What
relation were they?
Solution: The prisoner was the visitor's son.

WHAT KIN?

A BIG Indian and a little Indian sat on a log. The little

Indian was the big Indian's son, but the big Indian was not the little Indian's father. What relation were they?

Solution: The big Indian was the little Indian's mother.

POSSIBILITY

EXPLAIN how the following can be possible:

A man with no eyes
Went out to view the skies.
He saw an apple tree with apples on it;
He took no apples off,
He left no apples on.

Solution: He had one eye, the tree had two apples; he took one off and left one on.

THE CHINESE FOLDER

A VERY clever trick, which is said to be an old Chinese trick, can be worked out in the following manner: Take two pieces of goldenrod bond paper, twelve inches square, and fold these so that they make a square four inches on each side. After they have been carefully folded, paste the backs carefully together so that the fold will open on either side. This should be very carefully done, as it must appear to be only one fold.

Get three or four other colors of bond paper, as blue, green, and red, and make smaller folds in duplicate. In other words, make two folds out of the same color paper about three inches square. We will say that these are made out of red paper. Then make two folds, about two inches square, out of green paper; then make two folds, about an inch and a half square, out of the blue paper. Fold the blue fold into the green fold, then the green fold into the red fold, and last the red fold into the yellow or bottom sheet.

Now you are ready to do the trick. Open up one side of your fold, opening first the yellow, then red, green, and blue. Ask someone to deposit a coin or place a folded dollar bill on the green piece of paper. Fold this dollar bill up, turn the fold upside down and fold the green fold around it. Turn the green fold upside down and fold the red fold around, each time turning the fold upside down. Then place this in your last fold, fold it and turn it over. At this point put the index finger on the fold, and as you raise your finger give a low whistle and tell your spectators that you have made the coin or dollar bill disappear. All you have to do then is to start unfolding, and when you have unfolded all the folds, the coin or bill will not be in the last one. Of course, it is in the other side.

The coin or bill may be made to reappear in the same manner—that is, by refolding, turning the fold over, and unfolding the other side.

AGE AND TELEPHONE NUMBER

GIVE persons in the group pencils and slips of paper; ask each one to write down his telephone number. He is then told to multiply by two, add five, and multiply the result by fifty. He is then told to add his age to the total and add three hundred and sixty-five, the number of days in the year, to it. When this has been totaled up, subtract six hundred and fifteen from it. It will be found that, of the remaining figures, the last two will show their age and the first figures their telephone number. For example:

Telephone number	22430
Multiply by	2
	44860
Add	5
	44865
Multiply by	50

$$2243250$$

Add your age 33

$$2243283$$

Add days of year 365

$$2243648$$

Subtract key number 615

$$2243033$$

PROBLEM IN PUNCTUATION

ASK those in the group to punctuate the following sentence so it will make sense: that that is is that that is not is not is not that it is is.

Solution: That that is, is; that that is not, is not; is not that it? It is.

TOO WISE

Y Y U R Y Y U B I C U R Y Y for me.

Solution: Too wise you are, too wise you be, I see you are too wise for me.

NEW YEAR'S RESOLUTION

A MAN resolves to save a penny on January 1, two cents on January 2, and so on, doubling the amount saved on the previous day for the thirty-one days of January. How much would be saved in this way? Make a guess.

Solution: $10,737,418.24.

THE MAGIC BOTTLE

TAKE a tall flat bottle that would hold about one quart of water and fill it full of water. Get a small bottle, about one quarter of an inch in diameter, from the drug store and fill it about half full of water. Turn the small bottle upside down in the water in the large bottle, pouring a small quantity from the large bottle to leave an air space between the water and the cork. By pressing on the sides of the bottle, after the cork has been adjusted in the right place, the small bottle can be made to go up and down easily. This is caused by the air pressure between the water and the cork.

The one who is doing the stunt should tell his auditors that the small bottle is made to rise and fall by blowing on the large bottle. It would create a lot of good fun to have several try to blow hard enough to raise the small bottle. After several have tried, it would be well to explain how the trick is done, and let them all do it the right way.

TRICKS AND PUZZLES WITH MATCHES

Paper Match Trick

Take two paper matches, such as those given away for advertising purposes, and make a dot of ink on one side of each of these. Hold the matches with the thumb and index finger of the left hand, with the heads against the index finger and the dots up. Grasp them with the thumb and forefinger of the right hand, turn them over, so that the heads will be against the left thumb. The object, however, is to keep the dots up all the time. This may be accomplished by pushing with the right thumb toward the end of the right index finger and turning the matches over as the right hand turns over. It may be done so quickly that it will not be observed by onlookers and the trick will be very mysterious.

Make Nine

Lay six matches on the table about an inch apart. Add five to these and make nine. It may be done in the following manner:

MATCHES

WITH twelve matches, make letters that will spell what matches are made of:

Solution:

FOUR TRIANGLES

CAN you take six matches of equal length and with them make four equilateral triangles?

Solution: This can be done by using three matches to make a base, and with the other three matches constructing a pyramid. Each side of the pyramid is an equilaterial triangle.

EQUAL SQUARES AND TRIANGLES

WITH nine matches of equal lengths, form three equal squares and two equal triangles.

SYLLOGISMS

PENNY SYLLOGISM

To prove that a penny is a missionary:
A missionary is "One sent";

A penny is "One cent";
Therefore a penny is a missionary.

Train Syllogism

To prove that a train cannot run:
A train cannot run where it is;
A train cannot run where it is not;
Therefore a train cannot run at all.

Dog Syllogism

The dog with five tails:
One dog has one tail;
No dog has five tails;
Therefore, no dog has four more tails than one dog.

WORD MATHEMATICS
Dress and Insect

Add the bottom of a woman's dress to an insect and get a musical number sung by a church choir.
Solution: Anthem (ant-hem).

Girl's Name and Battle

Take a girl's name from a famous American battle and leave an ancient Roman garment.
Solution: Saratoga (Sara-toga).

Arrange the Letters

Arrange the following letters so that they will spell just one word: ENOTSUJDROW.
Solution: Spell with them "Just one word." The letters of these three words are merely jumbled.

One Word Contains Six

What word, beginning with an H and ending with an N, contains six words besides itself without transposing a single letter?
Solution: Herein—He, her, here, ere, rein, in.

WHAT IS IT THAT?

WHAT is it that, after you take away the whole, some still remains?

Solution: Wholesome.

SOWING WORDS

As we sow, so shall we reap: Sow unpopularity and what will come up? A wall flower. Sow contentment and what will come up? Heart's ease. Sow friendship and what will come up? Forget-me-nots. Bury the hatchet and what will come up? Sweet peas (Sweet peace). Plant grief and what will come up? Weeping Willow.

WORD DEFINITION

ASK your friends to define the following words and you will probably be amused at the gestures they make. Accordion, goatee, spiral staircase, hula-hula.

Accordion is usually defined by moving the hands back and forth like playing an accordion; goatee by stroking the chin like stroking a beard; spiral staircase by holding the index finger in a vertical position and moving it around in a circle; and hula-hula by shaking the body.

WORD TRANSFORMATION

ANY two words with an equal number of letters may be transformed by changing one letter at a time. For example:

Change PIG to PEN in two moves, as follows: Pig—Pin—Pen.

Change PUSH to PULL in two moves.

Solution: Push—Pulh—Pull.

Change FOOT to HAND in four moves.

Solution: Foot—Hoot—Haot—Hant—Hand.

Change BLACK to WHITE in five moves.

Solution: Black—Blace—Blate—Blite—Bhite—White.

PROVERB TRANSFORMATION

IN the following proverbs one letter in each word must be changed to find the proverb:

CALF A LOAD IF WETTER THAT SO BREAK. Half a loaf is better than no bread.

LETTER BATE THAT FEVER. Better late than never.

PAINT PEART NEWER SON PAIR LADS. Faint heart never won fair lady.

A SWITCH IS DIME RAVES MINE. A stitch in time saves nine.

SO NETS IF GOOF MEWS. No news is good news.

PIED PROVERBS

IN the following proverbs, each word is pied and the problem is to decipher both the word and the proverb.

KOLO FROEEB UYO PELA. Look before you leap.

RIBSD FO A HETRAEF LFCKO GOETTREH. Birds of a feather flock together.

KAME AHY HWELI EHT USN HESINS. Make hay while the sun shines.

SEANCEAPPAR REA FONET VIIGNEDCE. Appearances are often deceiving.

NOITAINTSARCPOR SI HET HITFE FO MITE. Procrastination is the thief of time.

MUSICAL TERMS

How much do you know about music? The following should be answered with musical terms:

People live in it—Flat; used in describing a razor—Sharp; used on a bow—Chord (cord); an insinuating remark—Slur; furniture in a store—Counters; often passed in school—Notes; a kind of fish—Bass; a person at ease—Natural; used in fishing—Lines; what one breathes—Air; what an ocean wave does—Swells; found in a saloon—Bar; a part of a sentence—Phrase; found on a fish—Scales; the name of a girl—Grace; another name for a cane—Staff; denoted by a clock—Time; what a policeman has—Beat; what we should do at night—Rest; what the carpenter does with his rule—Measures; what each side wants to do in a football game—Score; a kind of tar—Pitch; something to a door—Key.

CLOCK STROKES

IF a clock strikes every hour, how many strokes does it make in a day?

Solution: 156 times in 24 hours.

FIVE ON A SIDE

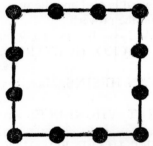

In the diagram on the left the dots represent twelve coins. In this position there are four on a side. The problem is to move four of the coins, and without using any more coins, arrange them so that there will be five on a side.

Solution: In order to do this, it is only necessary to pick up one of the coins on the line between the corners on each side and place it on top of the corner coin. Then, with two coins on each corner and one between, there are five on a side.

SIX ON A SIDE

IT is possible, in the same way and with the same number of coins, to have six on a side in the above puzzle. In order to do this it is only necessary to take both of the middle coins and place them on top of the corner coin. With three on each corner, there will be six on a side.

THE WOODCHUCK

If a woodchuck would chuck wood, how much wood would a woodchuck chuck?

Solution: A woodchuck would chuck all the wood he would chuck if a woodchuck would chuck wood.

DIRT IN A HOLE

How much dirt is there in a hole 18 inches square and 1 foot deep?

Solution: None.

TONGUE TWISTER

Six long, slim, slick, slender saplings grew in the woods.

THE SIFTER

A sifter sifting sand thrust three thousand thistles through the thick of his thumb.

THE STRONG MAN

A strong man can lift twelve hundred pounds in a circus. How much can he lift with a pulley and rope, the pulley fastened to the ceiling while he stands on the floor.

Solution: No more than his own weight.

THE WINDOW

A window is three feet high and two feet wide. On account of the brightness of the light, half of it is made opaque, but still the window is three feet high and two feet wide. How may this be done?

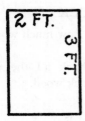

AT WHAT INTERVALS?

ONE man sees another man chopping down a tree 1,100 yards away. The man strikes the tree once every second. Sound travels at the rate of 1,100 feet per second. How much time lapses between two strokes of the woodman's axe, as the other man hears it?

Solution: One second.

BOY ON THE TRAIN

A BOY is on a train, which is moving at the rate of fifty miles an hour. He jumps straight up three feet. Where does he land?

Solution: In the same place from which he jumped.

PIGS IN PENS

USING matches to build the pens and coins to represent pigs, put nine pigs in four pens so that there will be an odd number in each pen.

Solution: Place three pigs in each of three pens and build a fourth pen around the other three.

HANDKERCHIEF AND TOOTHPICK

To do this trick have a toothpick concealed in the hem of your handkerchief. Show your friends another toothpick, and when you have finished displaying it, fold the handkerchief over it. Keep in mind the location of the toothpick in your handkerchief so that you can fold a part of the handkerchief over it and make it appear it is the toothpick you placed in the handkerchief. Hold the handkerchief and break the toothpick which is in the hem. It may be broken two or three times to produce a better effect, and then your friends will be surprised when you unfold the handkerchief and produce the toothpick placed there intact.

CHRISTMAS SAVINGS

WHEN a boy opens his Christmas savings bank he finds that he has just 100 coins in half dollars, pennies, and dimes. When he counted his money he found that he had exactly $5. How many coins had he of each denomination?

Solution: One half dollar, 39 dimes, and 60 pennies.

MOVING COINS

ARRANGE six coins as follows, using pennies and nickles:

A   B   C   D   E   F

(P) (N) (P) (N) (P) (N)

By making three moves and not moving more than two at a time arrange them so that they will be as in the following illustration:

(P) (P) (P) (N) (N) (N)

Solution: This may be done by first moving D and E to the right of F. Then move A and B to the left of F. Then move E to the extreme left.

HOW TO PREDICT THE ANSWER

WRITE down the digits from 1 to 9, omitting 8. After

this has been done ask someone to select one of these numbers. Suppose that person selects 4. You then multiply this 4 by 9, which gives you 36, and multiply the row of digits by 36. The answer will be 444,444,444. It will work the same way if any other number is selected. If three is selected, multiply 3 x 9 equals 27 and multiply the row of digits by 27 and your answer will be 333,333,333. For example:

You write down the digits as........1 2 3 4 5 6 7 9
Someone selects 4. Multiply 4 x 9 =   3 6
                                          ─────────────────
                                          7 4 0 7 4 0 7 4
                                          3 7 0 3 7 0 3 7
                                          ─────────────────
Your answer will be all fours, as....4 4 4 4 4 4 4 4 4

CANNIBALS AND MISSIONARIES

IN solving the following problem it is advisable to use three coins to represent the cannibals, one of these being heads and the other two being tails, the coin that lays heads to represent cannibal I, the other two coins to represent cannibals II and III. The problem is that three missionaries and three cannibals come to a river in Africa and desire to cross. The boat will only carry two. All the missionaries can row, but only one of the cannibals, cannibal I. The trips must be arranged so that the cannibals will never outnumber the missionaries. In other words, one missionary must never be left with two cannibals or two missionaries with the three cannibals. They were able to get across, but how was it done?

Solution: Cannibal I takes over one cannibal and leaves him. He then takes another cannibal and leaves him. When cannibal I returns with the boat two missionaries go over, one of them remaining while the other returns bringing a cannibal with him. One missionary then goes over with cannibal I. A missionary then returns with a cannibal, but leaves cannibal I on the other side. The two missionaries then cross over and turn over the boat to cannibal I, who makes two other trips over for the cannibals, bringing one at a time.

Perhaps the following arrangement will give a better understanding:

On the Trip Over	*On the Trip Back*
One cannibal and cannibal I —	Cannibal I
One cannibal and cannibal I —	Cannibal I
Two missionaries	— One missionary and one cannibal
One missionary and cannibal I —	One missionary and one cannibal
Two missionaries	— Cannibal I returns
Cannibal I and one cannibal	— Cannibal I
Cannibal I and one cannibal	

TWO CANARIES

A WOMAN had two canaries. One of these could sing 100 notes in ½ minute and the other could sing ½ as many notes in twice that length of time. How many notes could both birds sing in 15 seconds?

Solution: 62½.

MAKE THEM EQUAL 17

CAN you arrange the 9 digits on the three sides of a triangle so that the sum of the digits on each side will be 17?

Solution:

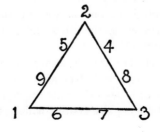

MAKE THEM EQUAL 20

PLACE the digits on the sides of a triangle as above, but in such a way that they will equal 20.

Solution:

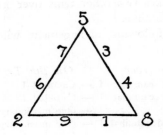

NURSERY RHYME RIDDLE

As I was going to St. Ives,
I met a man with seven wives;
Every wife had seven sacks,
Every sack had seven cats,
Every cat had seven kits.
Kits, cats, sacks, and wives,
How many were going to St. Ives?

Solution: One. Read it again and see.

SQUIRREL ON A LOG

A SQUIRREL is on the end of a log eight feet long and three feet in circumference. The log starts rolling and makes two complete revolutions, and as the log turns the squirrel stays on top and travels to the other end of the log. How far does the squirrel travel?

Solution: 10 feet. He travels along the hypotenuse of a right angle, whose base is 8 feet and height 6 feet, consequently the square of base—64—plus the square of the height ·—36—equals 100, the square root of which is 10.

ARRANGING AND ADDING

ARRANGE the digits from 1 to 7 so that they will add up 100.

Solution: 15+36+47+2=100.

HOW DEEP WAS THE RIVER?

A POLE resting on the bottom of a river sticks out of the water 6 feet. If the top of the pole is moved 12 feet to one side, it is even with the top of the water. The problem is to find the depth of the river.

Solution: The river was 9 feet deep. This answer can be easily proven by squaring this 9, which is the base of a right triangle which equals 81. Add to this the square of the other side of the triangle, which is 12 and which squared equals 144. These numbers added equal 225, the square root of which is 15, the length of the pole.

SECTION XII

Conundrums

100 CONUNDRUMS

1. WHAT is the difference between Congress and progress? Pro and con.

2. In what way are most of us like Columbus? He did not know where he was going when he started, he did not know where he was when he got there, and he did not know where he had been when he got back.

3. Where does all the pepper go? No one knows (nose).

4. How can you tell a single man from a married man? A single man has no buttons on his shirt; a married man has no shirt.

5. What is it that goes around a button (buttin')? A billy goat.

6. Who is the first man mentioned in the Bible? Chap. 1.

7. If the first man was Adam, who was the first woman? Madam.

8. What is the difference between stabbing a man and killing a hog? The first is assault with intent to kill and the other is killing with intent to salt.

9. When you see a woman walking, what do you wonder? You wonder if she is walking to reduce or if she is reduced to walking.

10. What should women use to clean their carpets? Their husbands.

11. What animal keeps the best time? The watchdog.

12. What is so rare as a day in June? Some days in March are pretty raw.

13. When will water stop running down hill? When it gets to the bottom.

14. Why did the boy stand on the burning deck? It was too hot to sit down.

15. When is baseball first mentioned in the Bible? Genesis 1:1: In the beginning (In the big inning).

16. At what time was Adam born? A little before Eve.

17. Who were the two noblemen of Bible times? Baron Fig Tree and Lord How Long.

18. How do wo know that St. Paul was a cook? The Bible says he went to Philippi (fill a pie).

19. What is it that can run and can't walk and has a tongue and can't talk? A wagon.

20. Is it cheaper to be married than single? At any rate one feels cheaper.

21. What is it that goes all around the house and makes only one track? A wheelbarrow.

22. Does a chair ever despise you? Yes, if it can't bear you.

23. Why is your nose in the middle of your face? It is the scenter.

24. Can one put his left shoe on first? No, if he puts on one shoe the other one is left.

25. Which side is a pitcher handle on? Outside.

26. If you would plant a puppy, what would come up? Dogwood (dog would).

27. What is the best bet ever made? The alphabet.

28. What was Joan of Arc made of? Maid of Orleans.

29. How do we know that Samson was an actor? He brought down the house.

30. What are the two smallest things mentioned in the Bible? The widow's mite and the wicked flee.

31. What tune makes everyone glad? Fortune.

32. What age will we reach if we live long enough? Dotage.

33. What is covered and yet seen? A book.

34. What are the little white things in your head that bite? Your teeth.

35. What increases in value when it turns upside down? The figure 6.

36. What grows larger the more you take from it? A hole.

37. What is the difference between a hill and a pill? The former is hard to get up and the latter had to get down.

38. What is both a time and a fruit? A date.

39. What is full of holes and yet holds water? A sponge.

40. Is there a word in the English language which contains all the vowels? Yes, unquestionably.

41. What has eyes and cannot see? A potato.

42. What has hands and never washes them? A clock.

43. What has legs and cannot walk? A table or chair.

44. What has pains and does not ache? A window.

45. What cannot talk, but nevertheless always tells you the truth? A mirror.

46. What is better than presence of mind in an automobile accident? Absence of body.

47. What is the merriest letter in the alphabet? U, because it is always in fun.

48. What is it that occurs once in a minute, twice in a moment, and not once in a thousand years? The letter M.

49. Why is E the most unfortunate letter? It is never in cash, always in debt, and never out of danger.

50. Why are some schoolrooms like an old-time flivver? They have a crank in front and lot of nuts behind.

51. What is the best kind of butter? A goat.

52. Why is the heart of a tree like a dog's tail? It is farthest away from the bark.

53. In what way does a confidence man live up to Bible teachings? When a stranger comes along, he "takes him in."

54. How do we know that the authoress of *Uncle Tom's Cabin* did not write it with her hand? Because it was written by Harriet Beecher's Toe (Stowe).

55. Why did they not play bridge on the Ark? Because Noah sat on the deck.

56. What is the best musical motto? B sharp and B natural, but never B flat.

57. Why does a duck go into the water? For divers reasons.

58. What is the strongest bird? The crane can lift the heaviest weight.

59. Why is O the noisiest vowel? All the others are inaudible.

60. How do we know that mosquitos are religious? First they sing over you, then the prey upon you.

61. What is it that has a mouth and never speaks and a bed and never sleeps in it? A river.

62. What is it that everyone has that he can always count on? His fingers.

63. What is it that always walks with its head down? A nail in the sole of a shoe.

64. Why is an egg like a young horse? It is of no value until broken.

65. What two numbers multiplied together make 7? 7 and 1.

66. Who are the two shortest men mentioned in the Bible? Bildad the Shu-hite and Ne-hi-mi-ah.

67. Who were the Tom Thumb Apostles? Peter, James, and John all slept on a watch.

68. When did Jacob sleep five in a bed? When he slept with his forefathers.

69. Why is a Dutchman's pancake like the sun? It rises in the east (yeast) and sets behind the vest (west).

70. Why is a Dutchman's napkin like a snake? He calls it a "viper."

71. What is always found in pairs? Scissors.

72. When was paper money first used? When the dove brought the green back to Noah.

73. Why did not the worms, like other creatures, go into the Ark in pairs (pears)? Because they went in apples.

74. In what order did Noah come from the Ark? He came forth.

75. Who was Jonah's guardian? The whale brought him up.

76. What is often in the hands of a receiver? A telephone.

77. What was it that Queen Mary had before and King William had behind and Queen Ann didn't have at all? The letter M.

78. What city may be represented by a mill, a sidewalk, and a door key? Milwaukee.

79. What nut is always cooked before eating? Doughnut.

80. What nut is always found at the rim of the ocean? Beechnut?

81. What can only walk when worn? Shoes.

82. What western city is a boy calling his mother and laughing? O-ma-ha.

83. What is the largest vegetable? A policeman's beat.

84. What is the largest sandwich? The sand which is on the desert.

85. Why is a long-winded man's speech like a cat's tail? It's fur to the end.

86. Why is a dry speech like an automobile wheel? The longer the spokes the bigger the tire.

87. What is it you haven't got (there are some exceptions), you don't want, and if you had it you wouldn't take a million dollars for it? Bald head.

88. What is it the average man frequently sees, the great man seldom sees, and God never sees? His equal.

89. What is the hardest soap manufactured? Castile (cast steel).

90. What is it that was given to you, belongs to you exclusively, and yet is used more by your friends than yourself? Your name.

91. How many wives does the English Prayer Book allow a man to have? Sixteen—"for (four) better for (four) worse, for (four) richer for (four) poorer."

92. What is the strongest day? Sunday. All the others are week (weak) days.

93. How may bookkeeping be taught in a lesson of three short words? "Don't lend them!"

94. What is it that Adam and Eve never had yet left to each of their children? Parents.

95. What kind of necktie should a sophisticated pig choose? A pigsty.

96. How is a dentist like a discouraged man? He always looks down in the mouth.

97. In what way are a girl's kisses like pickles in a bottle? After you get the first one the rest come easy.

98. What is a kiss? It is what a man struggles for before the wedding, and the woman struggles for afterwards.

99. When is a woman a live wire? When she is shocking.

100. What is it that has four legs and only one foot? A bedstead.

INDEXES

ALPHABETICAL INDEX

381

CLASSIFIED INDEX

STAGE STUNTS

STUNTS FOR SCOUTS AND CAMPS